The Burden of Traumascapes

Bloomsbury Advances in Sociolinguistics

Series Editor: Tommaso M. Milani

Since the emergence of sociolinguistics as a new field of enquiry in the late 1960s, research into the relationship between language and society has advanced almost beyond recognition. In particular, the past decade has witnessed the considerable influence of theories drawn from outside of sociolinguistics itself. Thus rather than see language as a mere reflection of society, recent work has been increasingly inspired by ideas drawn from social, cultural and political theory that have emphasized the constitutive role played by language/discourse in all areas of social life. The Advances in Sociolinguistics series seeks to provide a snapshot of the current diversity of the field of sociolinguistics and the blurring of the boundaries between sociolinguistics and other domains of study concerned with the role of language in society.

Titles in the series:

Becoming a Citizen, Kamran Khan

The Discursive Construction of Identity and Space among Mobile People, Roberta Piazza

Reterritorializing Linguistic Landscapes, David Malinowski and Stefania Tufi

Multilingual Memories, Robert Blackwood and John Macalister

Linguistic Landscapes beyond the Language, Greg Niedt and Corinne A. Seals

Making Sense of People and Place in Linguistic Landscapes, Amiena Peck, Christopher Stroud and Quentin Williams

The Tyranny of Writing, Constanze Weth and Kasper Juffermans

Remix Multilingualism, Quentin Williams

Voices in the Media, Gaëlle Planchenault

Negotiating and Contesting Identities in Linguistic Landscapes, Robert Blackwood

Intercultural Contact, Language Learning and Migration, Barbara Geraghty and Jean Conacher

The Burden of Traumascapes

Discourses of Remembering in Bosnia-Herzegovina and Beyond

Maida Kosatica

BLOOMSBURY ACADEMIC
LONDON • NEW YORK • OXFORD • NEW DELHI • SYDNEY

BLOOMSBURY ACADEMIC
Bloomsbury Publishing Plc
50 Bedford Square, London, WC1B 3DP, UK
1385 Broadway, New York, NY 10018, USA
29 Earlsfort Terrace, Dublin 2, Ireland

BLOOMSBURY, BLOOMSBURY ACADEMIC and the Diana logo are
trademarks of Bloomsbury Publishing Plc

First published in Great Britain 2022
This paperback edition published 2024

Copyright © Maida Kosatica, 2022

Maida Kosatica has asserted her right under the Copyright,
Designs and Patents Act, 1988, to be identified as Author of this work.

Cover image © Martin O'Neill

All rights reserved. No part of this publication may be reproduced or transmitted in any form or by any means, electronic or mechanical, including photocopying, recording, or any information storage or retrieval system, without prior permission in writing from the publishers.

Bloomsbury Publishing Plc does not have any control over, or responsibility for, any third-party websites referred to or in this book. All internet addresses given in this book were correct at the time of going to press. The author and publisher regret any inconvenience caused if addresses have changed or sites have ceased to exist, but can accept no responsibility for any such changes.

A catalogue record for this book is available from the British Library.

A catalog record for this book is available from the Library of Congress.

ISBN:	HB:	978-1-3501-3479-9
	PB:	978-1-3503-4170-8
	ePDF:	978-1-3501-3480-5
	eBook:	978-1-3501-3481-2

Series: Bloomsbury Advances in Sociolinguistics

Typeset by Integra Software Services Pvt. Ltd.

To find out more about our authors and books visit www.bloomsbury.com
and sign up for our newsletters.

I dedicate this book to all who suffer and to the memory of all the innocent lives taken.

Contents

List of Figures	viii
Preface	x
A Photographic Essay	xii
Introduction	1
1 Contemporary Perspectives on Traumascapes	13
2 Turbulent Graffscapes and Linguistic Violence	27
3 The Semiotic Production of Commemorative Performances	49
4 Waging War Online	77
5 (Un)Realities of War in Second-Generation Oral Narratives	111
Conclusion	149
Notes	160
References	163
Index	184

Figures

1	*Nermin come back* sculpture-installation © Maida Kosatica 2016	xii
2	*Tank graveyard* memorial © Maida Kosatica 2016	xiii
3	A façade of a club © Maida Kosatica 2016	xiv
4	Graffiti © Maida Kosatica 2016	xv
5	*Potočari* memorial cemetery complex © Maida Kosatica 2017	xvi
6	Still images taken from *The Scorpions – A Home Movie*, produced by Natasa Kandic © Humanitarian Law Center 2007	2
7	Detainees in the Manjača camp near Banja Luka © UN International Criminal Tribunal for the former Yugoslavia 2009	10
8	War video and photo exhibition in Mostar next to the Old Bridge © Maida Kosatica 2016	29
9	Residential building façade in Doboj © Maida Kosatica 2016	38
10	Residential building façade in Doboj © Maida Kosatica 2016	39
11	Residential portal space in Mostar © Maida Kosatica 2016	40
12	Muslim cemetery wall in Mostar © Maida Kosatica 2016	41
13	Park in Doboj © Maida Kosatica 2016	43
14	Hotel 'Rose' in Mostar © Maida Kosatica 2016	46
15	Still image of White House taken from the 'Crimes before the ICTY: Prijedor' video, directed by Petar Finci © United Nations International Residual Mechanism for Criminal Tribunals 2013	50
16	Monument to the fallen Bosnian Serb heroes in Trnopolje © Maida Kosatica 2017	52
17	Tourist boards in Prijedor © Maida Kosatica 2017	53

18	A man with a white armband standing on the main square in Prijedor © *Stop Genocide Denial* May 2012	60
19	Monument to the innocent killed citizens of Kozarac 1992–5 © Maida Kosatica 2017	129
20	Memorial room in Potočari © Maida Kosatica 2017	150

Preface

In this book, I write about different forms of remembering and its design follows my personal encounter with the prevailing ways the 1992–5 war in Bosnia-Herzegovina is being remembered. Taking a number of dynamic tours through painful sites and discursive terrains, the book is meant to delve into people's post-war traumas as part of their existence for years to come. In spite of today's prevalent trends towards requiring public apologies and genuine remorse for one's mistakes and actions, this book is not about forgiveness and reconciliation. I do not cover the notion of trauma from a clinical perspective, nor do I claim to offer great solutions to the ills of people. However, the exploration of different discursive and material-spatial processes in and around post-war Bosnia-Herzegovina allows me to form my own arguments about the complex nature of remembering. The book looks at the central role of (historical) trauma in explaining post-war landscapes and, in the broadest sense, places marked by violence. It is precisely the composited semiotic processes of remembering that constitute salient pieces of traumascapes, and thus my own building blocks in making sense of the Gordian knot suffocating Bosnia-Herzegovina for the longest time. In this light, the book is strategically arranged to progress from the material to more experiential ways of remembering. Only by sensibly bringing these together, we come to understand that there is no one single way to remember.

My work on this book owes much to dear people I want to thank. I would like to express my deep gratitude to my brilliant PhD supervisor, my mentor, the one who inspires me – Crispin Thurlow, for guiding me along this path with infinite enthusiasm, professionalism, and commitment. My sincere thanks go to the wonderful and thoughtful Tommaso Milani, the Series Editor, for continuously encouraging my academic work. Many thanks to Morwenna Scott and Laura Gallon from Bloomsbury Publishing for all of their guidance and patience. I am incredibly grateful to my parents for their unconditional support and encouragement. I thank my husband for selfless love. I thank my son – my light.

Chapter 3 is based on my paper, 'Emplacing Hate: Turbulent Graffscapes and Linguistic Violence in Post-war Bosnia-Herzegovina' published in *Linguistic*

Landscape (4: 1, 2018, pp. 1–28). I express my appreciation to John Benjamins Publishing for permission to reproduce this work.

Chapter 4 draws on my paper, '102: The Semiotics of Living Memorials' published in *Social Semiotics* (31: 5, 2021, pp. 738–56). I express my appreciation to Taylor & Francis for permission to reproduce this work.

The author and publisher gratefully acknowledge the permission granted to reproduce the copyright material in this book. Every effort has been made to trace copyright holders and to obtain their permission for the use of copyright material. However, if any have been inadvertently overlooked, the publishers will be pleased, if notified of any omissions, to make the necessary arrangements at the first opportunity.

A Photographic Essay

Figure 1 *Nermin come back* sculpture-installation © Maida Kosatica 2016

Father Ramo calls his son Nermin to surrender as soldiers said they will not do any harm to them. Father and son were found in a mass grave near Srebrenica in 2008. (Sarajevo)

A Photographic Essay xiii

Figure 2 *Tank graveyard* memorial © Maida Kosatica 2016

A memorial in Karuše made of two tanks and a transporter from the battle between the Bosnian Army and the Army of Serb Republic, assisted by forces of the JNA (Yugoslav National Army) in March 1993. (Doboj)

Figure 3 A façade of a club © Maida Kosatica 2016

Europe wasn't it enough? and UN-involved banners. (Sarajevo)

A Photographic Essay xv

Figure 4 Graffiti © Maida Kosatica 2016

'We are hungry' in three languages. (Sarajevo)

Figure 5 *Potočari* memorial cemetery complex © Maida Kosatica 2017

Graves of genocide victims. (Srebrenica, Potočari)

Introduction

This book has been in preparation for a long time, but I was not always mindful of that. There is a story behind it, which for many years, I was not aware I wanted to tell. I did not know why and how exactly I wanted to tell it. In other words, I did not know that I wanted to turn it into something more than my own memory episode. But now I do. Well aware of the heartfelt ethical responsibilities as I am writing about other people's trauma, it is only fair to first uncover one part of myself. My story may seem to be about violence, but I frame violence simply as an utter failure of human emotional faculties and the ability to empathize or compassionately rationalize. My aim, however, is not to establish new definitions, nor to offer famed ones by great thinkers. Rather, my objective is to show what we are left with after violence. This story is about unfathomable visuals and words that broke my reveries of people and filled my reality with darkness. Seventeen years ago, the television of Bosnia-Herzegovina (B&H) live-broadcast the 10th annual commemoration of the Srebrenica genocide. As in previous years, the ceremony was attended by tens of thousands of survivors and their local and foreign supporters, all listening to United Nations officials repeating their all-too-familiar, naïve statements of solidarity. As expected, the programme showed the collective burial of the remains of 610 individuals, a series of documentaries, testimonies of victims and witnesses, and other genocide-related content. Yet that year, there was something very different about the broadcast event. The programme included some disturbing amateur footage at which humanity shuddered (Figure 6). The footage, part of a two-hour video, was originally shown at the International Criminal Tribunal for the former Yugoslavia (ICTY) during the 2005 trial of Slobodan Milošević – the Serbian president charged with crimes against humanity.

In the video recorded to be a monstrous memento (aka a trophy or souvenir of the kills), a combat unit of the Serbian Ministry of Interior called the *Scorpions*

Figure 6 Still images taken from *The Scorpions – A Home Movie*, produced by Natasa Kandic © Humanitarian Law Center, 2007

trucked Bosnian Muslims (referred to as *packages*) from Srebrenica to distant locations, from which they were then parcelled out to be killed in small numbers. The footage showed the execution of six Bosnian Muslim civilians, four of whom were under eighteen and the other two under thirty. According to forensic documentation, the remains of six males shown in the video, identified as **Safet Fejzić (born 1978), Azmir Alispahić (born 1978), Smajil Ibrahimović (born 1960), Sidik Salkić (born 1959), Juso Delić (born 1970) and Dino Salihović (born 1979)**, were exhumed 160 kilometres from Srebrenica, in Trnovo municipality, in April 1999.[1] It seems that as if I always knew about genocide in Srebrenica, but as a sixteen-year-old I never imagined the mechanisms of mass killing – in what way exactly were these people murdered. Even when I was trying to picture what I thought was a quick and efficient movie-like killing, which was the only reference point I had – without blood and torture, I could not really visualize it. And even though I knew the edited video showed just a small part of the Srebrenica horror, this short stomach-churning spectacle of violence has stayed imprinted in my consciousness ever since. This was nothing like a Hollywood-quality production horror movie. This, I knew, is REAL. What was said after the video I did not hear. I did not even care to hear. The only thing existing were the images and words causing enormous pain. I could not care less about *who* exactly did what to *whom*; my story is not about *this* ethnic group killing *that* one. Politicized ethnonational narratives went far beyond the feelings as I remember them. The creatures of emotions all suffering from unimaginable hatred in very different ways, put my mind and body into perfect synchronization shouting the same thing – *It hurts endlessly*. The simple truth is, my soul was shattered. I have come to fully embrace what Michael Billig (1995: 1) poignantly claimed with the opening line of his *Banal Nationalism* published the same year the genocide in Srebrenica was committed:

> All societies that maintain armies maintain the belief that some things are more valuable than life itself.

And what I got to keep from all this is a wounding memory made of those feelings, images and words (in the precise order) I learned by heart, because 'only that which never ceases to hurt stays in the memory' (Nietzsche, 1899):

Scene 1: Tied and bloodied prisoners lying in the truck

Prisoner: (…)
Scorpion 1: Don't you worry about me
Scorpion 2: ((kicking a lying prisoner in the head with his foot)) Why are you shaking motherfucker?
Scorpion 3: (…) they smell like skunks
Scorpion 4: they shit themselves

Scene 2: Prisoners ordered off the truck

Scorpion 1: Do you have a lighter?
Scorpion 2: I have nothing. Fuck
Scorpion 3: GET OUT OF THE TRUCK. MOVE
Scorpion 3: Sit there line up there over there QUICKLY
Scorpion 2: Do your prayers like that motherfuckers
Scorpion 3: FASTER LIE DOWN
Scorpion 2: When you were killing Serbs you didn't wait motherfuckers
Scorpion 3: STRETCH OUT YOU TWO
Scorpion 4: Zekan go fast into the truck and get – my battery died fuck it

Scene 3: Prisoners lined up lying on the ground

   ((firing one shot above the prisoners' heads))
Scorpion 1: NO TALKING QUIET
Prisoner: (if you would give me some water)
Scorpion 2: What water fuck you
Scorpion 3: fuck off
   ((Scorpions laughing))
Scorpion 4: We're having guests ((three Scorpions approaching))

Scene 4: Prisoners standing on hillside
>((one by one four prisoners walk forwards))
>((short rifle bursts fired in the prisoners' backs and heads))
>((two prisoners move the corpses into a barn))
>((the two prisoners are shot in the barn))

Naturally, this projection of violence did not only touch people at the deepest level. It was also injected into the world by intense media coverage of what became a renewed national tragedy and disquieting testimony. It was treated as a form of mediatized evidence of the prolonged high-level involvement of Serbia in organizing the killing of Bosnian non-Serbs. The courtroom video testimony now heavily mediatized activated politicized narratives as the Guardian newspaper report shows:

Extract 1

[...] the 'smoking gun', for it is the final, incontrovertible proof of Serbia's part in the Srebrenica massacres in which more than 7,500 Bosnian Muslim men and boys were murdered. Until last week Serbian officials, both from the wartime regime of Slobodan Milosevic and since his fall in 2000, have argued that Serbia was not involved with the massacres. Now, the tape proves that to have been a lie.

(The Guardian, 2005)[2]

The video itself framed as a 'media event' intervening in the normal flow of broadcasting and our lives (Dayan and Katz, 1992), transitioned quickly from shocking and traumatic into an ethically remediated visual layering and accumulation of war memory (Hoskins, 2007). Speaking in terms of the global community, the video produced moral condemnation not only for one ethnic group in Bosnia's war, but the whole nation of Serbia was now held responsible for Bosnia's darkest chapter and 'Europe's worst atrocity since World War II'.[3] This type of discursive transition is organized around 'a denunciation mode of emotional commitment in relation to distant suffering' (Boltanski, 1999: 91). In Höijer's (2004: 522) terms, 'human suffering is considered unjust and compassion is combined with indignation and anger and turned into an accusation of the perpetrator'. Needless to say, the citizens responded anew to the video with condemnation and disgust. Apart from opening up a space for social critique, the visual representation of the executions revealed the voices that have been silenced for a very long time. The mother of one of the youngest victims, **Azmir Alispahić (sixteen years old)**, recalls the moment she saw the video:

Extract 2

When the truck came up, all that was there were rocks and bushes, I was at that place. The truck stops, they start throwing them out, three of them, when the fourth came, I screamed: 'There goes my Haska (Azmir)'. They took him out and asked him: 'Have you ever been with a woman?' He said: 'No sir', and they told him: 'Well you never will be'. My daughter was next to me, I cried out as hard as I could, and then I fainted.

(Nura Alispahić, 2017)[4]

As Halbwachs (1980: 51) notes, personal memory is not 'completely sealed off and isolated'. The moment Nura's words entered public space, her memory became socially relevant and synergic. In Kansteiner's (2002: 190) terms, 'individual memories assume collective relevance only when they are structured, represented, and used in a social setting'. Hence, a mother's story became a part of the collective trauma fused with the public memory, echoing in Bosnia-Herzegovina, and beyond, to this day. The grip is perhaps best explained by Cathy Caruth's (1991: 192) observation that 'trauma is never simply one's own because we are implicated in each other's trauma'. But besides crushing people's spirits, violence leaves marks on physical space as well, soaking in affect, emotions and feelings. Trauma, pain, the uncanny, are all deeply imprinted in the material world. Schramm (2011: 5) puts it simply like this:

> [T]he memory of violence is not only embedded in peoples' bodies and minds but also inscribed onto space in all kinds of settings: memorials, religious shrines, border zones or the natural environment.

Take, for example, the following instance of memory working its way into the social fabric and physical space more specifically. Every year on 17 July, local citizens visit the foliage which endures the act of execution. Today, the place is completely empty – not a single sign, a monument, a trace pointing to the brutal killings – nothing. It goes hand in hand with the contemporary genocide denial blazing in the country. Since no signs give voice to violence, visitors create a monument with banners showing the video stills and with flowers laid on the ground they call *blood-soaked*. It is precisely such concrete material sites marked by violence but deliberately left unrecognized by those who control the public space, that come to be established as an important part of Bosnia-Herzegovina's contemporary landscapes. Places that are discursively bound by traumatic repetitions like this one, Tumarkin (2001: 12) calls *traumascapes* – 'places marked by traumatic legacies of violence, suffering and loss'. Such sites are important and visited precisely because people know they are real as they link violence and the place of its occurrence – 'a kind of surplus of meaning, a symbolic power' (Violi, 2017: 194). In this sense, the places like the site of execution in Trnovo are not simply 'containers or screens to which memories are attached' (Argenti and Schramm, 2010: 25), but they powerfully work as memory on its own. This autobiographically informed short story aims at demonstrating how war memory is implicated in the production of complex, affect-filled spaces and discourses of remembering. Such discursive and semiotic manifestations of war memory have in common a particular function that I am interested in – they point to the existence and evolution of the sites of trauma or *traumascapes*. Bosnia-Herzegovina's burdens are everywhere to be found – in personal stories, material objects, empty space; and how they 'work' and what they 'do' is what this book is about.

Introducing Bosnia-Herzegovina: Pre- and post-war in brief

The answer to 'When did the Bosnian tragedy start?' is a difficult one. Violence and tragedies, deeply rooted in its ancestral differences, are something the whole history of Bosnia-Herzegovina is marked by. In order to understand the ethnic and religious divisions of present-day Bosnia-Herzegovina, one needs to go back in time to the period of the Ottoman Empire when Islam was brought to this part of the Balkans. From the fourteenth century onwards, the area of present-day Bosnia-Herzegovina was split between the Christian Catholic and Orthodox faiths, and Islam (Shaw, 1976). In the following section, I outline a brief overview of Bosnia-Herzegovina's history fully based on Glenny (2000). With the arrival of the Ottomans some of the population converted to Islam, while the others did not. This in turn created and maintained the tensions that we see to this day due to the class divisions within the Ottoman Empire where it was the Muslims that had certain rights and privileges that the Christian population was denied. The late Ottoman rule in the nineteenth century saw many uprisings both from the local Muslim landowners against the central power in Istanbul, but also in large part from the Orthodox Serbs. The uprisings led to a certain level of independence from the Ottoman Empire for the Serbs who had already started to develop the idea of Greater Serbia, encompassing all areas where the Orthodox Christians were present including Bosnia-Herzegovina and parts of Croatia, while the Croats also had their ideas of a Greater Croatia. The solution was the establishment of the Kingdom of Serbs, Croats and Slovenes, later becoming the Kingdom of Yugoslavia, after the First World War and the defeat of the Ottoman Empire. The unification did not stop the tensions, the legacy of centuries of religious division culminated during the Second World War. The Germans and Italians after occupying Croatia, Bosnia-Herzegovina and Serbia established the Ustashe puppet regime and the Independent State of Croatia which controlled both Croatia and Bosnia-Herzegovina with sections of the Muslim population collaborating with the Ustashe. This resulted in large-scale atrocities over the Serb population in Croatia and Bosnia-Herzegovina, with the Jasenovac concentration camp being particularly prominent. This cemented the hatred between the Croats and Serbs, but also the Serbs and Muslims whose conflict extends to the time of the Ottomans when religion determined a person's position in society and ethnicity was not as relevant. That is why when the Bosnian Serb general Ratko Mladić entered Srebrenica he spoke of revenge against the Turks, equating the Muslim population to the Ottoman Turks:

> We present this city to the Serbian people as a gift. Finally, after the rebellion against the Dahis [local janissary leaders], the time has come to take revenge on the Turks in this region.
> (Ratko Mladić quoted in Duijzings, 2007: 142)

The two major resistance groups to the Axis occupation were the communist Partisans starting in Serbia and expanding the resistance to Bosnia-Herzegovina and Croatia, and the royalist Chetniks primarily in Serbia. The Chetniks were concerned with saving the Serbian people and focused on defending majority Serb villages with their ultimate goal being Greater Serbia, in the end in an effort to avoid German retaliation they attempted to collaborate with the Nazi regime. The Partisans, on the other hand, were communists with their ultimate goal being a united Yugoslavia and therefore accepted Serbs and Croats, as well as Muslims into their ranks, unlike the Chetniks who hated the Croats equating them with the Ustashe and hated the Muslims for their collaboration and Ottoman past. The Chetniks and the Partisans collaborated in fighting the Germans up until the point the Chetniks realized that resisting the occupation was resulting in large-scale executions of thousands of Serbs by the Germans in occupied villages and towns. This was exemplified in the Kragujevac massacre and Hitler's orders to execute 100 Serbs for every German soldier killed, and execute 50 for every wounded. The rhetoric is eerily similar to the statement Aleksandar Vučić made in 1995, only in his case it was 100 Muslims for every Serb killed. The Chetniks blamed the Partisans for the massacres which led to a conflict between them. At the end of the war as the Germans were defeated and Partisans gained control of large parts of Serbia, Croatia and Bosnia-Herzegovina, the Ustashe regime and thousands of civilian Croats attempted to flee to Austria fearing retaliation by the communist Partisans. Their fear was justified as soldiers and civilians alike were considered Ustashe and tens of thousands were killed including women and children near the small Austrian town of Bleiburg. After the Second World War, the South Slavs attempted to unite once more, choosing their South Slavic origin rather than religion as the primary identity under the banner of communism and socialism with the Partisan leader Josip Broz Tito at the head of the Socialist Federal Republic of Yugoslavia. The Ustashe and the Chetniks were considered war criminals and were hunted down by the authorities, some were imprisoned, killed and many were released due to the very large number of those accused. Yugoslavia persisted throughout the post-war period and had also become an economic powerhouse in the region. On a diplomatic level it refused to accept Soviet hegemony with Tito often resisting Stalin when it came to international policy. Yugoslavia was also the founder of the non-aligned movement, bringing together many countries around the world that chose not to align themselves with either the Western powers or the Soviet bloc. Such a position between the East and the West enabled rapid economic development and the majority of the population supported the government, in particular the iconic leader Tito. Although the problems between the different ethnic groups persisted, it was Tito's power and popular support that kept nationalistic tendencies suppressed. The power was primarily manifested through the Yugoslavian secret police, although the fact that the majority of its officers were Serbs perpetuated the tensions. Another important factor in maintaining the tensions was the uneven economic development of the country with Slovenia and Croatia being the most developed. In fact, in the 1960s it was Croatia that was providing 40 per cent of Yugoslavia's foreign currency earnings mainly through tourism, but all revenue went to the central power in Belgrade to be distributed as the government saw fit. In 1971, over 50 per cent of the Zagreb city police force was Serbian while being only 15 per cent of Croatia's population. For the Serbs this was insurance against the resurgence of Ustashe, while for the Croats this represented the remnants of the Greater Serbia idea.

Due to the economic crisis in the 1970s resulting in hundreds of thousands of Yugoslavian guest-workers coming back from Western Europe, Yugoslavia was forced to borrow heavily, and the country was $18.5 billion in debt. Following Tito's death in 1980, many predicted the dissolution of Yugoslavia, however neither the NATO nor the Soviet Union were in favour of a destabilized Yugoslavia potentially in a civil war. With the fall of the Berlin Wall Yugoslavia became much less relevant. The heavy burden of the past atrocities remained somewhat repressed up until the 1980s, culminating in nationalist pre-war propaganda. The Serb population was propagandized with stories of Albanians in Kosovo attacking the minority Serb population, and also with the return of Ustashe in Croatia, while the Croat and Muslim populations feared the return of Chetniks. Up until the 1960s, the Muslim population in Bosnia-Herzegovina did not have a national identity, they were primarily considered by Serbs to be Muslim Serbs and for the Croats they were Muslim Croats. What happened during Yugoslavia was a national awakening among large parts of the Muslim population leading to their recognition as a separate nation in 1963. The move was intended to stifle the competition between the Serbs and Croats for the loyalty of the Muslims in Bosnia, however it resulted in Muslims essentially being considered Turks in the 1990s war and subject to hostilities from both the Serbs and Croats.

The war between Croatia and Serbia began in 1991 following massive nationalist propaganda, focusing particularly on the victims in Bleiburg and Jasenovac. For a time, Bosnia-Herzegovina remained relatively peaceful, all the while, even though already at war, the Serb leader Slobodan Milošević and the Croatian leader Franjo Tuđman planned its division between Serbia and Croatia. The president of Bosnia-Herzegovina, Alija Izetbegović at the time, with the encouragement of the United States, opted for a referendum on Bosnia-Herzegovina's independence from Yugoslavia which was boycotted by the Bosnian Serb population. Following the referendum, in 1992 the three ethnic groups were at war in Bosnia-Herzegovina, at first the Croats and Bosnian Muslims were loosely allied against the Serb aggression which was empowered by the Yugoslav National Army (JNA) weapons. This was mostly due to the fact that the majority of the officers in the army were Serbs and had prepared for the war by moving large amounts of weaponry and ammunition to the Bosnian Serb controlled areas. From late 1992 to early 1994 all three sides were engaged in battles against each other in different parts of the country, and in 1994 the Croats and Bosnian Muslims agreed to cease hostilities and focus on defeating the Bosnian Serbs. To add to this quagmire of hostilities in north-western Bosnia, some parts of the Muslim population were allied with the Serbs and fought against other Muslims. Overall, ethnic cleansing was rampant culminating with the genocide in Srebrenica in 1995 when the Bosnian Serbs and paramilitary units from Serbia massacred over 8,000 Muslim men.

Figure 7 illustrates only a fragment of war horrors brought to civilians who were affected tremendously by chronic and widespread deprivation, hunger,

Figure 7 Detainees in the Manjača camp near Banja Luka © UN International Criminal Tribunal for the former Yugoslavia 2009. Source: https://www.flickr.com/photos/icty/14377430247/in/photolist-nUu67p-peUaY5-8mENEZ

the loss of dignity, fear and trauma. It shows captured civilians in one of the notorious concentration camps run by Bosnian Serb forces which were set up for Bosnian Muslims and Croats located around the Prijedor area. And although the figure itself does not even begin to portray the scope and brutality of the crimes committed there, in such concentration camps, 'detainees were subjected to regular beatings' 'inflicted by fists, feet, batons, wooden poles, rifle butts and electric cables. In some cases the beatings were so severe as to result in permanent serious injury and deaths'.[5] The war finally ended with the signing of the Dayton Agreement in November of 1995 and the creation of the state of Bosnia-Herzegovina being composed of two entities. The Bosnian Serbs got their Republic of Srpska with 49 per cent of the territory and the Bosnian Croats and Bosnian Muslims formed the Federation of Bosnia-Herzegovina with 51 per cent of the territory, the entities were granted significant independence. The actual demographics remain highly contested to this day, with the first population census after the war coming only in 2013. The results of that census have not been accepted by the Republic of Srpska.[6] The Dayton agreement remains contested and discussed to this day, its inadequacies evident in the utter inability of Bosnia-Herzegovina politicians to agree on anything more than their desire to remain in power. And now, after the war, the holy trinity of victimhood is complete with the Serbs having their holy place of Jasenovac where Serbs were slaughtered, the Croats having their Bleiburg where Croats were slaughtered by the communists, and Bosnian Muslims have their Srebrenica marking the return of the Chetniks. With many citizens still unable to let go of the past (and many of them justifiably), the competition for victimhood and moral high ground sees no end in sight. Every election cycle is marked with the different ethnic political parties bringing back the memories of all these atrocities and stoking hatred and resentment towards the other groups. The parties present their respective ethnic groups as constantly endangered and threatened by the others urging the voters that they, the original ethnic party, are the only ones who can protect them from the vicious others. Such a political situation along with rampant corruption has led to massive economic stagnation with very high unemployment numbers and the continuing exodus of the young workable population. The country, in which an externally imposed peace deal has stopped the violence, rather than the free will of the leaders of different ethnic groups, is additionally burdened by its traumascapes. A fragile peace continues to be tested, particularly nowadays with ethnic tensions rising and public discourse marked by persistent discussions about 'independence' referendums, heating up ideas of a further breakup of Bosnia-Herzegovina and a new armed conflict.

1

Contemporary Perspectives on Traumascapes

Theories this book builds upon are framed as discursive and semiotic enquiries of remembering which predominantly, but not exclusively, rely on 'raw' material memory in physical space, and thus are situated under the umbrella of *memoryscapes* research. Back in 1984, Pierre Nora traced *the sites of memory* (*Les Lieux de Mémoire*) in French national culture, arguing that the nation is the primary framework for the constitution of collective memory, identity and imagined community of the nation. Nora (1984) argued that French national (collective) memory took the shape of institutions, events, memorials, a histography of landscapes and language – all meaningfully constituting sites of memory. Nora's influential body of work establishes the *terminus a quo* for understanding the perplexing interconnectedness of memory, space and language. This is why a critical engagement with Nora's theorisation is pivotal for the study of different kinds of *memoryscapes* (Weedon and Jordan, 2012). The term *memoryscape* comes from Appadurai's (1996: 33) explorations of global ethnoscapes, mediascapes, technoscapes, financescapes and ideoscapes 'inflected by the historical, linguistic, and political situatedness of different sorts of actors'. The notion of *-scapes* also works as a reference to 'a world of flows' which include 'ideas and ideologies, people and goods, images and messages, technologies and techniques' (Appadurai, 2001: 5). Along these lines, Phillips and Reyes (2011: 13) define memoryscape as 'a complex landscape upon which memories and memory practices move, come into contact, are contested by, and contest other forms of remembrance'. Following LaCapra (1998) who posited that the sites of memory are generally 'sites of trauma', I consider the role of trauma in shaping the physical environment and the ways people remember. In this sense, when a place has been hit by countless traumatic episodes, just like an individual overpowered by a deeply traumatic experience, it cannot function 'normally' and becomes what Maria Tumarkin (2005) calls a *traumascape*. But before turning to traumascapes thoroughly, I want to place the next section strictly within the literature that considers the multiplex ways remembering and trauma are bound up with language. It is in this way that I lay out the theoretical basis of the general approach I take, as well as ground my interpretations of traumascapes.

Language, discourse and remembering

It can be said that contemporary sociolinguistics and discourse studies' interests in language and remembering were initiated back in the 1970s when cognitive linguists attentive to explaining the creation of meanings rejected Chomsky's (1965) idea about the separation of the two phenomena. The main postulates of cognitive linguistics emphasize that language is not different from the rest of cognition; it is based on conceptual mechanisms, embodied and situated in the environment (Perlovsky, 2009). Thus, language is complexly correlated with many aspects of cognition, including memory – a cognitive process and a sociophysical experience whose nature is deeply linguistic/communicative (Levinson, 2003). A relationship between the two is an inherent property of human mental capacities and central to any research of remembering, as Edwards and Middleton (1987: 89) and Edwards and Potter (1992: 35) explain:

> [T]he importance of language is compounded as soon as memories are communicated, as soon as one person's remembering becomes another person's experience; joint versions of events are negotiated in discourse and are subject therefore to the dictates of whatever sort of discourse it is.
>
> For discourse analysis, remembering is studied as action, with the report itself taken as an act of remembering, and studied as a constructed, occasioned version of events. It is studied directly as discourse, rather than taken as a window upon something else.

Just as the two quotes above indicate, it is precisely through the processes of communicating and accessing memories that we get to understand this – the act of remembering and its mediation, in the broadest sense, is done and understood with the assistance of language and discourse (Achugar, 2008). Cognitive social psychology proposing clear-cut connections between language/communication and memory, focused on both individual (autobiographical) and collective memory, but the experimental studies did not rely on linguistic or discursive approaches which would complement the strict psychological perspective (Bietti, 2011). However, Edwards and Middleton's (1986) highly influential piece on memory (*Joint remembering: constructing an account of shared experience through conversational discourse*) introduced a new strand of analytical discourse exploration by recognizing that conversational discourse produces practices of memory-making that always emerge from experience situated in communicative interactions in which speakers perform remembering. This qualitative piece of discourse investigation in psychology, along with Potter and Wetherell's (1987) *Discourse and Social Psychology* which also had a major impact across the social and human sciences, is known as the key landmark in the field of discursive psychology. Analysing different forms of talk and writing, Potter's (1996) *Discourse and Cognition* and Edwards's (1997) *Representing Reality* established three main principles of future scholarly work: (1) discourse is constructed and constructive through linguistic building blocks like words, categories, idioms, repertoires, etc.; (2) discourse is action-oriented since while talking and writing we are primarily carrying out actions; (3) discourse is situated within a specific sequential environment since words are understood according to what precedes and follows them (Potter and Wiggins, 2007). The research on conversational remembering done by the leading discourse psychologists demonstrated that memory/remembering has its basis in discourse and human interactions understood as 'part of the essentially human activity of constructing shared mentality' (Edwards and Middleton, 1987: 90). Consulting the seminal pieces of cognitive social psychologists and discourse psychologists, Bietti (2011) introduced a new integrative approach to memory research which seeks to synthesize linguistic, discursive and cognitive perspectives exploring the ways in which processes of memory-making are situated and mediated in the 'real world' settings. Bietti's (2014) work which investigates the discursive acts of remembering related to the 1976–83 military dictatorship in Argentina, exhaustively brings these perspectives together. Drawing upon the tradition of discursive psychologists primarily interested in remembering in family conversational contexts, Bietti (2010) previously investigated the ways in which socially shared knowledge of the military dictatorship is communicated in private settings. His studies, in which he followed the lead of discourse analysts like Schiffrin (1996), Georgakopolou (2007), Tannen (2007) and van Dijk (2009), showed that the act of remembering is dynamic and malleable precisely by means of discursive epistemic strategies (such as *presuppositions, implicatures, justifications, rejections* and *reminders* of shared knowledge of the past). Studies like Bietti's pointing to the key role that language and the socio-physical environments in which people remember the past have in remembering processes, cannot be overestimated in positioning memory in the field of discourse studies, and semiotic landscapes, respectively. Needless to say, investigations of remembering processes related to periods of (political) violence provide an even more important theoretical ground for this book.

Recent years have seen the rise of widespread interest in memory and remembering practices and their relation to the (re)production of ideologies, power, dominance, political economies and inequality. How do the discourses of remembering constitute and transmit knowledge of the past; organize social institutions and exercise power; are employed in the construction of national identities and diasporic communities; affect conflict, amnesty and reconciliation; pervade local dimensions and counteract banalization; privilege some while subordinating others – these are only some of the questions regarding the 'grand memory narratives' which enriched and transformed the ways memory is approached discursively. In discourse studies in particular, scholars became interested in exploring broader contexts and various modes within which remembering, as a discursive, socio-cultural and political construct, is integrated into everyday life. In a number of contributions, this meant the extension of individual micro-processes of remembering in intimate settings (e.g. *oral histories* in Schiffrin, 2003) to collective forms of remembering in public spaces including whole assemblages of people and realized in a variety of modes (i.e. trials, tribunals, monuments, museums, commemorative speeches, protests, etc.) (e.g. Wodak and Auer Borea, 2009). In discourse studies, memory needs to be subjected to critical scrutiny because in recent decades, as Weedon and Jordan (2012) explain, collective memory shaped by specific interests and power relations has become a site of contestation for a wide range of different interest groups. Studies investigating the relationship between discourse, remembering and traumatic past have been compiled and published in the special issues and volumes like *Discourse and Human Rights Violations* (*Journal of Language and Politics*) edited by Anthonissen and Blommaert (2006) who bring together pieces that view language as an instrument of confronting a traumatic past, of negotiating conflict and of initiating processes of healing for individuals and communities. The discourses investigated by linguists and other scholars are generated during the hearings of the South African Truth and Reconciliation Commission (TRC) – a well-known Government-initiated reconciliation process. Interdisciplinary in nature, these studies focus on the micro and macro aspects of texts produced in/through the official processes of dealing with traumatic pasts. Anthonissen (2006), for example, explains that topics which relate to the uses and abuses of power give us an insight into how language mediates memory represented in the stories of humiliation, abuse, loss and trauma. The discursive construction of personal and national reconciliation, and its role in building 'a peaceful and unified future', appears in *Discourse, History and Memory* edited by Wodak and Richardson (2009) (*Critical Discourse Studies*). This collection investigates the politics of remembering by demonstrating how remembering is discursively constructed and promoted in the public sphere. Here, the focus is on the potential analytical use of the concepts like collective memory and trauma when exploring in-group suffering, as well as on the aspects of commemorative speeches in relation to political regimes. Another volume edited by Wodak and Auer Borea (2009), deals with the many aspects and consequences of commemorating the past through remembrance events. In this collection, authors discuss how European and non-European nation states manage or fail to come to terms with their traumatic pasts by exploring verbal commemorative practices, discursive realization of specific periods of history and how they are commemorated, and what the goals/consequences of commemorative events are. The studies in this collection mostly focus on the Nazi past, right-wing politics in Austria and the UK. The volume which is considered to be the most exhaustive one when it comes to exploring the multiple aspects of the discourses of remembering is certainly Wodak et al. (2009) iconic piece on the discursive construction of national identity. Wodak and colleagues' work analyses various discourses of remembering produced in/through Austrian post-war commemorative speeches and addresses, media texts, focus groups and qualitative interviews. Introducing the media constructions of public memory and national commemorative practices, they approach the spoken and written instances of remembering as the sites of collective memory that generate, reduplicate and question historically significant shared experiences. Their critical discourse analysis explains the remembering-nationalism relationship, pointing out that collective memory is an ideological representation of national identity. It also discovers a number of key linguistic aspects and forms (topics, discursive strategies and linguistic means) which are central to the construction process of national identities and brings to light the inextricable relationship between remembering and nationalism. Moving things to Latin America, in her work on the construction of memory in military discourse, Achugar (2008) analyses a wide spectrum of remembering texts about the Uruguayan dictatorship (from 1973 to 1985) (historical accounts, editorials from a monthly military publication, letters to the editor, press releases, a series of articles from periodicals and commemoration speeches). The study presents a detailed investigation of the public remembering approached as a discursive practice, a social practice and a mediation of other social practices, with a special focus on intertextuality, genre, lexicogrammar and discursive semantic levels. Achugar (2008) argues that the discourse she investigated is a principal semiotic system for the construction of institutional memories, but the mechanisms necessary for the transgenerational transmission of the web of these memories are complex and refer to other semiotic resources:

> Semiotic systems mediate between the experience and the memory of it. What is remembered is not the experience itself but its record through semiotic systems that allow us to attribute meaning to that experience. The process of remembering voluntarily is characterized by the use of semiotic elements that assist in the remembering. This process is dynamic and permeable to the context where it is constructed. The use of semiotic elements in the construction of memory makes the social always present even in individual memories.
> (Achugar, 2008: 198)

In a like manner, Wodak and Auer Borea (2009) explain that individuals do not remember on their own but through gestures, phrases, objects, visual images, architecture and landscapes that surround them as they grow up. In this sense, memory flows across language, space and bodies, without residing in a single place or a single moment. As any discursive phenomenon, whether accomplished in/through written or spoken discourse, memory interacts with other discursive modalities (Jaworski and Thurlow, 2010). Space and memory are especially enmeshed and mutually constitutive (McIlvennya and Noy, 2011). Associated with and embodied in public space, memory inevitably becomes objectified in monuments, museums, burial sites or ruins (Alexander, 2004), and thus a background feature of our everyday landscapes (Abousnnouga, 2012). Against this backdrop, the established field of linguistic landscapes (Landry and Bourhis, 1997) or semiotic landscapes (Jaworski and Thurlow, 2010) with space, multimodal and mediated discourse at the heart of investigation, gave birth to research focusing on the significance of the spatial dimension of memory and the affective experience of remembering. Following Jacques Leclerc (1989), Landry and Bourhis (1997: 25) propose that 'the language of public road signs, advertising billboards, street names, place names, commercial shop signs, and public signs on government buildings combines to form the linguistic landscape of a given territory, region, or urban agglomeration'. Collection which undoubtedly enriches the methodology when it comes to the investigation of memory and offers new ways of investigating remembering through its various modes and modalities, is certainly the special issue *Memory and Memorialization* published in the *Linguistic Landscape* Journal (2016). Ben-Rafael (2016: 1) opens the issue by stating that 'collective memory and remembrance are arenas of conflicts of political interest, clashes of ideologies or antagonisms of religious beliefs'. Studies dedicated to memory and (counter-) memorials offer a close-up examination of semiotic aspects and social contexts which imprint different ideologies, design regimes and discourses in public space – political, educational, as well as discourses of war, suffering, exclusion and contestation. In this sense, they suggest that memorials should be approached as the domains of struggle among competing political, nationalistic and ideological interests. Blackwood and Macalister's (2019) edited volume *Multilingual Memories: Monuments, Museums and the Linguistic Landscape* broadens the field by critically engaging with memory, remembering and multilingualism. Acknowledging the affective dimensions of remembering in public space, the volume examines how multi-layered and multidimensional memory places are complexly engaged with 'the multilingual realities of the communities that commission, construct and challenge them' (Blackwood and Macalister, 2019: 1). Semiotic landscapes, introduced more recently, intensely draw attention to the importance of looking at different meaning-making systems interacting with human intervention and experience when investigating signage in public space:

> [T]he richness of the public space demands attention to a broad list of components that participate in public spaces, interactively. These components include in addition to written texts in multiple languages also components such as visual objects, sounds, movements, geographical location, and people. These are not static but rather are parts of other layers that interact in the space as 'practiced', 'conceived' and 'lived' (Lefebvre, 1991) with all the complexities involved of power, domination, marginalization, contestations and negotiations.
> (Shohamy, 2015: 168)

Along the lines above, semiotic landscapes (Jaworski and Thurlow, 2010) emphasize the multimodal nature of landscapes and the delicate interconnectedness of language, (public) space, discursive modalities (visual images, nonverbal communication, architecture and the built environment) and affect (Milani and Richardson, 2021). In Jaworski and Thurlow's (2010) edited collection expanding linguistic landscapes, emerged studies that point us to the semiotic and communicative resources by which people remember. These studies indicate collective representations of the past as constituted in/through different semiotic resources and the complex politics of public remembering. Abousnnouga and Machin (2010) offer an examination of the First World War and contemporary British war memorials, demonstrating different discourses and legitimations of warfare, national unity, heroism and sacrifice. Elana Shohamy and Shoshi Waksman (2010) explore the meanings of the Ha'apala memorial commemorating Jewish migration to Palestine between 1934 and 1948. Through an analysis of its emplacement, design, the photographs, their titles and multilingual written texts, and the visitors who activate and negotiate the meaning, they reveal a range of competing narratives of migration, nationhood, ethnicity, collective remembering and exclusion. As an ideological, materialized text emplaced in a tourist and leisure spot the memorial is intended to tell different groups of visitors a story about an important period of migration for Jewish people who built a nation. At the same time, Israeli Arabs are not referred to in the texts at the site, and thus are completely excluded. Their non-existence is made evident by the absence of the Arabic language anywhere on the site even though Arabic was an official language in Israel for over seventy years (up until 19 June 2018), and is also the first language of Arabs living in Israel. Shohamy and Waksman explain that these 'controlled' tourist sites and such a presentation of 'historical truth' could potentially result in visitors objecting to 'being fed' and/or indoctrinated. Following Jaworski and Thurlow's (2010) compelling anthology, Abousnnouga and Machin (2013) brought out an in-depth multimodal critical discourse analysis of war memorials, focusing on the process of recontextualization through material semiotic choices. Considering the meaning potentials, they reveal how space is implicated in the construction, naturalization and maintenance of nationalism, collective ideals and moral order. The theme of commemoration also appears in *The Cultural Politics of Memory*, edited by Chris Weedon and Glenn Jordan (2012) (*Social Semiotics*). Drawing on theoretical insights by Halbwachs (1992), Ricoeur (2004), Nora (1989) and Hirsch (1999), studies in this issue focus on the role of cultural institutions and practices in constituting national collective memory which is 'challenged and augmented by a range of interest groups, often not previously included in hegemonic constructions of the nation, who are fighting to have their histories acknowledged, documented and commemorated, with the aim, in part, of reshaping national stories' (Weedon and Jordan, 2012: 144). The issue deals with the relationship between cultural and collective memory, cultural politics of memory, and what motivates nations to remember, especially regarding marginalized groups, as well as the concepts of counter-memory, post-memory and forgetting. Situating memory in the field of social semiotics, the contributions profile different semiotic, spatial and interactional resources that are inextricably linked to remembering practices. This is also evident in Richardson's (2021) study closely investigating the politics of applause at the 2019 Holocaust Memorial Day national ceremony in Britain, and showing how the discourse of commemoration and audience reactions are complexly intertwined affective practices. Setting the direction for this book, the above-mentioned theorizing and writing frames memory as a distinct aspect of discourse analytic, multimodal and semiotic enquiry. The key methodology of this book is based upon the kinds of principles proposed in the foregoing contributions accentuating remembering as a significant form of discourse approached and analysed in myriad ways. The book is placed precisely within such body of work defining the discourses of remembering as organic assemblages of different modes pointing to tense and precarious spaces.

Trauma-scapes

Brought to people primarily through extensive media coverage (e.g. images of forced migration, natural disasters, terrorist attacks), trauma (industry) has permeated our everyday lives and the contemporary humanistic social sciences, becoming one of the interdisciplinary idioms along with the cognitive constructs of remembering, healing and forgetting. Especially in the fields of history, literature, cultural studies and fine art, trauma is privileged as a route through which scholars examine 'cultural issues of experience, memory, the body, and representation' (Wallis and Duggan, 2011: 1). The way it is universally embedded in media discourse is nicely captured in the remark by anthropologist Alexander Hinton (2002: 22) who observes how one of the tropes of genocide is that it travels through civilizational boundaries, foregrounding our needs to 'witness', consume and make sense of (our own) trauma:

> In the mass media, the victims of genocide are frequently condensed into an essentialized portrait of the universal sufferer, an image that can be… (re)broadcast to global audiences who see their own potential trauma reflected in this simulation of the modern subject.

The emergence and mediation of trauma within different discursive terrains broadens and complicates the already perplexing concept. The very idea of trauma is becoming incrementally knotty and the word 'trauma', as Di Nicola

(2018: 25) notes, has become 'too (am)bivalent and polysemous, too deterministic and fatalistic an idea'. One of the most famous proponents of trauma studies, Dominick LaCapra (2001: 96) argues, 'no genre or discipline "owns" trauma as a problem or can provide definite boundaries for it'. For this book's purposes, I draw on the scholarship increasingly attentive to the spatial, affective and material dimensions of trauma. Accordingly, I do not address trauma as used in the domain of psychiatry, psychology, psychoanalysis and clinical context. In Cathy Caruth's (1996: 4) terms:

> Trauma seems to be much more than a pathology, or the simple illness of a wounded psyche: it is always the story of a wound that cries out, that addresses us in the attempt to tell us of a reality or truth not otherwise available.

Caruth (1995: 4) herself is 'interested not so much in further defining trauma, that is, than in attempting to understand its surprising impact: to examine how trauma unsettles and forces us to rethink our notions of experience'. At the same time, we might ask which experiences exactly come under the category 'traumatic'? Nonetheless, all this makes the concept especially thought-provoking for language scholars who are challenged to clarify theoretical and methodological aporia, and the ways in which all of us are delicately entangled in trauma, as LaCapra (2016: xxxi) poetically suggests:

> There is an important sense in which the after-effects – the hauntingly possessive ghosts – of traumatic events are not fully owned by anyone and, in various ways, affect everyone.

Although principally associated with clinical uses to approach an individual's overwhelming experience of psychological suffering, trauma studies scholars like Shoshana Felman (2002), Judith Herman (1992) and Lawrence Langer (1991) – to name just a few, treat trauma not only as a psychological, but a socio-political category and ultimately, a discursive act. Notably, trauma is organized and produced through testimonies as a genre that 'cuts across the oral and the written' (LaCapra, 2016: 381). To be even more thorny, trauma subsists as a certain event is being recalled (even when denying the impact of that experience). Theoretical underpinnings of testimonies as trauma narratives come to be understood through the recognition of a victim's voice in a courtroom. In her seminal work on trials and traumas in the twentieth century, Felman (2002) puts the whole history of Nazi genocide and persecution of European Jews through a critical examination. Observing the relationship between justice and trauma,

Felman scrutinizes the 1961 trial of Adolf Eichmann which was different from all the Nuremberg trials prosecuting Nazi officials precisely because it privileged the oral testimony of victims. This trial is of crucial importance since it represents the first historical revolution by the victims and how their voices came to be heard for the first time. Ultimately, it shows how people can confront their violent history in a public space through the expression of collective injury which is extremely hard and sometimes impossible to express in the first place. Inspired by such observations, trauma theorists convincingly argue that testimonies produce a particular kind of life narrative filled with 'the potent mixture of words and images as survivors publicly recount their most private experiences' (Schiff et al., 2001: 163). Frequent failure to rigorously define the linguistic mechanisms of trauma is indisputable and perhaps a result of (language) scholars avoiding the commitment to engage such a messy concept. However, concrete grounds for a discursive approach to trauma seem to be laid by Caruth (1996) who reminds us that victim narratives do not simply point to the unjustified violence done to the innocent but reconfirm the significance of those who listen to these stories and who are affected by them (also called *supplementary witnesses* (Levin, 2006)). By rethinking its (therapeutic) relation to language, Caruth (1996) proposes that trauma is inevitably implicated in the so-called *discourses of healing* conceptualized as dialogues in which people attempt to recount their experiences via the written or spoken word (Thompson, 2004). More importantly, it is precisely through such considerations that we come to recognize storytelling as the key to accessing trauma as a valid articulation of (in)direct trauma memories in language. In the field of linguistics, the legitimization of storytelling as a narrative structure of past experience is due to Labov and Waletzky (1967) who enabled scholars from a wide range of humanistic disciplines, and beyond, to explore complex socio-cultural processes through such a form of communication. Perhaps even Labov (1972) himself inadvertently set the ground for further work on trauma narratives with one of his influential papers on how black youth in New York dealt with difficult experiences in their stories. Drawing heavily on Labov and Waletzky's (1967) influential model of narrative privileging the personal, the emotive and the experiential dimensions of a storytelling event, narrative research was especially fruitful in analysing trauma discourse during the 1990s (e.g. life stories of Holocaust survivors (Dwork, 1991), war memories of young Israeli men (Lomski-Feder, 1995), traumatic experiences of captivity (Lieblich, 1994), life stories of raped refugee women (Agger, 1994)). A limited number of contemporary discourse studies exploring Holocaust narratives (e.g. Schiff et al., 2001; Schiffrin, 2002) reconfirmed that trauma stories are not simply one's attempts to work through difficult experiences. Accomplished as 'socially mediated attributions' (Alexander, 2004), life stories are not only useful in order to grasp the consequence and meaning of trauma in people's lives, but to learn more about the complex disruptive forces of the social milieu in the long term. In other words, stories show how personal experiences of everyday life and reformulations of the past intersect with broader domains of socio-political and moral meanings (Schiffrin, 2002). In the same vein, Leydesdorff and colleagues (2002: 13) straightforwardly observe the richness and complexity of this genre:

> It gives the opportunity to explore the relation between personal and collective experience, by focusing on remembering and forgetting as cultural processes. It also offers a means of making sense and interpreting the experience of marginalized peoples and forgotten histories. It allows us to explore the relation between individual memories and testimonies, and the wider public contexts, cultural practices, and forms of representation that shape the possibilities of their telling and their witnessing.

Considering its social significance, trauma does not exclusively arise from a single traumatic event but also from a persisting social condition (Erikson, 1994) and it is only fully evident from a different place and time (Caruth, 1991). In LaCapra's (2001: 186) terms, 'trauma cannot be localized in terms of discrete, dated experience'. Thus, trauma needs to be situated in larger contexts and histories of violence (Schwab, 2010). What particularly makes the generally accepted understanding of trauma problematic is how it is inter- or trans-generationally transmitted to the descendants of both victims and perpetrators whose voices need to be critically attended to. Recognizing that trauma is discursively constructed, and that landscapes are 'discursive terrains' (Daniels and Cosgrove, 1993: 59), we might ask then how is physical environment infused with trauma and how people make sense of trauma in terms of 'lived space' (Lefebvre, 1991) or 'a context for human action and socio-political activity' (Jaworski and Thurlow, 2010: 6). Looking beyond storytelling and narrativity, we find trauma located in space. Violi (2012: 37) introduced the notion of *trauma sites* into the field of semiotics to indicate that trauma is a culturally and semiotically constructed event:

> [Trauma sites are] places characterized by a specific semiotic trait: an indexical link to past traumatic events [and which] exist factually as material testimonies of the violence and horror that took place there.

Violi (2017: 191) explains that the sites of trauma are a result of the process of the 'spatialization of memory' or a semiotic transformation of a public nature where 'a given portion of space is invested with value, semiotically marked and institutionally recognized as a sign of the event in hand'. Through such processes, the places of imprisonment, mass-murder, detention centres or concentration camps, are subsequently transformed into museums or memorials to exhibit and conserve the memory of that particular tragic past. Of course, not all sites of trauma are accomplished and 'exposed' as the sites devoted to memorialization where people learn not to repeat the mistakes of a violent past, as Violi (2017) argues. By trauma site, Violi specifically means a memorial. Since I am interested in more than institutionalized traumatic sites, in a much broader notion of trauma spatialization, in disputed sites of trauma, as well as in the tangible persistence of trauma across time, space and generations, I draw on Tumarkin's (2005) term *traumascapes* as the more appropriate analytical concept unveiling the complex spatial, material and personal articulations of trauma. Tumarkin (2005: 233) argues that traumascapes are physical places realized by ongoing remembering experiences of traumatic events and their aftermath is quintessentially recognized in Bosnia-Herzegovina:

> There are the physical sites of terror attacks, natural and industrial catastrophes, genocide, exile, ecological degradation, and communal loss of heart. They are part of a scar tissue that stretches across the world, from Hiroshima to Auschwitz, Dresden to *Srebrenica, Sarajevo* to New York, Bali, London, Jerusalem, and New Orleans.

Mazzucchelli et al. (2014) also looked at the processes of spatialization or 'the spatial turn' of collective memories of war in Europe. Reconceptualizing their work through a productive feedback between semiotics and other disciplines, they argue that the predominant European war memory represented and recalled is traumatic and linked to political, cultural and ethnic violence. In this regard, the European sites of memory have been named *terrorscapes* defined as 'the places where terror, political or state-perpetrated violence has happened or was prepared – seeking to understand both what happened as well as how the spacetimes of terror are collectively remembered or forgotten' (van der Laarse, 2013). However, as Tumarkin (2005: 12) emphasizes, the concept of traumascapes carries a notion of continuity:

> Full of visual and sensory triggers, capable of eliciting a whole palette of emotions, traumacapes catalyse and shape remembering and reliving of traumatic events. It is through these places that the past, whether buried or laid bare for all to see, continues to inhabit and refashion the present.

Indeed, traumascapes are bound by endless repetitions and thus opposed to closure and forgetting (Tumarkin, 2001). The notion of *–scapes*, as never uniformed or fixed, but rather emergent and constantly (re)produced by people engaged in memory work (Schramm, 2011), is especially related to the dynamic nature of discourses of remembering. Considering the level of competition and contestation around the war memory in Bosnia-Herzegovina (Moll, 2013), the term *–scapes* is crucial in setting the main concept of the book as it indicates complex discursive terrains 'across which the struggle between the different, often hostile, codes of meaning construction has been engaged' (Daniels and Cosgrove, 1993: 59). In this sense, the concept of traumascapes, understood broadly as physical spaces and places marked by traumatic legacies of violence in which the sense of trauma establishes its meanings, comprehensively encompasses the theoretical grounds of this book. Although Tumarkin juxtaposes specific material locations with purposefully created sites of memorialization, she emphasizes a profusion of visual and sensory triggers. Traumascapes 'get to us' differently, as Tumarkin (2019: 5) poignantly writes, stirring 'everything from awe to unease, from fear to epiphany, from a burst of involuntary memories to a sense of deep, all-powerful transformation'. However, just as some locations affect us more than others, a range of traumascapes are marked by the non-existent, the absent, the unwritten and the unsayable in lieu of visual and sensory opulence, as she maintains. The exceptionally contested nature of trauma makes places marked by traumatic legacies of violence sometimes concealed and a place needs more than a monument, a ruin, or material remains, to be designated and valorised a traumascape. Dawson (2016: 137) sees working of traumascapes through the relevance of myriad personal and interpersonal experiences:

> Not all places where traumatic violence has occurred are memoryscapes inscribed with tangible meanings of the past. Some are invisible and subject to material erasure and redevelopment, and to silencing and forgetting within cultural practices; yet they may remain significant in the psychic and somatic experience and living memory of victims and perpetrators, witnesses and the bereaved.

Akin to Dawson, the fact that trajectories of traumascapes are not clear-cut is a very salient theoretical point of this book. This is nicely captured in Aleksandar Hemon's (2013) *The Book of My Lives*, narrating the ruination vignettes of the author's hometown as he traumatically organizes his own diasporic existence. It is his thought-provoking memoir about 'wandering' Sarajevo, wondering 'which buildings would provide good sniper positions' and envisioning himself 'ducking under fire', that remind me to always think 'depth over surface' as people's traumas continue to travel.

2

Turbulent Graffscapes and Linguistic Violence

The beginnings of violence

In the pre-war landscapes of Bosnia-Herzegovina, before urbicide, massive graveyards and war monuments, it was often violent language that took the place of heavy artillery. Words were a weapon for generating hate. As the Bosnian columnist in Extract 1 recalls, in the pre-war period the country's spatial narrations intimated danger on the horizon:

Extract 1

> In Sarajevo, just before the war in Bosnia, no more than 50 meters from Markale Market, at a post office I passed every day on my way to school, graffiti appeared one day: 'This is Serbia'. The very next day, someone added: 'This is the post office, idiot'.[1]

The Guardian extract points directly to the complex nature of Bosnia-Herzegovina's *graffscapes* – that dimension of the linguistic/semiotic landscape constituted by graffiti, typically unauthorized and seen/treated as 'transgressive' (see Pennycook, 2010). Importantly, the same kind of graffiti are still a significant feature of the country's post-war landscape. The piece mentioned above appeared in the centre of the capital where two major massacres occurred during the war. If such graffiti were to appear today on the same façade, 50 meters from what is now known as *Markale Massacre Memorial*, it would almost certainly be promptly removed. Before the war, the country's graffiti attracted much attention, eliciting strong emotional responses, and raising concerns about the potential for deep social disruption. Another newspaper report in Extract 2 gives a different post hoc sense of the intensification of these spatial narrations:

Extract 2

> Many saw it coming. Ethnically charged graffiti began appearing on buildings around town. The local newspapers published the locations of bomb shelters. A classmate told me not to sleep in my bedroom because it faced military barracks. I dismissed these warnings, just as I ignored all other signs of coming doom.
>
> (*New York Times*, 2015)[2]

While some citizens lived in hope that a violent conflict could be avoided, ominous signs started appearing around different cities, carrying messages of social fragmentation. And, as I mean to show in this chapter, the same divisions persist to this day. Like pre-war Bosnia-Herzegovina, words are again the weapon of choice, and, once again, especially in the way they are deployed in space. The divided post-war Bosnia-Herzegovina lacks clear and obvious political boundaries, apart from the 'obligatory' road signs indicating to the travellers that they have entered one of the two largely autonomous entities, the Federation of Bosnia-Herzegovina and the Republic of Srpska. Nonetheless, its three constitutive peoples are undoubtedly separated, and their spaces paint a complex social reality reflected in stories of violence and loss. Forbidding landscapes likewise tell a story of the illusory social unity of these people and their unwillingness, or inability, to come to terms with their violent past. Visual aspects of the divided frontiers, viz. the Serb Republic, Brčko District, central Bosnia and Herzegovina, summon a memory as a present experience, one which is marked in the material spaces of everyday life. Today, in Mostar, the largest city in Herzegovina, the southern region of Bosnia-Herzegovina, one is certain to run into tangible signs of war: riddled façades, dilapidated structures or informal border zones. Even Mostar's number one attraction, the Old Bridge, the soul of the city, has lost its main function of connecting people; instead, it divides the city and its citizens in two: in the west, the Croat part, and in the east, the Bosniak part. Yet, on the surface, we find Mostar as one of Bosnia-Herzegovina's most popular tourist destinations whose past suffering is commercialized through postcards, tourist guidebooks and maps, as we see in Figure 8.

This *dark tourism* (Lennon and Foley, 1996), in a city inundated with eerie leftovers from the war, offers a confusing dichotomy of cordiality and tension. Apart from the commodified suffering which engages people with the busy

Figure 8 War video and photo exhibition in Mostar next to the Old Bridge © Maida Kosatica 2016

tourist spaces of Mostar through exhibitions and video projections for one euro, empty bullet souvenirs, or military uniform pieces, other shadows are cast over this city. Looking beyond the highly visible scars of Mostar and Bosnia-Herzegovina's tourism sites, however, we find evidence of an uncommercialized but emotionally charged form of messaging communicated in/with space: graffiti. In Bosnia-Herzegovina's contested zones, the linguistic landscape produces texts which disturbingly resemble war-period public discourses, and function at the same time as the potential causes and consequences of a generally tense social climate. As one key resource in the linguistic landscape, I examine the graffiti appearing in disputed areas of Bosnia-Herzegovina whose territorial status has been made clear by the Dayton Peace Agreement, but which remain highly contested by different ethnic groups. This chapter aims to bring theoretical and empirical additions to the field of linguistic landscapes by exploring graffiti which manifest and materialize *discourse of violence* – 'language accompanying, reporting and reclaiming acts of violence, possibly leading to violence, or that is itself a violation' (O'Connor, 1995: 309). In this regard, and to briefly clarify my terms, I understand violence as a complex phenomenon; it is both intended and unintended acts which lead to physical, psychological/emotional or symbolic abuse, pain, injury. Along these lines, the graffiti I examine here are not necessarily causal in their effect – this I do not document and cannot prove – but rather they contribute to the *affective regimes* (Wee, 2016) layered into Bosnia-Herzegovina's linguistic landscape. Likewise, through their appropriation and/or disruption of spaces – sometimes careless, sometimes strategic, they render the landscape *turbulent* (Cresswell and Martin, 2012; Stroud, 2016): unsettled and uneasy. The graffscapes of Bosnia-Herzegovina thereby help sustain – in both symbolic and material ways – a regime of mutual hatred, distrust, fear, anger or disgust, which may cause people to (re)experience, (re)imagine, and in some cases even (re)desire violence. Despite its apparent political unification, everyday semiosis of Bosnia-Herzegovina reveals that this state is far from being a peaceful one. Indeed, its linguistic landscape confirms that peace is not merely the absence of physical violence. Perhaps it is this which makes it all the more surprising that Bosnia-Herzegovina's graffscape has not yet been the object of scholarly attention. Before turning to the analysis at the heart of this chapter, I want to establish more thoroughly some of the key terms and notions which frame my analysis and ground my interpretations of the graffscape in Bosnia-Herzegovina. Specifically, I start by locating the study in linguistic landscape research addressing both conflict zones and graffscapes. I then address the thorny issues of hate and 'hate speech', linking them to my preference for *linguistic violence* as a way to better understand the workings of graffiti in a place like Bosnia-Herzegovina.

Turbulent graffscapes: Moving beyond words and beyond 'hate speech'

It is almost a truism that graffiti are often culturally charged. Within institutional frameworks in particular, graffiti are often viewed as transgressive, intrusive or simply unauthorised (cf. Scollon and Scollon, 2003; Karlander, 2016) – signs which are 'out of place and must be erased in order to return the social space to its proper condition' (Young, 2005: 55). Notwithstanding these common hegemonic dismissals, Lynn and Lea's (2005: 40, 51) study of racist graffiti demonstrates how threatening and oppressive graffiti can indeed be, especially when 'singling out specific groups of people as objects of hate or anger, and encouraging others to the same view'. Following Lynn and Lea's (2005) lead, however, the significance or meaning of a graffiti can only be understood in terms of its location, time of creation and authorship; in other words, knowing when, where graffiti appeared and by whom it was created. Of course, acts of removal must also be understood in these terms: when and by whom was it removed, and how long the graffiti was there before removal. Graffscapes in Bosnia-Herzegovina are layered upon and help produce multiple conflict zones; these are even more tangible and charged if the 'right graffiti' is placed on the 'right spot' – on walls or buildings which are widely perceived as 'ours' or 'theirs'. Take, for example, the following instance reported as an act of vandalism, damage to a property and messages of inappropriate and threatening content by Klix.ba, an online news website. In this case, it was the spraying of a nationalistic symbol on the façade of the Muslim Association building in a small town in Herzegovina, Trebinje. In the comments section of the Klix.ba report from March 2014, the following anonymous message was posted:

Extract 3

Necessary ingredients:
1–2 16-year olds well versed in nationalistic additives,
1 spray can,
1 religious building.
Preparation time: 1–2 minutes.
The stew for comments and dissemination of hate is ready.

The recipe-like style points to the apparent ease and speed with which an affective charge is produced. It is perhaps not surprising that teenagers are the first suspects, a generation born after the war but nonetheless well educated in the conflicts of the past. And these posted comments quickly escalate the affective charge, releasing less playful responses as we see in Extract 4.

Extract 4

Genocidal men keep committing genocides in old places, this time psychologically.
What else can be expected of monsters and fiends who destroy and pollute everything they touch.
It is about time we expel these primitive scumbags from Bosnia.

The extracts provide a glimpse into the strength of feeling towards graffiti, evincing the power of the linguistic landscape to establish and/or contribute to wider *affective regimes* (Wee, 2016). We witness how affect as an embodied meaning or experience is inextricably constituted as something semiotic and discursive (cf. Wetherell, 2012). By the same token, we see also how different kinds of affect are materialized in these already contested sites. Apart from insults or accusations which produce competing pre-post-war messages of mutual distrust and hatred, graffiti seemingly cause people to (re)experience, (re)imagine or even (re)desire violence and trauma. Graffiti being left in places where they will undoubtedly be seen clearly illustrate that they are not just simple acts of vandalism. Since the walls are carefully chosen (e.g. mosques, churches, schools, cemeteries, etc.), graffiti such as this can be interpreted as strategically provocative and/or deliberately insulting. It is meant to unsettle and disturb. And since disorder, as Mary Douglas (1966) famously observed, symbolizes both danger and power, the removal of graffiti is regarded as an act of re-ordering the environment, not simply of cleaning it. The instance of graffiti described above was indeed buffed the next day. The prompt removal of graffiti creates – or is intended to create – an illusion of safety and comfort (Moreau and Alderman, 2011). The 'silent' façades and cleaned-up spaces apparently assure citizens of a well-ordered, hate-free society. But the feeling is often temporary, just as the buffing is only ever provisional. Indeed, the appropriation and regulation of these turbulent spaces – the tussle between order and disorder – proves the case that linguistic landscapes are always emergent and under revision (Karlander, 2016). The shifting nature of the landscape points not only to the turbulence of space, of course, but also to the turmoil and uncertainty of social and political life. As Cresswell and Martin (2012) explain, turbulence nicely describes contexts of contest and division, and accounting for competing discourses about how place/space should work, what it should look like, or who should own or control it. In turn, Stroud (2016: 15) argues, 'turbulence is the disruptive "revolutionary moment", where different orders and regimes of understanding may come together through moments of dissonance, disagreement and contest'. Considering Bosnia-Herzegovina's recent history and the nature of the graffiti investigated here, such irruptive moments do not necessarily lead to positive change. Nonetheless, through the shifting graffscapes, citizens continue to engage with the environment, display their resistance to sharing the space. In the words of Ley and Cybriwsky (1974: 505), the walls and public spaces of Bosnia-Herzegovina are 'more than an attitudinal tabloid; they are a behavioural manifesto'. In the face (and wake) of war trauma, people's experiences of, and stories about, recent history often result in strong or provocative language, as the following 2012 statement by the Organization for Security and Cooperation (emphasis mine) attests:

> In the post-war period, bias-motivated incidents ranged from physical and *verbal attacks* to material damage and the destruction of religious objects with the resulting frequency posing potential risks to Bosnia-Herzegovina's stability.[3]

These so-called verbal attacks are frequently referred to as hate speech, especially under the frameworks of different international institutions or organizations. For example, the Council of Europe's Committee of Ministers' Recommendation 97(20) defines hate speech as 'all forms of expression which spread, incite, promote or justify racial hatred, xenophobia, anti-Semitism or other forms of hatred based on intolerance, including: intolerance expressed by aggressive nationalism and ethnocentrism, discrimination and hostility against minorities, migrants and people of immigrant origin'.[4] Quite understandably, language publicly inciting or inflaming national, racial or religious hatred, discord or hostility among the constituent peoples, is criminalized in Bosnia-Herzegovina (Criminal Code of Bosnia-Herzegovina – Article 145a).[4] Nonetheless, what actually constitutes these crimes is open to debate. What exactly are 'the most harmful forms of expression in the country' (Smith, 2014)? These are unspecified, ambiguous and left open to interpretation depending on which ethnic group is evaluating them. What, one wonders, for example, is inherently hateful about the phrase *This is Serbia*? The simple fact is that hate is not simply or neatly linguistic. When sprayed on the wall of a religious structure, however, *This is Serbia* becomes hateful through its emplacement. Even then the relationship between hate and speech is a complex one. As Butler (1997: 12) has famously argued, 'the notion that speech wounds appears to rely on the inseparable and incongruous relation between body and speech, but also, consequently, between speech and its effects'. Words themselves do not necessarily injure as they are spoken (or written); the embodied-performative aspect is crucial. As Butler (1997) further explains, some utterances wound under certain circumstances, but the circumstances alone do not make the utterances wound; the effect of vulnerability is contextual, but not fully. In the case of graffiti, symbolic acts wound through the inseparable and incongruous relation between emplacement and content (words). Just as the body amplifies the spoken words, it is their emplacement that helps realize graffiti's meaning and power. Indeed, a simple inspection of the graffiti – like any verbal expression – is insufficient, especially if we consider more subtle rhetoric delivered through in-jokes, subtle humiliation or euphemisms (e.g. *Clear the tall trees, Finish the work* in Tirrell, 2012). Hate speech, as a relatively broad, often confusing juridical-political notion, fails to incorporate such symbolic forms of violence embodied in language itself (cf. Bourdieu, 1991; Žižek, 2006). Many nonverbal or multimodal forms of violence are effective/affective precisely because they are not as loud and obvious as hate speech. But they are as significant because they naturalize violence as 'an inevitable, unavoidable fact of life' (Colaguori, 2010: 391). Most importantly, these symbolic acts may establish the conditions for non-linguistic, physical violence. Although distancing myself from the term hate speech as something politically convenient but analytically and theoretically inadequate, this does not mean that I reject the term *hate* which clearly has empirical and experiential value. What becomes apparent from my study of Bosnia-Herzegovina, however, is that graffiti may not appear as obvious hate speech, nor are they necessarily motived simply or exclusively by hatred. For these reasons, I privilege the notion of linguistic violence which subsumes hate speech and encompasses a spectrum of semiotic tactics (e.g. spaces, words, images), emotions and experiences. Tirrell (2012: 176) argues that linguistic violence is 'enacted or delivered through discursive behaviours constituting social or psychological damage, and generating permissions for physical damage, including assault and death'. This, however, is not a simple case of verbalized attacks; it is not simply a matter of *verba volant, scripta manent* – especially not in the case of ephemeral signs like graffiti. The composition, configuration and emplacement of graffiti can render its linguistic violence more subtle or more blatant. As with all language, meaning is generated partly by *who* produces the words, but also by *when* and *where* the words take place. As one last point before turning to my data analysis, linguistic violence is nowadays more readily set in motion via the remediating practices of new/social media. In 2015, at the twentieth commemoration of the Srebrenica genocide, a banner displaying 'For every dead Serb we will kill 100 Muslims!' appeared in the crowd. It was a quote from a recorded statement made in 1995, and available on YouTube, by the Serbian prime minister who was also at the commemoration in 2015, and who was elected to be the President of Serbia in 2017.[5] This is a perfect example of the way war-time rhetoric, made accessible via YouTube, continues to circulate long after the war is ostensibly over. And most certainly, the words had lost none of their charge in the meantime. On the contrary. The prime minister was struck in the face while being attacked with stones, bottles and other objects. That these same words can appear in different modes (speech/written text), affecting different audiences, shows how language that was most likely unknown to Bosnian Muslims in Bosnia-Herzegovina at the time of their original speaking (communication lines were cut off during the war), continues to work across time and space. To sum up, linguistic violence is much more than hate and it is also more than simply speech per se, more than the spoken word. The hatefulness and violence of language – and, of course, graffiti – hinges partly on its content but just as much on its emplacement in a particular space, at a particular moment and for a certain amount of time. It is this which we see clearly in my analysis, organized around three different spatialities, three different word-space relationships.

Graffscapes and/as linguistic violence: Innerspaces, banal spaces, restricted spaces

The two datasets at the heart of this study represent different kinds of bottom-up (unofficial) signs (Ben-Rafael et al., 2006). The first comes from the *Supergrađani* (Supercitizens) initiative which was launched by the OSCE Mission to Bosnia-Herzegovina in cooperation with Foundation for New Communication *Dokukino*. The initiative was established as a response to hate crimes and bias-motivated incidents, with a website for reporting perceived instances of hate speech, offensive graffiti, physical violence or damage to property. Citizens submit anonymous reports that OSCE verifies and then adds to the online database. Reports made are divided into what are labelled *cohesions* and *conflicts*; and conflicts have been divided further into *incidents*, *spaces* and *public events*. Offensive graffiti are listed under the category of *incidents*. The OSCE reserves the right to remove all unrelated, biased, incorrect or unverifiable content. At this point, it should be mentioned that citizens of Bosnia-Herzegovina refer to themselves as Bosniaks (Bosnian Muslims), Croats (Bosnian Catholics) and Serbs (Bosnian Orthodox Christians). Apart from the two official entities the Federation of Bosnia-Herzegovina and the Serb Republic, the country has another self-governing administrative unit, Brčko District, which falls under dual sovereignty of the two entities. With regard to its language policy, there are three official languages – Bosnian, Croatian and Serbian languages, and two scripts – Latin and Cyrillic. The so-called different languages are varieties of one language referred to as Serbo-Croatian before the war (cf. Kordić, 2010). Although the Republic of Bosnia-Herzegovina, Croatia, Serbia and Montenegro have their own official languages now – Bosnian, Croatian, Serbian and Montenegrin, respectively, the official languages of these countries are a single polycentric language. Bosnian Muslims and Croats use the Latin, while Bosnian Serbs use both scripts, mainly Cyrillic.

The second of my datasets was obtained during my own fieldwork in May 2016. Apart from a few exceptions, most of the graffiti were photographed during a systematic exploration of four sites: (1) Doboj, (2) Sarajevo, (3) East Sarajevo and (4) Mostar. These sites were chosen for their contested nature and status reflected in their history of mass killings, ethnic cleansing, siege and destruction, as well as in today's complex ethno-national politics utilized among different ethnic groups who live in these places. The data collected is not all-inclusive and constitutes a snapshot of the graffscapes at a certain time and place. Other graffiti were undoubtedly missed, especially since many are being removed periodically and new ones written in their place. I actively looked for examples readily characterized as provocative, including those expressing violent, nationalistic texts or symbols targeting a specific ethnic group. Most studies of graffscapes, especially the few addressing conflict zones, point to graffiti as a site/resource for experiencing socio-economic crises (e.g. Zaimakis, 2015), and for inciting political resistance and social change (e.g. Hanauer, 2011). In these studies, it seems that violent events (e.g. terrorist attacks) produce a kind of anti-conflict protest through graffiti messages of peace, unity, resilience and hope, such as those honouring victims and/or commemorating events (e.g. Rubdy, 2015; De Ruiter, 2015). As will become evident shortly, the graffscapes in Bosnia-Herzegovina's conflict zones are somewhat different; rather than conveying reconciliatory messages, we find messages which sustain linguistic violence. The unspeakable atrocities of the past are expressed as painted outbursts across the contemporary landscape. Grounded in long-standing and these more recent approaches in linguistic landscape research, I treat Bosnia-Herzegovina's post-war graffscapes through the foundational principles of emplacement and indexicality: 'all semiotic signs, whether embodied or disembodied, have a significant part of their meaning in how they are placed in the world' (Scollon and Scollon, 2003: 205). In this sense, I adopt a multimodal/social semiotic approach (e.g. Kress and van Leeuwen, 2001; Kress, 2010) in focusing on textual content and style, script, composition, layering, scale. It is in this way that I highlight three overlapping spatial themes: the graffiti of innerspaces; graffiti in banal spaces; and graffiti in restricted spaces.

The graffiti of innerspaces – Turf wars

I turn first to graffiti found within spaces marked explicitly or understood clearly to belong to one or other ethnic group, mostly on the walls of residential buildings or abandoned structures, and less frequently on the public walls of border areas. The meanings of graffiti marking the territory are explicitly space/place dependent, and they are realized through their deliberate and strategic staging. However, these graffiti do not simply reflect territorial boundary marking; they also show post-war changes in the country's ethnic composition. Here we see how graffiti also act as statements of supremacy, demonstrating the power of materialized, spatialized messages to demarcate places in the ominous post-war ambience. In 2015, graffiti reported to the Supercitizens in Brčko District was written on the wall of what seems to be a derelict structure right next to the Fifth Elementary School. The school which was completely devastated in 1992, and reopened in 2000, has been described as the first, post-war, multi-ethnic elementary school in Bosnia-Herzegovina. As a true border city, located next to Croatia and the Serb Republic, after the war, Brčko was formed as a single administrative unit since a different agreement in Dayton was not possible. Unlike the violent claims on Brčko (e.g. through ethnic cleansing, mass murders and torture), the city is today claimed by both Bosniaks/Croats and Serbs in seemingly more peaceful but still turbulent ways – not least through its 'turf wars'. The graffiti reads 'The Army of B&H (acronym, Bosnia-Herzegovina)/Brčko will never be "брчко" (in Cyrillic)'. In simple, lexically speaking, terms, a straightforward claim over space is made. Letters on the left side form an acronym indicating that a Bosnian Muslim individual or group produced the message, especially considering the location of graffiti: a part of Brčko populated by Bosnian Muslims. The code-/style-switch into Cyrillic lettering is pointed because it is the script used by Serbs. Regarding the scale, the lettering is relatively large, covering the entire wall. The primary red colour is pronounced on a white background, while the yellow is a layered attempt at disputing the original message. The word *never* appears to have been vigorously disputed. This kind of layering and use of vibrant colours make the graffiti especially prominent. Its emplacement means that the school children are the likely and perhaps intended audience (they may even be the producers). On a route to and from the school, this graffiti has a constantly returning audience, and only because it has not been emplaced on the façade of the school itself, had not immediately been removed. Another innerspace example of turfing is the graffiti which reads 'Serb Republic our country!!!' (in Cyrillic), appearing in an almost exclusively Bosnian-Serb residential area of Doboj in the Serb Republic (Figure 9). The pronoun *our* indicates that it was produced by a Bosnian Serb individual or group. Considering this area's ethnic composition, other Bosnian Serbs are most likely the intended audience. To some extent this is straightforward territory marking, but seemingly non-violent graffiti may also convey a somewhat more

Figure 9 Residential building façade in Doboj © Maida Kosatica 2016

aggressive, intimidating provocation for other ethnic groups. Nowadays, such claims and any discussion about the status of the Serb Republic within Bosnia-Herzegovina result in social tensions and public discourse which resembles the pre-war political rhetoric. The neatly sprayed message of average size is similar in colour and style to other graffiti found in the residential areas of Doboj. This example is not especially prominent and neither is any other graffiti in these residential areas which generally do not contain violent messages. However, the amount of graffiti found within a few meters of each other makes these innerspaces remarkable. Literally every residential façade contains at least a few graffiti, whether nationalistic symbols or written messages. This, it has to be said, is a space already covered with garbage, either discarded carelessly by the residents or simply falling out of overfilled containers not collected by the authorities – an all too familiar scene across Bosnia-Herzegovina. All of which leaves the impression of an area marked by its poverty and bigotry. As Ley and Cybriwsky (1974) observe, charged graffiti often become denser the closer one gets to the core of a certain group's turf.

The physical proximity, individualized orthography, size and colour, reveal a certain level of consistency, suggesting that much of the graffiti is produced by the same person(s) or group(s). This is particularly evident in East Sarajevo, although the pattern of similarity repeats across my other fieldwork sites as well. Graffiti commonly indicate supportive, in-group messages of dominance, unity and power, in some cases expressed through nationalistic, war-related tags or so-called bombers (Figures 10 and 11). These war-related symbols are to be found in public parks, on the walls of abandoned structures, and on roadside walls along the roads, informing out-group members of the territorial limits of their own space (Landry and Bourhis, 1997). In Figure 10, the nationalistic symbol with four 'S' (C in Cyrillic script) and the Cross of St. Sava refer to the phrase *Samo sloga Srbe spašava* (Only unity saves the Serbs). During the war, this symbol was frequently inscribed in villages and towns captured by the Bosnian Serb forces. As a result, the tag is considered equivalent to the nationalistic sign of Chetniks, a pejorative term commonly used by Bosniak and Croat groups to refer to those Serbs who committed atrocities against the non-Serbs.

The Ustashe symbol (Figure 11), with the letter 'U' and the Catholic cross above, symbolizes a Croatian fascist organization which was active between 1929 and 1945, and which committed atrocities against non-Croats, specifically targeting Serbs. The symbol indicates a clearly anti-Serb ideology, and a belief in

Figure 10 Residential building façade in Doboj © Maida Kosatica 2016

Figure 11 Residential portal space in Mostar © Maida Kosatica 2016

the holiness and sanctity of the Croatian state (McCormick, 2014). Regardless of these aggressive associations, they are often regarded by those using them as badges of honour. Marking and claiming territory this way therefore provides not only a sense of status but also of security (Ley and Cybriwsky, 1974).

Other examples found outside residential areas, contain hostile, outwardly directed messages such as the one in Figure 12. Deliberately emplaced on the wall of a Muslim cemetery (i.e. a Muslim innerspace), the graffiti reads 'In this city you are only a guest' with a crossed Ustashe symbol below. The message is directly intended for Bosnian Croats as unwanted neighbours who, it is believed, do not belong in Mostar and should leave not only the city but the country of Bosnia-Herzegovina itself, since they openly express their 'special Croatness' by using the Ustashe symbol throughout Mostar West. It could be argued that if Bosnian Croats produced a graffiti of similar content in the same location (e.g. 'Muslims, in this city you are only guests'), it would most probably be reported as an act of vandalism, resulting in quick removal since it would be considered an insult in 'our own backyard'. As Wee (2016: 107) suggests, 'different feeling and display rules are to varying degrees enforced and/or observed by the authorities and inhabitants associated with a given site'.

These examples of graffiti in what I am calling innerspaces reveal how central spatiality is to meaning-making. The significance of these messages cannot be only about the words since their discursive content is neither extreme or surprising; instead, it is where they are and in their close proximity that the

Figure 12 Muslim cemetery wall in Mostar © Maida Kosatica 2016

graffiti make sense. They are most certainly not sprayed on these particular walls haphazardly. Territorial graffiti persist and are partly sheltered by the innerspaces which help preserve their message in space and time. Consequently, unreported graffiti are not being removed, perhaps creating a sense of justice and righteousness, and ultimately, the space in which a group feels extremely comfortable asserting its rights to the territory. In Ley and Cybriwsky's (1974: 494) words, 'to make a claim of primacy for oneself and the conquest of territory, even in fantasy, is always an act performed for an audience'. In this regard, messages concerning Bosnia-Herzegovina's territorial structure are akin to the nationalist propaganda discourses on the territorial status of Bosnia-Herzegovina which preceded the war. In turn, these visual-material turf wars are just as capable of invoking the all-too-familiar feelings of superiority and territoriality which preceded the war before.

Graffiti in banal spaces – Everyday provocations

I turn now to looking at the occurrence of graffiti in more territorially ambiguous spaces, and where emplacement appears to be more random and incidental. These types of graffiti are found mainly in pedestrian zones and other banal places – different parts of public infrastructure. The strong content of the graffiti and their spatial dispersion point to their provocative purpose. This is how contested sites of Bosnia-Herzegovina articulate the kind of affective regimes they wish to maintain. In fact, we see here how the 'regime of understanding' (Wee, 2016) established is one of enduring, mutual hate. Unlike graffiti marking the territory, graffiti in these banal spaces are occasionally reported and removed. As such, content-space/place relationship is more variable, and the message itself is often prioritized as a meaning-making resource, although not exclusively. More specifically, the following examples show how the words and symbols stand out against the background, becoming the focal points since the space itself is easily accessible. Slogans and symbols produced by the three ethnic groups are similar in their rhetoric and style, requiring an audience already acquainted with the 'historical truths' of each ethnic group. In more practical terms, graffiti involve those who know the language, scripts and the historically relevant 'local code' (Lynn and Lea, 2005). In my first two examples, a rhetoric of violence is produced through well-known slogans in which lexical choice adds an additional rhyming element. Here we see also the strong layering of affect into the graffscape: words performing their violence by promoting overt nationalism and explicitly invoking the brutal methods previously used to eliminate others. The graffiti which reads 'Serbs on the willows' appeared on the very borderline of Sarajevo and East Sarajevo within the territory of the Federation of Bosnia-Herzegovina. Emplacement is not entirely accidental; however, the graffiti is sprayed on an otherwise nondescript roadside wall. Note how it is layered on top of a previously buffed piece. The slogan originates in a poem written by Slovenian author Marko Natlačen (1914), published in the Slovenian language journal *Slovenac*.[6] The borrowed wording expresses an unapologetic but subtly encoded anti-Serb sentiment, and was largely used as a 'licence to kill' during the war by the Army of Bosnia-Herzegovina and Croatian Army members. (The willows in the slogan refer to the trees from which Serbian people should be hanged.) As it appears on this roadside wall, the slogan expresses hateful feelings towards Serbians, Bosnian Serbs and the Serb Republic – an administrative entity referred to by some Bosniaks as a *genocidal creation*, in other words, established through genocide and ethnic cleansing. The graffiti was not roundly supported even within the supposed ingroup; it was in fact reported by someone who had himself been the person to remove the initial graffiti just a few days beforehand. Soon after being reported this second time round, the new graffiti was removed yet again. Although it appeared in an otherwise relatively banal but high-visibility place, the content itself was deemed sufficiently violent for it to be reported, logged online and removed again. This kind of graffiti unapologetically promotes the idea expunging – territorially and completely – another ethnic group. In a similar example of banal emplacement, another graffiti from 2013 shows a stylistically identical provocation reading 'The knife, the barbed wire, Srebrenica'. This low-lying piece of graffiti is marked along the concrete base of a wood-top bench in a pedestrian, park-like zone in Doboj. The pink wall and red lettering make the graffiti even more prominent. The message contains a Serbian slogan glorifying the genocide in Srebrenica. (The Supercitizens website says nothing about its removal and during my fieldwork, I was not able to locate the place to check if it was still there.) The choice of *knife* and *barbed wire* appear discordantly threatening and sinister given the ordinariness of the setting – a spot where young people and children sometimes hang out. Speaking of children, another graffiti found during my fieldwork in the same city, shares many of the same banal spatial properties (Figure 13).

The graffiti can just be made out on the end of a bench behind the seated boy's leg. It is the same nationalistic *Samo sloga Srbe spašava* marking from the previous section. The same symbol, the same graffiti, but emplaced in a very different kind of space. Where the one above was a case of explicit boundary-marking, the 'turfing' here is, in some ways, more violent for its random, incidental nature – its casual backdropping of a place where these children are found playing and socializing. It is a passive-aggressive enculturation into the wider affective regimes and conflicted histories of Bosnia-Herzegovina. As such, in a moment where discursive content might appear to outweigh spatial location, we are reminded

Figure 13 Park in Doboj © Maida Kosatica 2016

that the meaning of graffiti is not less dependent on the particularities of its emplacement. It is not clear what effects banal emplacements such as these have on the development of prejudice and discrimination, as Wilson (2014) notes. Nonetheless, it seems reasonable to suppose that the ubiquity and persistence of these pejorative messages have negative ramifications. In much the same way, Thurlow (2001) explains how the social-psychological toxicity of homophobic pejoratives lies in their persistent, carefree circulation and normalization. The linguistic violence of graffiti in Bosnia-Herzegovina likewise produces a kind of *ambient hate* by which prejudice is silently and/or passively endorsed as part of people's everyday social lives (cf. Wilson, 2014). Besides, these types of graffiti appear alongside far bolder, more spectacular instances.

Graffiti in restricted spaces – Bold incursions

The last category of graffiti – the third language-space relationship – I want to consider concerns examples strategically emplaced in otherwise monitored, regulated and surveilled spaces. These graffiti are found mainly on the façades of public infrastructure such as educational buildings and religious structures, or on private properties. In these cases, emplacement undoubtedly amplifies the content, but the significance of the words (discursive content) and their emplacement (space/place) are otherwise impossible to tease apart. It is their emplacement that also conditions their ephemerality, with graffiti often reported and removed immediately. As such, these are especially dynamic, turbulent spaces. These graffiti also regularly end up in the media. Prior to the war, everyday social life was awash with narratives of victimhood on all sides, along with the identification of oppressors. These ethnic conflicts were, and still are, justified by, as Pratto and colleagues (1994: 741) indicate, 'appealing to historical injustices, previous territorial boundaries, religious prohibitions, genetic and cultural theories of in-group superiority, or other such ideologies'. In this regard, contemporary post-war narratives are no different, although sometimes going beyond hateful feelings to the overt incitement of physical violence. This is exemplified in the following two examples appearing on school walls. The first graffiti reads 'I know about the knife – I feel the wire – I will fuck your mother for Srebrenica', again with a religious symbol indicating its producer(s). It appeared on the façade of an elementary school in Potočari, 6 kilometre north-west of Srebrenica in the Serb Republic entity. This almost 'meta-affective' message (a statement about affect) is an overt expression of revenge.

An unusually long message, the graffiti seems to have been carefully sprayed on what looks like the entire wall to the left of this school's entrance. This school-wall message purposefully re-inscribes the linguistic violence of the well-known slogan 'The knife, the barbed wire, Srebrenica'. In this one moment, in this one slice of the Bosnia-Herzegovina graffscape, we see the expression and materialization of public *historical traumas* (Brave Heart and DeBruyn, 1998) intended for a whole new generation born long after the war had ended. In this way, we find graffiti laying bare an inherited or adopted victimhood, re-opening wounds which, it seems, may be unlikely to ever heal. The next example shows just how far into the past the linguistic violence of the contemporary landscape can reach. In Cyrillic, the graffiti from 2015 reads 'To a Turkish man's head do not ever raise a gun, you can do it so much better, since the cattle are slaughtered with a knife!!! Serbs'. Here we have a reference to Ottoman occupation and the belief that, as descendants of the Turks due to the religion, Bosnian Muslims carry a historical blame for past wrongdoings. This rhetoric is all but identical to pre-war nationalist propaganda, seeking to legitimize and justify bloodshed and genocide in response to, or revenge for, ancient conflicts. This current-day graffiti – with its poetic style and provocative emplacement – mobilizes anew these deep-seated animosities and prejudices. Overly intense lexical quality does not only create a correspondence of sounds between the words filled with details (men's heads, a knife instead of the gun, cattle should be slaughtered), but enables easier repetition and a greater understanding of the restructuring of historical events, i.e. Bosnian Muslims as Turks. Certainly, not all graffiti appearing in restricted spaces take this kind of poetic form and style; eclectic profanations also include smashed windows and demolished monuments. As Schmidt and Schroder (2001) argue, any violence without an audience is socially meaningless. In this respect, the poeticized approach is less about aesthetics and more about tactics – designed for memorability and repeatability, like the 'venal poetry' of advertising (Hayakawa, 1946). The producers of the graffiti will be well aware that their messages will otherwise be short-lived in its current material-spatial form. Through their strategic emplacement, graffiti in restricted spaces are deployed for their specific locational advantages and affective charge. Space/place is key. The truth is, if anything appears on the facades of school buildings and the like, then it will be considered an act of vandalism and more than likely be removed immediately. This does not mean the discursive content of graffiti is irrelevant. Just as the spatial properties of emplacement 'carry' the meaning in one moment, in others it is the words that do the work – that bear the illocutionary force, as it were. 'The knife, the barbed wire, Srebrenica' would seem to be unambiguous and unequivocally charged wherever it were emplaced. In these restricted spaces, however, the meanings and violence of written graffiti hinge inseparably on the language-space interplay.

Conclusion

Just before entering the historical centre of Mostar whose narrow footpaths lead to the Old Bridge, there it stands, place appropriate – on a vertical construction, enclosed by a rusty fence, an aesthetically pleasing red rose with a message carefully stylized and captured in paint – 'War is not over' (Figure 14).

This time a graffiti in English, as if to address all locals and foreigners alike, setting up a universal spatial reminder of past conflicts. Indeed, this graffiti seems to capture nicely the essential truth of Bosnia-Herzegovina's turbulent graffscapes as

Figure 14 Hotel 'Rose' in Mostar © Maida Kosatica 2016

cultural forms of violence [...] in fact deeply meaningful, recalling the histories that shore up the conflicts in which antagonists are engaged and forcing the nightmares of the past into the waking realities of the present.

(Whitehead, 2004: 10)

In short, and to follow Raymond Williams (1977), the linguistic landscape and, specifically, its graffscapes work constantly and relentlessly to *structure* the feelings of the country.

After the war ended, physical violence subsided but was replaced by a ubiquitous, persistent distrust and hate. This is especially visible in contested areas which portray current conflicts resulting from the loss of life and the right to live in peace. Graffscapes in Bosnia-Herzegovina acknowledge these disputed territories, entities and experiences, proving how the past still has a firm grasp on the present. In this chapter, I initially sought to point out that, when it comes to controversial communicative acts such as graffiti, the notion of linguistic violence is a broader one than hate speech, and therefore opens up new ways of analysing and interpreting complex graffscapes such as those in Bosnia-Herzegovina. Linguistic violence helps separate out the hate from the speech; it also helps emphasise the role of space/place as a meaning-making resource. Hate is a fully embodied and multimodal experience or accomplishment. In the linguistic landscape of areas marked by a history of extreme violence and in which conflicts still exist, graffscapes also vary between those that are incidental and those that are more strategically produced. Although the design, content and location of graffiti are extremely important, its significance – in terms of meaning and consequence – depends also on emplacement as a temporally framed as well as spatially framed act. The visually materialized violence of (some) graffiti is a key contributor to the wider affective regimes of Bosnia-Herzegovina linguistic landscape, driving constant efforts by different ethnic groups to disrupt and/or appropriate space. The linguistic landscapes themselves play an important role in understanding the rhetorical significance of graffiti as an embodiment or materialization of post-war distrust. In examining how contemporary forms of conflict are constituted and sustained, graffiti may be viewed as a response to, and an expression of, a continued lack of consensus regarding the war and the territory. The ubiquity and nature of Bosnia-Herzegovina's graffscape suggests that the level of linguistic violence is higher in some sites than in others, but it is difficult to ascertain whether one ethnic group or party is more involved than another. Importantly, spatialized violent discourses structure the mobility of people who often avoid entering areas (sometimes within their own cities) which they perceive as hostile – not least through the assertive, explicit marking of space. This, in turn, means the three constitutive peoples end up having less interaction, merely intensifying ingroup-outgroup dynamics and societal divides (cf. Chick, 1985, on apartheid South Africa). Linguistic violence in the form of graffiti which acquire and sustain their symbolic power through/ in the intersection of language and space ultimately become inculturated into contemporary social space. It is, as Neil Whitehead (quoted above) suggests, a case of past nightmares making their way constantly into the waking present. Indeed, the Bosnia-Herzegovina graffscape sustains old and new ethnic prejudices which were arguably more supressed before the breakup of Yugoslavia. Politically speaking, Bosnia-Herzegovina is one state, but essentially it is divided in a complex manner; and, even though the armed conflict is over, its causes and ramifications are very much present. In Bosnia-Herzegovina we find provocative graffscapes which continue to generate experiences of the war, invoking remnants of the past and dictating commands in the present. They partly function through graffiti with clearly interpretable meanings – delivering messages of territorial marking, assertions of ethnic pride or dominance and the glorification of methods for expelling or eliminating others. Unlike in the country's pre-war graffscape, the spatial narrations of contemporary Bosnia-Herzegovina seem sometimes far more explicit, and, perhaps, point worryingly to the potential for even more extreme physical violence once again. The overriding inscribed in and carried across the linguistic landscape is this: the war in Bosnia-Herzegovina is not over. This message is literally etched, scrawled and sprayed on walls which themselves are still scarred with shell holes and shrapnel.

3

The Semiotic Production of Commemorative Performances

> Can you imagine a monument for Nazis in
> front of Auschwitz?

It is difficult to find the right words for the White House – one of the most disheartening places in Bosnia-Herzegovina, yet inescapable in understanding the people's strong commemorative needs (Figure 15). After the Serb forces took control of Prijedor, a town in north-western Bosnia-Herzegovina, thousands of non-Serb civilians were imprisoned in Omarska, Keraterm and Trnopolje concentration camps.[1] The International Criminal Tribunal for the former Yugoslavia gives a short background on the most notorious concentration camp in Bosnia-Herzegovina, Omarska (emphasis mine):

> Within the area of the Omarska mining complex that was used for the camp, the camp authorities generally confined the prisoners in three different buildings: the administration building, where interrogations took place and most of the women were confined; the garage or hangar building; *the 'white house,' a small building where particularly severe beatings were administered*; and on a cement courtyard area between the buildings known as the 'pista'. There was another small building, known as the *'red house', where prisoners were sometimes taken but most often did not emerge alive.*[2]

There is almost nothing to retell about what happened in the red house from the Case No. IT-95-4-I indictment – only one person survived it. The red walls soaked up all the blood a long time ago. It is Ed Vulliamy, a former Guardian journalist, who keeps revisiting Omarska and telling its story to the world, loudly revealing the sickening horrors of Serb concentration camps. On 5 August 1992, together with Penny Marshall and Ian Williams, Vulliamy reached Omarska and Trnopolje camps, and reported on the imprisoned Bosnian Muslim and Croat

Figure 15 Still image of White House taken from the 'Crimes before the ICTY: Prijedor' video, directed by Petar Finci © United Nations International Residual Mechanism for Criminal Tribunals 2013

men. At least thirty-six to thirty-eight women held in Omarska were repeatedly raped and sexually assaulted by the guards.³ Danner (2009: 55) remarks Omarska bears comparison with Auschwitz:

> In Omarska as in Auschwitz the masters created these walking corpses from healthy men by employing simple methods: withold all but the barest nourishment, forcing the prisoners' bodes to waste anyway; impose upon them a ceaseless terror, subjecting them to unremitting physical cruelty; immerse them in degradation and death and decay, destroying all hope and obliterating the will to live.

In the wake of Vullamy's first eyewitness report intensely circulating the world media, the Omarska camp ceased operating on 21 August 1992. Due to an outcry by the International Community, other concentration camps were closed in the same year. Today, these places are *unmarked sites of violence*, as Bosniaks call them. Every year on 6 August, together with their families and other visitors, the survivors visit the former Omarska camp complex, building their own short-lived monuments that commemorate those who were brutally killed. As a survivor told the Guardian, people need these sites to be accessible for public commemoration:

Extract 1

We would be pleased if there could just be some kind of memorial, maybe that the white house might be fenced off. We just want something to ensure that the memory is preserved, and in the smallest way to awaken the conscience of the Serbs. Because if we don't awaken that conscience, we might as well forget everything. And that would be the saddest thing of all – to forget what happened and what could happen again tomorrow. Yes, tomorrow.

(*The Guardian*, 2004)[4]

The call for a memorial highlights the importance of not turning a blind eye to the possibility that the same atrocities might repeat. At the same time, Extract 1 provides an insight into the despairing commemorative needs: *some kind of a memorial* – just a fence, perhaps. However, the building of a memorial had still not taken place. Not so long ago, the bodies were hidden in mass graves around Omarska. Today, violence is being denied with the absence of memorials. Bosniaks' appeals continue to be ignored and one cannot find a single stone in the city representing an official monument.[5] Nonetheless, a large stone eagle with an Orthodox cross placed on the left side of Trnopolje camp commemorates 'the fallen Serb heroes who gave their lives for the foundation of the Serb Republic' (Figure 16). Those asking for a memorial which would commemorate civilians killed in the former camps feel defeated and a camp survivor asks *Can you imagine a monument for Nazis in front of Auschwitz?*[6] Bosnia-Herzegovina's war memory as its contemporary heritage is a part of the country's everyday landscapes, and the public recognition of violence that had occurred is immensely important for different moral-cum-political reasons. In this sense, the country is a rich site for investigating and understanding the relationship between memory and public space. Different commemorative activities continuously altering public space may appear far from disputed. However, the simple fact is that the majority of memorial sites simultaneously shift between two completely different impressions. On the one hand, they are a way to mourn, pay respect, claim rights and proclaim the truth. On the other hand, they provoke, deepen divisions and destabilize the armistice over two decades long. Today, more than ever, denial and oppression are (re)inscribed in Bosnia-Herzegovina's landscape.

Take, for instance, the institutionalized discourse of denial in contested zones like Prijedor, where the Liberation Day celebrated on 30 April for Bosnian Muslims and Croats stands for nothing else but the beginning of the campaign

Figure 16 Monument to the fallen Bosnian Serb heroes in Trnopolje © Maida Kosatica 2017

of ethnic cleansing of non-Serbs in the area. This blends nicely into the textbook example of Prijedor's cityscape pointing to the dynamics of polarizing narratives accomplished through systematic policies of denial (Subašić and Ćurak, 2014). And this often happens in the most banal ways, through surfaces which are a permanent part of the cityscape, as people pass them by every day. Figure 17 shows one of the tourist boards in the city, produced by the Ministry of Trade and Tourism of the Serb Republic, Town of Prijedor and Tourist Organization of Prijedor. There is not a single line addressing the 1992–5 war events, not a single word about any twentieth-century events. The public space has been 'spared' such stories and the war is simply erased – as if it had never happened. Prijedor seems to be a peculiar place where the war in general is literally skipped over in the collective historical narrative, and the voices of the minority ethnic groups are unheard.

Although Bosnia-Herzegovina's post-war memorials have not received much scholarly attention, the few authors shed some light on the predicament of monuments (e.g. Mannergren Selimovic, 2013; Ristić, 2013). Sokol (2014: 121) explains how

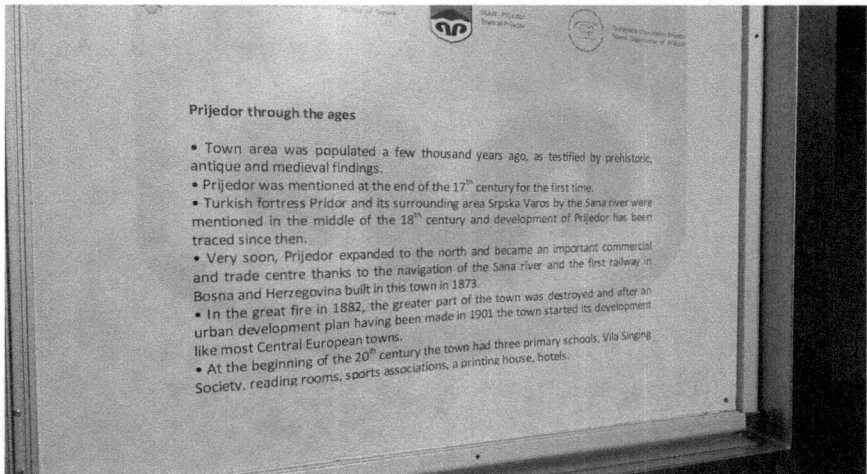

Figure 17 Tourist boards in Prijedor © Maida Kosatica 2017

Monuments in Bosnia and Herzegovina construct and reinforce mutually exclusive narratives that are part of the ethno-national identities, and as such are instruments of identity building. Memory initiatives are very rarely directed towards civic nation-building that would include all the ethno-national groups. Instead, identity consolidation is carried out on the level of the ethno-national groups, within which monuments only serve to strengthen divisions.

Regardless of how they are materially realized (in plaques, walls or stones), memorials in Bosnia-Herzegovina 'are mainly reflected through the voices of victims, warnings, and more experiential aspects' (Kosatica, 2019: 161). Especially disturbing, however, are those commemorating and glorifying convicted war criminals and political leaders promoting genocidal ideologies. Along these lines, the construction of official memorials is often obstructed, monuments are vandalized, while some places have been reported as unsafe for commemorative activities (Kosatica, forthcoming). In this sense, memorial sites act as a means of perpetuating the conflict and of symbolically defining and marking the ethnicization of territory (McDowell and Braniff, 2014). But it is the absence of monuments in particular that reveals the workings of power and uncovers even more complex, and fierce conflicts of memory in post-war Bosnia–Herzegovina. Here, I refer to the material absence of a monument as a physical element within the landscape (i.e. something that never existed in the first place). By the same token, this also refers to the non-existence of public and civic displays of information addressing and recognizing the violence and offering compassion. Of course, the absence of sound/speech/physical elements does not mean the absence of (specific) messages being conveyed. In this sense, absence and (visual) silence, understood as pragmatic and discursive strategies which achieve communicative goals (Jaworski, 1993), are acts of minority suppression that produce intensely charged places/spaces. Consider the people who witnessed the murders of their loved ones but are in one way or another prevented from commemorating their deaths publicly. What about the people who are still filled with dread, but also eager in a way for the exhumation and identification of the corpses of those missing since the war? How and where they commemorate goes beyond our understanding. Their struggles are multi-layered and complexly reflected in public space. The brief story about Omarska introduces this chapter which attends to the relationship between commemoration, performance and the semiotics of public place. Combining social semiotics and multimodality approaches, I look at a range of semiotic resources and modalities of performance (Bell and Gibson, 2011) used in post-war commemoration events fuelled by the violence and suffering that has taken place. Social semiotics is not only concerned with what people do with and use semiotic resources for, but it also considers how some groups have much greater power than others in defining public semiotic resources (Machin and Abousnnouga, 2011). In this regard, the chapter demonstrates how the weaker 'others' layer their voice into public space. The commemorative events analysed here are not simply about remembrance, nor about filling the 'empty' space; rather they produce a global message of warning conveyed by particularly visible and vocal *living memorials* (Allen and Brown, 2011). Here, I look at the ephemeral memorials and the ways public space is being performatively experienced, reinvented and appropriated.

Between commemoration and performance: Living memorials

Wodak and de Cillia (2007: 339) understand (official) commemoration as historical narratives 'discursively and visually (re)constructed, changing and shifting due to contexts and diverse, often contradicting and conflicting, political interests'. Commemoration typically involves remembering of the past (Duncan, 2014), and therefore is primarily discursive. Unlike monumentalization or memorial media occupying a single material form or specific location and representing inert matter (as in Figure 16), commemoration should be understood as a set of memorializing activities involving physical locations, artefacts, a variety of media and human bodies (Allen and Brow, 2011). This is precisely why commemoration as a rich semiotic system allows us to step away from our standard practice of analysing static and more traditional public signage, becoming in this way integral to the development of semiotic landscapes research and *corporeal sociolinguistics* (Peck and Stroud, 2015; Bucholtz and Hall, 2016). In this chapter, I am inspired by polysemous memorializing activities, (re)mediated and (re)consumed in/through time, space and language, and experienced in a variety of different ways. My interest is specifically with what Allen and Brown (2011) call *living memorials* commemorating the life of victims through a fleeting assemblage of people, things and narratives which are arranged in complex networks of activities. The idea behind living memorials is not only that people 'shape the meaning of a memorial through their own actions and energies' as Linenthal (2003: 134) argues, but that people themselves make a memorial. Following the lead of Massumi (2002) and Clough (2007) in arguing that the material body transforms into an event as the body itself becomes a memorial, Allen and Brown (2011: 314) further explain (emphasis mine) that a living memorial (and therefore commemoration in more general terms), has *the body as its centrality* that 'makes the space for meaning-making and reflection possible through its capacity to *affectively connect with other elements*' in that memorial. This view on the embodied activities making space certainly resonates well with Thurlow and Jaworski's (2014: 464) observation that spaces 'emerge in the ways we move through them, interact in them – and interact with them'. In the same vein, Pink (2007: 245) argues that 'the experiencing body is central to the production of place'. Such perspectives emphasize that space, discourse and embodied experiences are interconnected, and it is the corporeality of those present in the space that lies the performativity of commemorative events. Indeed, commemoration is a multimodal practice and social performance including symbolic, indexical and iconic semiotic dimensions, as Reisigl (2017) notes. It embodies speeches, written word, visuals, music, place arrangements, architecture, ceremony, art and the processes of collective action or interaction (McDowell and Braniff, 2014; Reisigl, 2017). Understood this way, commemoration is analysed through the prism of performance by the scholars of drama and performance studies, as well as memory, cultural and media studies (e.g. Brady and Walsh, 2009; Plate and Smelik, 2013). Critical theory, anthropology of language and social semiotics research, had also addressed the fact that semiotic processes and events are firmly linked to performance (e.g. Butler, 2015; Kitis and Milani, 2015; Helbo, 2016). The performative turn taken in this chapter does not mean that I view commemoration as a merely acted and staged event in the sense of theatrical and imaginative pieces. This is especially not the case with what I am looking at here. From the aspect of performance studies, in Spangler's (2009: 102) terms:

> To call something a performance is thus not to malign it as artificial, for the lens of performance attends to the very real narratives of memory and history that such symbols constitute, sustain, subvert, critique, or naturalize.

After all, performance 'encompasses more modes of social [...] behaviour than acting ever could' (Lampe, 1988: 182). Likewise, and as my data demonstrate, performance does not necessarily serve political elites – quite the contrary – nor is it always commodified (in Debord's terminology, 1995). However, I argue that it does widen the category of commemoration in many other ways, and as Connerton (1989) claims, it is the only act that truly preserves memory. In classic Husserlian terms, I am concerned with affective complexity or the production of emotional connections between the bodies and the narrative. And here, performance invokes much more than *représentation*, interactive street theatres and outbursts of public emotion.

There are two understandings of performance that inform this chapter. First, performance is 'an embodied behaviour that privileges body over speech, presence over absence, and praxis over product' (Plate and Smelik, 2013: 9). Second, performance is (artistic) communication in focused interaction (Bauman, 2011). These 'simple' definitions are akin to the way Butler (2015: 83) discusses the performance of bodies that speak politically not only in vocal or written language – 'both action and gesture signify and speak, both as action and claim: the one is not finally extricable from the other'. In other words, bodies are both material and discursive. Aligned with Goffman's (1959) frame of reference on the performing bodies that communicate through/with themselves, Butler's work demonstrates how bodies (understood as beyond biological organisms) are complex active processes that (affectively) communicate in/with the world. And such notions underpin some current developments within the field of linguistic landscapes (Milani et al., 2018) which analyse how the bodies performatively bring into being spatial turbulence in interaction with other bodies and the materiality of urban environments (e.g. protest performances). It is this focus on the body and the bodily experience that has uncovered, for the semiotic landscapes scholarship especially, not only performative but also affective and emotional dimensions negotiated and layered into place/space (e.g. Peck and Stroud, 2015; Wee, 2016; Milani, Levon and Glocer, 2019). In Milani's (2015: 445) terms, 'performances cannot be fully captured without considering their highly affective component'. The emergent 'embodiment' turns focusing on affect and experience is what the recent investigations of memoryscapes have caught up with as well, such as memorial museums or concentration camp memorials. Here, bodily pragmatics and embodied semiotics work as a strategy to convey the experience of human hardship 'created by somatic sensations, positions, attitudes, and senses' (Goh, 2016: 5). Such work ultimately tells us that to deal with the body is to deal with the viscerality of politics, be it in the form of protests or commemorative practices. By the same token, Sheller and Urry (2006: 216) remind us that the body is 'an affective vehicle through which we sense place'. As such, our bodies become part of commemoration, 'turning our ears, eyes, and senses' (Birdsall and Drozdzewski, 2017: 5). In fact, the bodies affect and are affected, and when people move their bodies, 'they do so with feeling and emotion' (Stroud and Prinsloo, 2015: xi). For all these reasons, the body is a compelling site (or a resource) for gaining insight into the performance-memory nexus. Commemorative events analysed in this chapter focus on the 1992–5 violence marking the regions of Prijedor and Srebrenica, but are not limited to these places, and appear in other cities across Bosnia-Herzegovina and other countries. By this token, all data are directly related to what happened at the sites of concentration camps, ethnic cleansing and genocide. There are two types of commemoration events I am looking at here: commemorative initiatives and commemorative public art installations. The first type is organized by the local citizens mostly through grassroots initiatives, where memorials are temporarily being built with/through a large compacted body composed of the many participating human bodies. Also called *grassroots memorials* such type of commemorative practice, as Truc and Sánchez-Carretero (2019: 36) explain, is performative in nature with a direct material arrangement pointing to 'levels of social distress experienced in response to a particular event in ways that other memorials might not; they signal an event that is felt as traumatic by a group'. On the other hand, public art installations are originally created by artists, where the commemorative moment is fully accomplished once people interact with them. The character of these commemorative events shares some elements of protests which Kitis and Milani (2015: 274) define as 'performances in which people engage with the spaces they intentionally occupy, orienting their bodies towards transgressing and reconstituting space by affecting its materiality'. Both commemorative initiatives and public art installations are ephemeral in character working like anniversaries 'constructed in relation to silences' and 'materialised in who gets to be commemorated and by whom, and this in turn is at the base of the conflicts of memories and the polarisation process of memorial sites' (Truc and Sánchez-Carretero, 2019: 35). Traveling and moving, being massively (re)mediated and visited, commemorative events I look at become 'big' and popular objects of public attention (Carr and Fisher, 2016), and result in a plethora of digital media resources such as photographs capturing the events available on social networking sites and artists' official websites, professional video recordings and interviews with the participants available in online media outlets, amateur videos uploaded on YouTube and Facebook. Consequentially, I have collected multimedia/multimodal data, namely videos and images that were culled from electronic sources mentioned above. Such diversity of sources attempts also to reduce what Kitis and Milani (2015: 273) call 'the partiality of the point of view'. Combining social semiotics and multimodality approaches, as well as performance theories, I analyse a range of semiotic resources and modalities of performance such as set, sound, appearance, movement and gesture (Bell and Gibons, 2011) at a transdisciplinary level (Halliday, 2001; McMurtrie and Murphy, 2016). The transdisciplinary approach, as Chiapello and Fairclough (2002: 206) explain, creates a dialogue between disciplines and theoretical-analytical frameworks 'through a process of each internally appropriating the logic of the other as a resource for its own development'. Therefore, it aims to understand multiple meaning-making systems (e.g. language, movement) and 'transcend disciplinary boundaries to achieve the kind of integrated focus necessary to research' (Unsworth, 2008: 8–9). Although we can imagine how multimodal commemoration is, a transdisciplinary analysis allows for investigation, inter alia, how chosen modes for commemorative expression affect the dynamics of performance and the role of audience interacting with the installations/participation in commemorative events. As McMurtrie and Murphy (2016: 450) explain, the transdisciplinary approach is not only about what those who perform say, but 'whether and how performance can enable social change through enabling movement'. Stroud's (2016: 10) notion that 'place take the shapes of the bodies that inhabit them' while the place 'incites bodies to become' brings me to a convenient organization of this study which follows the two types of commemorative events identified in the next section: commemorative initiatives and commemorative public art installations. I look at two commemorative events: *The White Armbands Day* and *Što te nema* (Why are you not here), relying also on other commemorative events which present contemporary (but by no means exclusive) commemorative events in Bosnia-Herzegovina and beyond.

Commemorative initiatives

The struggle for memorials in Prijedor officially started in 2012, when a man whose brother and father were imprisoned in the Omarska camp was denied a visit to the former camp by the guards of ArcelorMittal company – the current owner of the Omarska complex. On that day, several activist associations in Prijedor planned a public gathering to commemorate the women and girls who were killed in the area but were prohibited by the local authorities. Determined to answer the prohibitions, the man put a piece of white cloth around his left arm and stood silently alone in the city's square with a white body bag at his feet for couple of minutes (Figure 18). Meant to protest and provoke, this man's act introduced a new language of commemoration in Bosnia–Herzegovina and became an instrument of resistance aimed at raising awareness. Extract 2 shows his own interpretation of this 'intervention' and his emotional state in particular:

Extract 2

It was a very weird feeling, an overwhelming feeling of dehumanization, the same one I remembered from 1992. I was once again marked as 'the other' in the city where I was born. Victims in Prijedor aren't seen, and I wanted to show them, 'You can't erase me'.

(*The New Yorker*, 2015)[7]

Clearly responding to a personal trauma, here we see what Truc and Sánchez-Carretero (2019: 35) characterize as 'a communicative gesture that asks for action', commemorating victims, expressing emotions and protesting. What is

Figure 18 A man with a white armband standing on the main square in Prijedor © *Stop Genocide Denial* May 2012 (reproduced with permission)

remarkable about this case is how the act of one individual armed only with the tranquillity of his own body, feeling a burden of responsibility to commemorate, became an affective performance in just a couple of seconds, promoting the rights of those in body bags and highlighting a very present social and spatial marginalization. Quite literally, this man could have easily ended up in one of those bags had he not been expelled from Prijedor when he was a child. One could argue that his embodied performance 'screams' without a single spoken word that the bodies refusing to be silenced will find a way to commemorate. Through a banal marking – a piece of white cloth, this centralized body became both powerful through the man's courage and the refusal to be 'erased', and vulnerable at the same time as he relives those feelings he experienced as a child. The act also makes intertextual references to the period when Serb forces began to ethnically cleanse Prijedor of its non-Serb residents. After the Serb forces took control of the Prijedor area, a decree was issued via local radio for all non-Serbs to mark their houses with white flags and to wear white armbands when leaving their homes. The white armband marking of the man works as the reperformance or restaging of the dehumanization practices dating back to 1992, serving again to reach back into the past, both as a speech act – the voice for those that were killed, and as an act of confirmation – protesting and standing up for those who crave public recognition. Here, the body roughly presents itself in what Goh (2016) defines a *tithenal* posture (from the Greek *tithenai* – to put in place) since the man places himself in a bodily position analogous to that of the suffering bodies (i.e. marked for death and vulnerable). Hence, white armbands work as deictics which allow the man to assume and even relive the experience. At the same time, a *synecdochal strategy* (from the Greek *sun* and *ekdekhesthai* – to take up together) is accomplished by the display of a white armband whose 'nature is physically connected to suffering bodies' (Goh, 2016: 11). In this sense, the armbands evoke both bodily and intimate experiences. The one man's personal protest is known today as the first commemorative initiative in Prijedor. Posted and shared online, this story entered the digital space and received much attention. On 5 August 2012 (the 20th anniversary of Vulliamy's Omarska camp exposure) the story got its sequel when different local associations organized a peaceful walk throughout the city, carrying 102 empty school backpacks with the names of the children that were killed. With these backpacks activists wrote 'GENOCIDE?' on the main square which resulted in one of the associations' directors, who initiated this act, being taken into custody. Four months later, the local Commemoration Committee planned to organize a gathering to bring attention to human rights violations in the Prijedor area on 10 December, International Human Rights Day. The event was banned without any legal reason being given, and as a response to it, seven people walked through the city with white tape over their mouths and a banner reading 'When human rights are violated, civil disobedience becomes a duty'.[8] The following year on 31 May, the local authorities once again did not give permission to activists to organize a commemoration event. Nonetheless, dozens of people gathered in the city's square, peacefully standing above 256 neatly arranged white body bags with the names of the women and girls that were killed. In this sense, the commemoration works as an embodied reaction to the political pressures in which the bodies are symbolically 'pressed against the bodies representing authority (the police) in an attempt to reconfigure space' (Kitis and Milani, 2015: 274). Nonetheless, it does not produce what Kitis and Milani (2015) identify as 'confrontational encounters' in sense that human bodies in these commemorations do not perform any violent force. Initiated through the association *Jer me se tiče* (Because it concerns me), the commemorative gathering is known today as *The White Armbands Day*, with the number of participants/supporters growing every year. Although it had been previously claimed that the commemoration threatened the stability and peace of the Prijedor area, to this day, no violent incidents have taken place. The name of the commemoration and the date are directly related to the day the radio decree about white armbands was issued. The spokesman for the *Killed Children of Prijedor* Association explains that a request for the construction of a monument for all killed civilians had been submitted to the local authorities. As consent had not been given, in 2014 the association asked for at least a monument for the 102 killed children (96 Bosnian Muslims, 4 Bosnian Croats and 2 Bosnian Serbs). What was then proposed is a monument outside the city. As with graffiti whose significance depends on emplacement, once again, we are reminded of the role of space/place as a meaning-making resource. As with graffiti whose significance depends on emplacement, once again, we are reminded of the role of space/place as a meaning-making resource. Needless to say, to those asking for a monument the emplacement outside the city is not negotiable as it would essentially denote accepting the rhetoric of denial and agreeing to hide the most painful consequences of the war from the public eye. After several proposed and rejected locations, in 2021, the association and local authorities agreed that the monument be built in the city park. *The White Armbands Day* event usually starts around noon in the city centre where armbands and roses are given to participants, mostly activists of different local associations and family members of the victims. The visitors from other parts of Bosnia–Herzegovina and abroad join the participants, while the representatives of local authorities do not attend *The White Armbands* events. Slowly and silently, almost without a word, the crowd marked with armbands walks through the main pedestrian area carrying roses and banners with different slogans and short messages calling for solidarity (e.g. *Don't deny it, Solidarity is our weapon*). The annually repeated messages primarily convey empathy and non-violently appeal for a change-based discourse, understanding and agreement regarding the violent past, without any emphasis on religious or ethnic divisions. These messages are also a part of the final short speeches given after a monument is symbolically constructed, in which the representatives of different associations address the authorities asking to build a monument to children killed in Prijedor without further delay. The focus on children and the justice storyline never changes, but those responsible for the absence of a monument are nonetheless heavily condemned. *The White Armbands Day* is purposefully, though not exclusively, characterized by verbal silence. As an important modality of performance (Bell and Gibson, 2011) such sound configuration has its own potential. Participants are intended to remain silent throughout all stages of commemoration, and especially when their walk is 'interrupted' by the slowly but loudly echoed 102 names, interchangeably pronounced by a male and a female voice. The soundscape generally scales between complete silence (laying roses on the ground), whispers (parents instructing children how to interact with installations), and ambient noise (different layers of background sounds). Indeed, 'silence is no absolute' (Jaworski, 1993: 159), and here, it does not indicate any sort of suppression of emotional expression, but dignity, respect and empathy. As we all know, silence is a familiar strategy used to create memorializing atmospheres that evoke affective reflection (see Wee, 2016 on cemeteries), make the dead present and 'bring us back to ourselves' (Brown, 2012: 247). Therefore, when non-participants laugh or loudly greet each other as evident in some online footage, it is interpreted as the absence of solidarity with those who mourn, a rude interruption of the moment of silence for the dead. Likewise, the initiative acknowledges when the spectators respect the silence. Silence, as Birdsall and Drozdzewski (2017: 11) explain, is 'part of a wider assemblage of commemoration and a contributor, if not a vehicle for performing the spectacle of memory'. In the same way white armbands and other semiotic means unify mourners, such soundscape produces 'a smoothing of the jumble of multivocality, bodies and language into one "voice"' (Stroud, 2016: 8). In Allen and Brown's (2011: 316) view, it is precisely 'the organization of a transient mass of bodies into a silent collective that affords the possibility of formal commemoration'. The climactic point of the event is being realized when the collective reaches the square, and a symbolic construction of a monument begins – a defining moment in the memorial production and the initial purpose of *The White Armbands Day*. Allen and Brown (2011: 314) explain, 'the centrality of embodiment is one of the key media through which living memorials perpetuate themselves'. Indeed, without the supporting bodies a monument could not be constructed. The creation of the monument is clearly a *bodily feedback* (Goh 2016) to unmarked sites of violence. When participants reach the square, they walk to the centre and at a prearranged location start laying the roses in the shape of a circle (the so-called *Rose Ring*). This moment illustrates how Allen and Brown (2011: 319) understand a living memorial – there must be an active involvement in commemoration, done through embodiment rather than a symbolic connection. Once the roses have been placed, the ring is vacated. There is no agreement on who places the first rose, it is rather a spontaneous activity. While the bodies lay down the roses, the surrounding participants stand framing and supporting them. Their appearance is what Butler (2011: 87) calls

> a morphological moment where the body risks appearance not only in order to speak and act, but to suffer and move, as well, to engage other bodies, to negotiate an environment on which one depends, to establish a social organization for the satisfaction of needs.

Indeed, the roses are only powerful against the background of regimented bodies. Like a choreography, unrehearsed, yet learnt as it repeats every year, we see here the actual 102 uniform bodies. What really alters the site of agony, are the *bodies in alliance* (Butler, 2011) making the performative moment possible in the first place. Such embodied uniformity we find in other living memorials. Take, for instance, the commemoration in the former camp of Omarska where mourners take hundreds of white balloons from the White House before the culminating act of releasing them into the sky. Sailing through the blue canvas for a couple of minutes, the *balloon monument* disrupts and occupies space, to some extent. In these culminating moments artefacts and bodies do not ever work as separate entities, rather they are mutually constitutive in the production of symbolic and ephemeral, but nonetheless powerful monuments. Kress and van Leeuwen (2002: 354) remind us that colours are also signifiers of associative symbolic and emotive values. Accordingly, delicate means for the construction of monuments work quite straightforwardly – balloons and roses in this case, conveying the messages of mourning and innocence (white), and bleeding and violence (red). Embraced with a white name tag wrapped around its thorny stalk, each rose at *The White Armbands Day* represents one innocent body. Likewise, the balloons represent the exhumed bodies from the mass graves found in the area. In a quiet, yet visually eloquent way, both means allow us to actually see the scale of loss and make a greater sense of the number of victims. Participants at *The White Armbands Day* use a variety of semiotic means such as body markers, banners and accompanying artefacts such as school bags, shoes or toy blocks all symbolically representing the innocence of children. The bodies interact with these elements affectively through touch as a resource for making meaning (Bezemer and Kress, 2014). In the words of Cranny-Francis (2011: 470), touch is not only a physical or intellectual, but also an emotional practice which 'places the toucher in an intimate relation to the touched, an acceptance of "being with" that creates the opportunity for an empathetic relationship between the two'. Whether cutting a white piece of cloth into hundreds of armbands or wrapping name tags around the stalks of roses, people are constantly interacting with the artefacts, and with each other. Here we see various touchpoint activities that create tangible interactive systems we find both in the body-to-bod (e.g. tying armbands around each other's arms) and in the body-to-an object (e.g. writing the names on the artefacts) relationships. As *The White Armbands Day* is highly (re)mediated and mediatized, the global community learns about its backstory – who is the monument for, why has it not been erected, who is preventing this and how? In the midst of websites, online news portals and television appearances, a particular way of how *The White Armbands Day* is remediated is evident in photographs shared on Facebook. These photographs illustrate how at the same time 'the body both remediates and is remediated' (Bolter and Grusin, 2003: 238). Supporters use *spectacular self-locations* (Thurlow and Jaworski, 2014) and the nature of photography itself is performatively corporeal. However, these are much different from everyday tourist performances. Here, people use mega-popular sights in order to communicate where the support comes from and the event's worldwide reach. In this sense, posing a marked body in front of the Eiffel Tower could be interpreted as a strategy of visual scaling since we are being told how far the event has travelled in space and time through a huge number of supporters. These visuals show how commemoration circulates on social media networks through worldwide assemblages of living memorials. Photographs also centralize the vulnerable bodies marked with white armbands. Knudsen and Stage (2016: 8) note that 'exposing one's own vulnerable body has become a way to capture the interest and political attention of the global public sphere'. In other words, these vulnerable bodies are not simply out on a limb. They show a support to those who are at the real sites of commemoration, remediating offline living memorials on a global scale. What this tells us is that size matters – the number of posted and shared pictures is as important as the number of bodies walking together to the main square in Prijedor. Heavily remediated, this is seen equally as a shared experience and united bodily performance producing a virtual living memorial. Most certainly, other examples of living memorials have a more pronounced bodily dimension, sensory modality, synchronized choreography and a strict design, like *The living flower of Srebrenica* event performed during the annual Srebrenica Genocide commemoration. Taking place at different locations, it carries monolithic assemblages of bodies that build the symbol of the genocide with eleven petals standing for the date when it began (11 July 1995). The synchronized bodies, performing at the *Place des Nations* square in Geneva in 2015, follow the empowering artistic representation of memory, the oratorio *Srebrenica Inferno* (Softić, 2011). Through the voice and image of an orphan as a metaphor for all the people who lost someone in the genocide, the oratorio emphasizes the feelings of inconsolability and loneliness. Such a soundscape guides bodies through the stages of the performance. As a video excerpt shows, when the oratorio starts, the bodies are facing the ground and encircling a red centre, illustrating the dead bodies bleeding into a pool of blood. The oratorio is then interrupted with a prayer in accordance with the traditional Islamic funeral. During the second aria, the bodies roll over on their backs facing the sky as if to manifest the exhumed bodies recovered at last to be buried with dignity. At this point, the red fabric is removed, revealing the green flower centre, while a section of the audience waits for the signal to release the white balloons. The others (*audience as witness*) actively watch in order for the event to succeed (Beeman, 1993). Just like the mothers, wives and sisters hugging the green-draped caskets under the July sun in Potočari, memory performers surrounding the flower centre display the collective funeral gestures we see during the annual burials. Working as a tithenal-synechdochal strategy, the performance relies on the performers firstly acquiring the specific physical feature of bleeding bodies and then pragmatically embodying the suffering bodies of women bidding their final farewell. As Goh (2016) observes, such practices evoke affective discomfort in the audience. In other instances, the flower is built with a massive number of the bodies in white where the performance includes other elements, such as the number of genocide victims – *8372*. Delivering a hypermediated picture of the annual commemoration, *The Living Flower of Srebrenica* works as both a political message and also a protest against the denial of genocide, nationalism and violence. This is precisely why platforms are of crucial importance – the *Place des Nations* square in Geneva or a football stadium conveniently chosen for capturing the performance on a colossal stage. Turning back to the *White Armbands Day*, it is by no means a coincidence that the participants of the event occupy the main pedestrian area of Prijedor, and that the roses are left in the centre of the city's only square. Equally staged and similar in scale, the multi-city *White Armbands Day* is propagated to other places across the globe (e.g. Canada, Sweden, Switzerland, Australia, the USA, Turkey, France, Austria, Denmark). During the 2015 commemoration in Geneva, the white armbands were tied around the bars of the fence of the United Nation's complex, the leading intergovernmental body responsible for promoting and protecting human rights. Here, place 'embeds the event as an international political symbol and enhance its commemorability' (Conway, 2010: 101) and expands its meaning – it is a call for civil rights and justice as much as it is a reminder to the 1990s crimes that happened in the Prijedor area. Once again, we are reminded that place is key. It is precisely the commemoration platforms that show the performative quality and significance of place, empowering the mourners with 'increased visibility for their actions and message of protest' (Kitis and Milani, 2015: 280). *The White Armbands Day* is a living memorial accomplished through performative bodies inviting to share such platforms with others – everyone is welcome to join the unified body in asking for a monument. However, those who the space is shared with choose to prolong the rhetoric of denial for which the minority group still suffers enormously. During the 2021 *White Armbands Day* event in Prijedor, not far from the square where the Rose Ring is being built, a local organization put up posters reading *Stop the Serbophobic lie about the made-up white armbands! The lie shall not pass!* How the denial of violence is countered through art performance in and beyond Bosnia-Herzegovina, I demonstrate in the next section where I turn to another form of memorializing activities where the embodied interaction with artefacts enhances the experience of commemoration.

Commemorative public art installations

When a painful memory is indescribable, and words are simply not enough, the memory is faithfully and meaningfully brought to us through art which intensely captures and reveal those who suffer(ed). Possibly, the biggest (in terms of the actual size and public response) and most memorable commemorative public art performance in Bosnia-Herzegovina was the day-long event *Sarajevo Red Line* dedicated to the civilians killed in the capital during the 1992–6 siege. Performed as a one-time only event on 6 April 2012 (the date the war broke out in 1992), it occupied 800 meters of Sarajevo's main street with 11,541 red chairs arranged in 825 rows (the official number of civilians killed) to create 'a river of blood'. For a short while only, the emplacement of chairs just in front of one of the city's major landmarks, *The Eternal Flame* (a memorial to the victims of Second World War) caused a proper disruption of space and everyday life amplifying the impression left by the extraordinary experience. It is quite emblematic, since on many occasions during the war, Sarajevo's main streets were literally stained with blood. The event is scalar because it fosters variables such as the size of the performance and the variety of media – convenient since it is precisely this place that fits over 11,000 chairs and strategic because it enables the producers to control this part of the city (car-dominated street closed to traffic). All this, as Kitis and Milani (2015: 280) observe, indicates that the producers want 'increased visibility for their actions and message'. But perhaps even more importantly, this profoundly changes the spatio-affective experience for citizens. In many ways 6 April 2012 was indeed the day the city of Sarajevo stood still. Yet, for the visitors, the recognizable off-limits, exclusive space for vehicles was suddenly redesigned as a space of increased physical mobility where they could move between the chairs in no right or wrong direction. Such an approachable platform did not only change the space visually, but also influenced the way people moved and affectively interacted with the artefacts, accomplishing the event to its entirety. In art performances, as Giovannucci (2013: 449) explains, 'the use of multiple mediums enhances the ability of an audience to connect, thus giving people an opportunity to relate to the tragedy whether it directly affected them or not'. The most powerful modes of communication at the *Sarajevo Red Line* were the three-dimensional objects and music. Although music as a semiotic mode (van Leeuwen, 1999) 'conveys meaning potentials' (Machin and Richardson, 2012: 329), systematic analysis of sound is beyond the scope of this section, nonetheless there are a few relevant particularities of the event's soundscape, especially since the performance was envisaged as a concert (not in the typical sense) for those who are no longer here to attend it. On the red stage, choirs, soloists and actors delivered poetry and traditional Bosnian songs through the highbrow representations of oriental Bosnian music, yet still associated with melancholy. The soundscape made the audience attentive and silent, but more importantly, it allowed for a musical experience that is essentially a bodily experience (Eyerman, 2002). As we know, music is much more than sound, but it is not only 'a correlate for bodily movements' (Zbikowski, 2013: 114). It induces affect (Juslin and Sloboda, 2011), 'communicates high emotion' (Machin and Richardson, 2012: 338) and confirms collective identity, as Eyerman (2002: 450) explains:

> Collective experience, listening with the whole (individual and collective) body is more important than the cognitive experience of the text, at least in the opening stages, but probably all along the way. The music encourages bodily movement and contact, and collective experience. This emotionally loaded experience will be talked about, remembered and embodied as powerfully emotional, thus linking the individual to the collective.

Visually speaking, cheap plastic chairs which were imported from Serbia at dismay of many spectators were the strongest visuals allowing the audience to understand the brutality of the killing and the scale of loss. The artefacts were strategically chosen by the author as they 'represent a future presence; they are never just chairs; someday they will be filled again' (*New York Times*).[9] Yet, the seats were never filled, paradoxically emphasizing the presence of the absent civilians. During the programme, the audience physically interacted with these artefacts, as anticipated by the author – *They would walk up and down and choose a chair and that would become the chair of someone lost. They left flowers or a message and by the end of the day all chairs were filled* (Haris Pašović for *New York Times*).[10] As Connolly (2011: 616) explains, 'effective trauma narratives require a particular form of artistic representation' recreating spaces for dialogue. A particularly strong example of this is perhaps most evident in the heightened state of intimacy and close encounters with 643 smaller chairs representing the dead bodies of children. With the missing buried bodies and their headstones, chairs themselves were approached as graves and sentiments at work here are similar to those appropriate to the ambience of a cemetery. Children in particular were encouraged to decorate the chairs with toys. In this sense, as the audience would place flowers, letters and objects on the chairs, it was evident that audience treated the installation as a cemetery. Ultimately, *Sarajevo Red Line* illustrates how the semiotics of space incite the bodies *to be* (Stroud, 2016), in other words, how bodies present in the public space are animated by strategic artistic invitations in order to manifest a memorial to its full potential. Although the affective experience described above remains localized and only really experienced by the visitors themselves, Giovannucci (2013: 449) suggests that 'the immediate impact of the memorial affected not just those seeing it with their own eyes, in person, but those watching it through news coverage around the world'. Again, we have a remediated experience. *Sarajevo Red Line* was reported mostly through lexical scaling moving between past and present, where the narrative circulating was no more about the event itself as about what preceded it all those years ago. Different newspapers delivered the story in similar ways: *the longest siege* is not measured in years but months and days – *44 months*, the number of victims killed is constantly repeated in the reports, as well as the exact number of citizens living under *330 shells a day* falling on the city, with *the daily record of 3777 grenades* (Daily Mai).[11] Similarly, the event is identified as a global event *sending a message to the world*, the rows of chairs are described as *endless*, measured in miles – *stretched half a mile down Marshal Tito street* (New York Times),[12] visited by *tens of thousands of passers-by overwhelmed by the length of the red river* who are witnessing the consequences of *slaughter and an unspeakable horror* (Independent).[13] As Carr and Fisher (2016: 138) argue, scalar discourse that emerges in the mediation of events has a power to establish them as big 'with even bigger implications about the past and for the future'. It is precisely through these scalar strategies in written language that readers come to visualize the war and consume the presented enormity of the violence and the importance of *Sarajevo Red Line* which introduces us to more contemporary art installations (produced for people generationally distant from the trauma or those who have not witnessed a traumatic event).

Perhaps one of the most perennial so-called nomadic monument is *Što te nema* (as in an old Bosnian song in translation *Why are you not here*). The installation had its debut in Sarajevo in 2006. Apart from its third instalment presented in the city of Tuzla (Bosnia-Herzegovina, 2008), it has been performed abroad: 2007 – The United Nations Headquarters in New York City, 2009 – Het

Plein in The Hague, 2010 – Norrmalmstorg in Stockholm, 2011 – Church Street in Burlington, 2012 – Taksim Square in Istanbul, 2013 – Washington Square Park in New York City, 2014 – Yonge-Dundas Square in Toronto, 2015 – Place de Saint-Gervais in Geneva, 2016 – Copley Square in Boston, 2017 – Daley Plaza in Chicago, 2018 – Helvetiaplatz in Zurich, 2019 – Serra dei Giardini in Venice. In 2020, marking the 25th anniversary of the genocide, the memorial was recreated in Srebrenica, and this version will remain permanently at *Memorial Center Potočari*. Organized every year on 11 July, *Što te nema* is directly connected to the Srebrenica Genocide annual commemoration. As the site of genocide has been turned into a cemetery and memorial centre (including a museum and other memorial sites), the *Što te nema* memorial is not a performative expression attempting to realize a non-existing monument. It aims to publicly counter the still and more-than-ever existing denial of the genocide. Organized in cooperation between the artist and the transnational diaspora, and often sponsored by local institutions, the installation mainly occupies cities' 'outdoor assembly spaces' (Martin Rojo, 2014). The choice of prominent locations for the exhibition in the cities may give the events a more long-term visibility and support in different ways (Conway, 2008). Indeed, high-quality platforms have a potential for social actions like no other places, providing increased visibility for signage and interactions, while also affecting the size of the events (Kitis and Milani, 2015).

Simple in content and design, *Što te nema* consists of an ever-growing collection of small porcelain coffee cups (traditional Bosnian *fildžani*). It starts with empty cups neatly arranged on the ground in the shape of a circle along with the traditional pots (*džezve*) filled with freshly hand-made Bosnian coffee placed on the perimeter of the circle. Donated mostly by diasporic Bosnians, every cup is different – 'some are marked with a name of the family that donated the cup, others have cracks from age and use, while still others were bought and donated specifically for the purpose of the project' (Karabegović, 2014: 469). The number of cups corresponds to the number of the people whose remains were exhumed from the mass graves, identified and buried in the Potočari cemetery. The setting is described as minimalistic and free of national markings as Karabegović (2014) claims – there are no signs, flyers, flags, banners, speeches, nor donations. However, sometimes the smallest details bring out almost unnoticeable moments of nationalism. A cup with the coat of arms of Bosnia and Herzegovina (usually representing the Bosnian Muslim Army), or the participants wearing the Bosnia-Herzegovina flag around their shoulders, ever so slightly remind other diaspora members of their true background and nationhood. It is precisely these subtle moments that point to the relationship between remembering and (public displays of) nationalism. As Wodak and colleagues (2009) demonstrated in their analyses of commemorative speeches, the narratives of remembering are constitutive elements of *imagined communities* (Anderson, 1983), and thus of the discursive construction of national identities. Nationalism necessarily always draws on narratives of the past (Wodak and de Cillia, 2007), and if that past is tragic, as in this case, it is not surprising that commemoration is extremely contested by, and inevitably provides, a certain dose of ethnonationalism. Unlike commemorative initiatives where embodied activities constitute the physical basis of a memorial (Allen and Brown, 2011), here, the body plays a different role and has a somewhat different status. As Shohamy and Waksman (2013) explain, any public space is a dynamic and fluid, and people in it simply *do* things. Consequently, participants' engagements with the installation change and constantly shift in one way or another – they pour the coffee, move around the installation, partake in the conversations, take pictures, watch in silence, cry. Just like the participants who symbolically approached and decorated the red chairs as graves at the *Sarajevo Red Line* event, here, people crouch in prayer over the cups as they would do when visiting a Muslim cemetery. A bizarre emplacement of coffee cups on the ground provokes passers-by to stop around the installation, pour coffee into the cups and take a moment to reflect. This becomes a shared performance where people pour the coffee immediately with the volunteers instructing them, or they repeat it after watching others. Once poured, the coffee remains un-drunk while the participants immerse themselves in conversation. An especially important 'invitation medium' is the intense aroma of Bosnian coffee occupying the squares and spreading 'outwards into the surroundings' (Lefebvre, 1991: 198). Pennycook and Otsuji (2014: 196, 200) argue that smells apart from intersecting with other senses, 'evoke memories and places' and 'make central the capacity of the senses to connect across time and space'. They invite us to focus on a broader domain of the unintended aspects of *smellscapes* (Pennycook and Otsuji, 2014), but just like with the deliberately chosen platform, unintentionality seems not to be the case here. Hence, the strong smell of coffee could be interpreted as a 'welcome sign' (Jaworski, 2014), indeed a 'dark attraction' (Golańska, 2015), which is 'above all associational' and does 'a great deal of semiotic work' (Pennycook and Otsuji, 2014: 208–9). Yet, how exactly does the coffee enable people to commemorate? Apart from the method of preparation (similar to the Turkish coffee) and serving, there is nothing extraordinary in this simple drink known to everybody. However, as Croegaert (2011) explains, the peculiarity of Bosnian coffee lies in its authentic deep-rooted socio-cultural ritual. Closely linked to the concept of *ćejf* that 'involves senses of time: slowing time, transcending time, to enjoy life without hurrying' (Alexander, 2006: 407), it is an integral part of everyday Bosnian life. A dosage is taken several times a day and every time for a different occasion: compulsory morning one, noon coffee, guest coffee, coffee for special occasions, cigarette coffee. Moreover, people never drink coffee by themselves, and here we find the paradox of un-drunk coffee sitting on the ground. Symbolically, the Bosniak women of Srebrenica are waiting for the men to join them in the coffee drinking ritual, but they will never come and therefore the coffee stays un-drunk and cold. In other words, the women are waiting for the bodily remains of their loved ones to be exhumed while the coffee gets cold and the sensation of *ćejf* times with their families can never be brought back. As we have already seen in the previous section, the synecdochal strategy of displaying the artefacts whose nature is intimately connected to the suffering bodies of survivors is both important in understanding the scale of loss and moving the participants affectively. Simple yet effective, the cups of coffee as well as the survivor's memories remain full and very personal, particularly to those who continue to suffer still awaiting some kind of closure. They represent, at the same time, the victims and survivors of Srebrenica, indeed, of the entire Bosnia-Herzegovina as Extract 3 shows:

Extract 3

I'm not from Srebrenica. However, I did lose my father during the war in 1993. He was taken to Omarska and he was murdered. So I'm actually here to commemorate him as well as everybody who was lost during the Srebrenica genocide. My father's body was never recovered. We, for the past 25 years, have not had a grave to mourn over. It's just a dark cloud that's been hanging over my head all this time and I was three years old when this happened.

(*Što te nema*, Chicago 2017)

Marianne Hirsch (2002: 98), who focuses especially on visual art, writes that 'the challenge for the post-memorial artist is precisely to allow the spectator to enter the image, to imagine the disaster in one's own body'. Hirsch (1997) uses the term *postmemory* to refer to a powerful form of memory mediated through an imaginative investment and creation. It seems that the concept of postmemory also aligns with Goh's (2016) synechdocal and tithenal bodies. Indeed, it is through the bodies' close engagement with a strategically produced material-spatial media that we see these strategies at work. This is comparable to other nomadic memorials like the *Prijedor 92* installation designed to amplify the anxiety and discomfort with a confined space and the hanging pictures of the victims.

The second integral part of *Što te nema* is manifested through Bosnian coffee, as already pointed out, the invitation medium of the installation. However, quite literary, Bosnian coffee is an invitation for a conversation. Croegaert (2011) explains that the process of preparation and drinking coffee accompanies certain sorts of conversations. Here, coffee has an important role in inviting people to express their thoughts and feelings. As video recordings available on the *Što te nema* Facebook page show, participants, volunteers and the organization team members seem to be standing and talking to each other in every stage of the event. Karabegović (2014: 467) already made a point of the volunteers who answer participants' questions about the war – 'in turn, participants share their own stories or stories they connect in relation to the topic or ask further questions'. As Croegaert (2011: 645) puts it, coffee is a mnemonic device:

> The talk surrounding Bosnian coffee emphasizes memory and distinctions of time (before the war and after), place (here and there), and people (those who left and those who remain).

Conversations at *Što te nema*, specifically about Srebrenica, work as affective interactions and deep emotional interconnectedness leading people to come to learn, imagine and understand the pain of distant suffering bodies. The embodied performance of pouring the coffee in cups juxtaposed against loud bodies that discuss and react to a past that they themselves did not witness, yet able to feel the suffering deeply, brings us closer to the meaning of the participatory commemoration that intensifies the experience of affective identification (Extract 4):

Extract 4

I'm not Bosnian. I've done volunteer work with Bosnia for 20 years and what happened in Srebrenica bothers me to this day, and anything I can do just to try to share the burden of the survivors and to commemorate those people whose lives are lost, I'm more than happy to participate. Every July is very painful for me because there hasn't really been justice for people from Srebrenica... there has been a lot of denial of crimes.

(*Što te nema*, Chicago 2017)

Extract 4 shows how public art commemorations are actively implicated in a veritable transmission of the Bosnian Muslims' narrative beyond the boundaries of Bosnia-Herzegovina, perhaps in an attempt to gain recognition elsewhere since in Bosnia-Herzegovina itself the rhetoric of denial stands in the way. As people inevitably feel the need to place blame and to name those who inflicted the injustice, the inevitable 'politicization' attempts to achieve a consensus outside in the hope of obtaining consensus within Bosnia-Herzegovina through external pressure. In the minds of the participants and spectators, a question almost certainly arises, 'Who did this'? And if the answer is given, the (Bosnian) Serbs, then the direction in which the animosity ought to go becomes clear. Whether this is the only way to counter the denial of violence or not, commemoration sites allow multiple reading positions adopted by outsiders who are inevitably engaged in debating and rethinking the personal and collective stories embedded in these sites (Shohamy and Waksman, 2010). At this intersection of semiotic landscapes and commemoration we see that the spaces of art performance work as a means of communication and a very efficient form of remembering bringing to the fore people's investment in the historical, national and emotional narratives (Sohamy and Waksman, 2010). These spaces come to be understood as extensions and reproductions of Bosnia-Herzegovina's traumascapes which remain deliberately unrecognized. The movement of traumascapes is crucial for local ethnic minorities in order to receive transnational support and recognition from outsiders. Thus, spaces of commemoration outside Bosnia-Herzegovina are an integral component of its traumascapes active in defying the imposed local regimes of memory and remembering.

Conclusion

Gaining momentum amongst language and discourse analysts, performative activities (such as demonstrations, protests, public assemblies) (see Martin Rojo, 2014; Milani 2015; Stroud, 2016) offer interesting critical enquiries especially as they convey important (political) messages and 'raise awareness about specific issues in order to influence people and obtain public recognition of particular problems and positions' (Waksman and Shohamy, 2016: 56). In some places, such as Bosnia-Herzegovina, they call attention to human rights and unspeakable violence affecting almost all people from the country, and even beyond, in one way or another.

In this chapter, I have sought to analyse the discourse of remembering taking the form of commemorative initiatives and public art commemoration. More specifically, I have tried to show how the performative and experiential body is key in the production of more-than-visual/verbal memorializing activities – commemorative performances. How powerful the body is becomes instantly apparent in the first example (Figure 18 and Extract 2) where only one body through authentic war marking acquires new significance (Stroud, 2016) and ultimately reacts to a non-existing monument. The analysis of commemorative events in this chapter suggests that performative practices are central in highlighting the deaths of the innocent, the issue of the rhetoric of denial and the sites of memory, as FitzGerald (2009: 86) indicates:

> The construction of monuments is itself a deeply performative act: it is the action of commemorating agents which brings the monument into being in the first place, and their vigilance which sustains it against the forces of time, decay, and forgetting.

In this sense, commemorative performances are central aspects of placemaking, and key in understanding how traumascapes are semiotically re-organized and interactively accomplished. They reveal the space moves and extends and yet another burden of Bosnia-Herzegovina's traumascapes – the sites of violence still remain unrecognized and denied. They also point to the dynamic entanglement of place/space, body and memory, and ultimately to the transitory nature of memoryscapes (cf. Hanauer, 2013). In the wake of ethnic domination and inequality, placing a semiotic-cum-performative introspection at the heart of the analysis of Bosnia-Herzegovina's memoryscapes is crucial for understanding what sites of memory provide and mean to people. They are not only about the recognition of violence nor are they simply places of mourning. Rather they represent a resistance to the imposed memory regimes and marginalized status that people have in their own country. The symbolic construction of monuments through living memorials employs many experiential elements that performative bodies bring into public space and place making processes. These performances are neatly organized in stages, performed on carefully chosen platforms; they are engaging, affective, heavily mediated and mediatized. We have seen moments where the participants are placed in imaginable and similar physical positions to those of the suffering bodies (both victims and survivors), and consequently evoking intimate and affective experiences. This further creates different touchpoint activities manifesting tangible interactive systems found both in 'the-body-to-body' and 'the-body-to-an object' relations that allow people to understand the scale of loss and the importance of memorializing activities. Examples presented in this chapter show how the commemorative performances are dynamic, moving locally and globally (e.g. when *Što te nema* installation went to a different city every year), and also shifting, moving internally (e.g. engaging with the artefacts, moving around the installations, having conversations, reflecting emotionally). The scaling qualities of commemoration emerge in the moments of (re)mediation of the performances, elevating their importance. Embodied performances turn into almost spectacles through the strategic selection of the platform affecting the size of commemorative events, a variety of media and public descriptions which establish them as big and relevant. From small local initiatives to global performances about *slaughters-horrors-genocide*, affective dimensions of commemoration continue to grow as they are scaled in real as well as virtual spaces. However, all this would not be accomplished had it not been for the bodies that were themselves performative: 'invested, marked, trained, tortured, forced to carry out tasks, to perform ceremonies, to emit signs' (Foucault, 1977). In the context of post-war Bosnia-Herzegovina, commemorative events call attention to human rights and unspeakable violence affecting almost all people from the country, and even beyond, in one way or another. They are not simply memorializing activities, but often global movements achieved through affective, monolithic, massive body and its experiences. Ironically enough, such monumentalized bodies speak louder than any, so greatly desired and needed, stone inscribed with the names of the victims that many would pass by without even noticing it. The idea dates back to Robert Musil (1987) who said that 'there is nothing in this world as invisible as a monument'. In other words, if the preservation of a specific memory and the drafting of a message that warns of the consequences of war is exactly where a monument's importance and significance lies, isn't the absence of the monument precisely that which keeps the memory alive, accomplishes global reach, and alerts us to Bosnia-Herzegovina's past, present and future? Parents in Prijedor still do not have a monument for their children that were killed, but if they wish to draw attention to the violence, those who are responsible, and those who keep denying it, then performative reactions to 'empty' public space might actually be the best possible way of accomplishing this.

4

Waging War Online

Nationalism in Bosnia-Herzegovina's media

Along the ever-present echo of the 1992–5 war, nationalism[1] in Bosnia-Herzegovina has 'a crucial role as the very foundation of "the social"' (Finlayson, 1998: 114). To comprehend and put into words the nature of ethno-nationalist divisions and post-war national rebirth in the country is a rather laborious task. In this respect, to say that the country's three constitutive peoples link themselves to and identify exclusively with their ethnicities, reduces the task in complexity and extent. Robinson and colleagues (2001) conclude on a more specific note that a nation's cohesive elements and forces are ethnicity, culture, territory and citizenship. Along these lines, Cvitković (2006) argues that Bosnian Croats, in the political sense, are the citizens of Bosnia-Herzegovina (most of them Herzegovinians – regional identity), while in the national-cultural sense, they are Croats who primarily identify with their Croatian identity. In terms of the state affiliation, Bosnian Serbs belong to Bosnia-Herzegovina, and in terms of national affiliation to Serbian people. Both Bosnian Croats and Serbs, as Robinson et al. (2001: 964) explain, link themselves to a Croatia and Serbia respectively, while Bosniaks' identity has been defined by their religion and 'a territorial dimension related to the former Yugoslav Republic of Bosnia-Herzegovina that includes large areas dominated by Croats and Serbs'. Correspondingly, Bosnian Muslims have been 'ethnicised' by the effects of war and embraced the category Bosniak established to denote a separate Muslim category of Bosnians as opposed to Croats (Catholic) and Serbs (Orthodox) (Robinson et al., 2001). Thus, when Wodak (2018: 403) says that nationalism and nationhood are 'projects of modernity, related to the centralising tendency towards the homogenisation of populations', Bosnia-Herzegovina is proof that in places marked by trauma nationalism is simply a response to a burdensome socio-political reality controlled by the legacy of loss and violence. Bosnia-Herzegovina's media scene is divided along the above referred ethnic lines in terms of both their content and the audience they target, and is fully representative of the socio-political situation in the country (Janićko, 2015). Generally speaking, Bosnia-Herzegovina media with underdeveloped policies supporting the monolithic media arena (Udovičić et al., 2001) are deeply affected by ethnocentrism and political clientelism (Open Society Foundations, 2012). Such milieu routinely reproduces nationalist zeal particularly because of its functionally strong links with political spaces (Schlesinger, 2000). In this regard, nationalism has been the topic of interest and concern among many international human rights organizations as well as local agencies and associations (e.g. United Nations Educational, Scientific and Cultural Organization (UNESCO), Organization for Security and Co-operation in Europe (OSCE), South and East Europe Media Organisation (SEEMO), Press Council in Bosnia-Herzegovina (VZS), BH Journalists Association). Their monitoring studies mainly focus on the media representatives supporting nationalistic sensationalism in the chase for 'readers' clicks' and publishing biased or misleading information. Recommendations and appeals specifically concern political parties promoting nationalistic sentiments to garner support for separatism as they 'exploit virulent nationalistic rhetoric, fostering divisions between the various constituent peoples and ethnic groups living in Bosnia-Herzegovina' (ECRI, 2011: 22). As put out in the last available ECRI Report on Bosnia-Herzegovina published in February 2017, there has not been much progress and the levels of inter-ethnic tensions in the media space are still high. The report points directly to the problematic nature of media outlets, and especially online platforms that promote and condone the prevalence of inflammatory rhetoric defined as 'hate speech' which continuously pollutes the digital space (ECRI, 2017). As a matter of fact, it seems that supreme political authorities themselves are seriously challenged by the interactive writing spaces in the form of readers' comments, which again highlights the scarce research on the production of fertile soils for communicating national hegemony.

Supported by the emergence of so-called independent outlets in the post-war period, media texts influence citizens' perceptions (Taylor and Kent, 2000) 'constructing ideologically motivated versions of reality which are aimed at persuading people that certain phenomena are good or bad' (Baker et al., 2013: 3). Unlike the 1990s period when the media was influential 'to the extent that what average Yugoslavs believed depended almost entirely on what their media were telling them' (Bennett, 1995: 95), nowadays, however, the citizens rely on their personal experiences and deeply rooted distrust of the Other's intentions which they do not hesitate to express publicly. Consequently, reader comments sections in particular seem to constitute important everyday meta-discursive and participatory sites/resources for delivering hateful sentiments. Online news sites worldwide have adopted a variety of strategies to deal with unwelcome comments, including 'turning "comments off", not archiving comments, and adopting moderation policies' (Hughey and Daniels, 2013: 333) or by stating something like: *You agree not to use language that abuses or discriminates on the basis of race, religion, nationality, gender, sexual preference, age, region, disability, etc.* (*New York Times*).[2] The latter is often adopted by the online news portals in Bosnia-Herzegovina which represent a virtually inexhaustible source of nationalistic attitudes that readers freely share in a relatively anonymous and unconstrained setting/space. In general, it is considered that comments are an integral element of a web portal, they provide feedback from and interactivity with the public, thereby preserving freedom of speech and expression.[3] This is quite understandable – after all, the suppression of people's sentiments already turned out to be a poor decision for this country (Tito's policy in the Yugoslav republics). Additionally, as Loke (2012: 241) explains, news organizations adopt comments sections for economic reasons since 'stories with comments attract more page views and page views are a strong selling point in luring advertisers to spend more money'. It has been only recently that the Communications Regulatory Agency BH (RAK) started to urge the media outlets to adjust their program content when covering commemorative and other war-related events announced by the Council of Ministers of Bosnia-Herzegovina. In June 2017, for example, the Agency appealed to all the media providers to carefully and professionally select the program content for the 11 July which will not disturb the memory of Srebrenica Genocide victims, and to show appropriate sympathies to their families. This mainly resulted in the disabling of user's comments on the genocide–related reports, as well as monitoring comments sections. It should be indicated that the self-regulatory body for print and online media, Bosnia-Herzegovina Press Council, implemented the Press Code in August 1998, but the Council cannot impose any sanctions to the media outlets. The Communication Regulatory Agency, on the other hand, implemented the Broadcast Code of Practice which applies only to television and radio broadcast stations and their staff. However, it is not my intention to engage with the question of Bosnia-Herzegovina media regulations or the conditions under which media outlets operate, but to examine a particular case of user-generated content and computer-mediated discourse (CMD) (Herring and Androutsopoulos, 2015) – online comments emerging from the reports around *the acts of vandalism and the messages of inappropriate/threatening content* (Klix. ba) appearing through graffiti, memorial sites (museums and monuments) and memorializing activities (commemorative events). Complementing previous chapters, this study seeks to address citizens' attitudes as a way of consulting different voices present in semiotic landscapes (Jaworski and Thurlow, 2010). Positioned at the intersection of mediascapes and public space, online comments illustrate how personal(ly) mediatized representations and understandings of the physical environment relate to the practices of nationalism 'flagging' that goes beyond the simple 'We vs They' rhetoric, creating resonant public debates which contextualize the endemic socio-political instability of the country.

Banal nationalism – everyday and mediated

One of the key thinkers on the subject of nationalism, Benedict Anderson (1983) and his observations inspired the work of many scholars investigating nationalism in media discourse. For example, Law (2001), Bishop and Jaworski (2003), Higgins (2004) and Costelloe (2014) form their basic assumptions necessary for the investigation of questions of nationalism (nationality, nationhood, national identities) on his seminal work on *imagined communities*. Anderson (1983: 15) primarily argues that nations are imagined because 'the members of even the smallest nations will never know most of their fellow-members, meet them, or even hear of them', and as they are limited by having 'finite, if elastic, boundaries, beyond which lie other nations'. It is specifically the education systems and media that have the key roles in these processes of imagining. As a matter of fact, Anderson (1983) identifies mass media as the primary agents of the imagining of a nation. Similarly, Costelloe (2014: 323) argues that the media 'implicitly encourage those living in a defined geographical area to imagine other readers simultaneously consuming and reacting to the same media products, thus encouraging a sense of national belonging and comradeship'. Web technologies in particular create imagined communities and introduce large assemblies of readers to everyday expressions of nationalism as they talk about imagined communities and belonging in constantly changing space-time structures (White, 2015). As White (2015: 629) explains, it is precisely the internet that opens up 'opportunities to consume and reproduce the forms and symbols of banal nationalism, and to observe those processes at work'. By this token, digital media texts come under scrutiny as an especially rich site articulating, framing and promoting the discourse of nationalism. Michael

Billig's (1995) *Banal Nationalism* is certainly inspiring for reflecting on nationalism regularly 'flagged' (i.e. communicated) in media, education systems and other institutionalized domains. However, that nationalism is contingent in nature and not a conscious daily choice operating through banal practices as an everyday discursive phenomenon, is something Anderson (1983) has known for quite some time, famously observing that a nation's existence is the performative of the *daily plebiscite* (after Renan, 1882). Similarly, as Stuart Hall (1988: 8) has written, nationalism as every other ideology needs to 'naturalise itself out of history and into nature and thus to become invisible, to operate unconsciously'. In this chapter, I refer to everyday nationalism aiming to invoke the 'not so banal' ways in which it is (re)produced. In order to do so, I need to step away from the media context shortly and address the critical reviews of Billig's term. The term *banal*, potentially considered as insignificant and innocent, is not problematic as it has been emphasized that it most certainly does not imply that banal is benign. However, it is separated from 'hot' processes that reproduce nationalism, and thus is potentially viewed as dealing exclusively with the mundane and barely noticed contexts. By referring to hot nationalism as a recognizable phenomenon reflected in extreme social movements, Billig (1995) indicates that 'the banal' and 'the hot' are understood as linear. Indeed, for Billig (1995), the banal exclusively stands for unnoticed, unnamed and therefore unidentifiable as a problem. However, not all scholars follow this 'banal-before-hot' pattern. Hutchinson (2006: 298), for example, argues that hot nationalism which 'instils the idea of the nation as a sacred and transcendent object of worship and sacrifice', operates together with banal nationalism through an interactive, fluid relationship. In their study of bilingual road signs in Wales, Jones and Merriman (2009) also illustrate that banal and hot elements reproducing nationalism are rather merged. They privilege 'the everyday' and emphasize how nationalist discourses and practices incorporate a variety of hotter 'differences and conflicts' affecting people's lives on a habitual basis. Contexts and discursive levels of everyday nationalism vary, and its materialization is more than representational, especially in Bosnia-Herzegovina where red-hot nationalism professedly 'cooled down' but the peace agreement left the country in an extremely fragile form. Everyday nationalism is semiotic in nature and encompassed in all sorts of public expressions: monuments, museums, buildings or street names (e.g. monuments to Chetnik leaders in the Serb Republic, the Coat of Arms of the Republic of Croatia on the buildings in Herzegovina) (see Torsti, 2004), and not only flags, banknotes, or coins (Billig, 1995). Billig (1995: 93) argues that people are subtly reminded of their national place through low key nationalist elements, vague in nature and perceived as harmless – 'prosaic, routine words, which take nations for granted, and which, in so doing, enhabit [sic] them'. Nationalism, as Neiger and Rimmer-Tsory (2012: 724) note, 'is characterized by a "friend or foe" discourse that brings to the fore the conflictual interactions between Us and Them'. However, everyday nationalism is not solely about deictic language (personal pronouns, demonstratives or markers of time and place), 'tiny' words or jokes (Billig, 2001). Just as national identities are 'dynamic, vulnerable and ambivalent' (Triandafyllidou and Wodak, 2003), they are being delivered differently as the contexts change; at times even through extremely 'hot' elements. However, discourse relation to nationalism is not 'necessarily malicious' (Costelloe, 2014) as nationalism 'comes in manifold forms, some benign and reassuring, and others terrifying' (Calhoun, 1997: 3). Within discourse studies, it has been traditionally argued that nationalism and national identities are 'discursively, by means of language and other semiotic systems, produced, reproduced, transformed and destructed' (de Cillia et al., 1999: 153). Discourse analysts, although building analytical frameworks upon the 'We vs They' rhetoric, propose different strategies by which nationalism, nationhood and national identity are realized in discourse (e.g. Coupland, 1999; Bishop and Jaworski, 2003; Wodak, 2006: Li, 2009). Janíčko's study from 2015 is the only discourse analysis of Bosnia-Herzegovina's media content on the topic of nationalism. In his analysis of Bosnia-Herzegovina's daily print newspapers, Janíčko (2015: 47) reveals that in the Bosniak and Serb media 'a concrete representation of those seen as guilty of the crime' prevails, realized through accusations, denials, promotion of patriotism and abstraction. With the rise of new media technologies, the traditional focus on nationalism in the context of the print media has been replaced by the exploration of 'nations thriving in cyberspace' (Eriksen, 2007) and enacting national identities on a global scale. Skey (2009) in particular calls for investigations of everyday nationalism along the emergence of the digital media and 'virtual ethnic communities' which, as Conversi (2012: 1360) notes, should be understood as 'a multi-dimensional expansion of Anderson's imagined communities'. In his exploration of *internet nationalism* (Skey, 2009) or 'long-distance' nationalism (after Anderson, 1992), Conversi (2012: 1371) focused on the concept of 'netizens who use digital technologies to promote hostility, aggressive patriotism, xenophobia, conflict, ethnic exclusion and, eventually, war'. Regardless of being produced in closed virtual spaces, language promoting such sentiments nonetheless takes place in real time, without any delays, and has 'an oral, spontaneous quality' (Eriksen, 2007: 8). Furthermore, online communication is no different than the language of everyday life. It is just as political discourse 'rigorously categorical, dividing the population into mutually exclusive ethno-national categories, and making no allowance for mixed or ambiguous forms' (Brubaker and Cooper, 2000: 27). In recent years, user-generated content has received considerable attention from communication scholars and discourse analysts. A handful of contributions orienting towards a discourse analytic approach have been in the investigations of reader comments with regard to ideologies and problematization of socially meaningful power relations embodying very revealing aspects of digital discourse and the society producing it. Loke (2012), for example, examines how race is articulated behind an anonymous space and reveals patterns of modern racism suggesting that race tolerance has been greatly exaggerated in today's modern society. Collins and Nelich (2014) explore aspects of deliberation in user comment threads in response to articles on climate change taken from the Guardian. Their findings reveal that whilst some aspects of online discourse demonstrate 'incivility', user comments also show potential for engaging in dialog and high levels of interaction. Erjavec and Poler Kovačić (2013) did a critical discourse analysis of offensive reader comments on Slovenian news websites, revealing general attacks on human dignity, on personality based on the supposed political orientation of a journalist and a media company. Prior to this study, they published a discourse analysis of hate speech in news web sites' comments (Erjavec and Poler Kovačić, 2012) revealing a type of a nationalist discourse concerning national groups from the former Yugoslavia and Roma people. Baruh and Popescu (2008) investigated Turkish nationalism in online discussions in which the participants construct the Turkish motherland based on the collective memory of sacrifice. Media Plan Institute, an independent organization on Bosnia-Herzegovina media development, in cooperation with the Konrad Adenauer Foundation's Media Program for South East Europe, offered a pioneer analysis attempt of the online comments posted on influential web portals in Bosnia-Herzegovina. The results suggested that, contrary to a popular belief about comments exclusively illustrating the level of national hate, intolerance and vulgarity, comments are 'usually free of political connotations in the sense of ethnic, national or religious conflicts, but mostly coming in the form of insulting someone's character' (Media Plan Institute, 2010: 62). Yet, five years after its publication, the OSCE Mission in Bosnia-Herzegovina in co-operation with the Ministry of Security, called for continued monitoring by governmental institutions and media representatives of online content used for inciting violence realized primarily in/through online reader comments.[4] One of the main problems in Media Plan Institute's study is that it fails to employ a well-founded analytical framework for approaching online comments. Needless to say, there is no official document central to the issue of online comments (including the reproduction and evolution of online nationalism) as this has never been empirically demonstrated. The expansion of digital technology also facilitates the articulation and remediation of the national collective memory (Weedon and Jordan, 2012) residing in physical space. As Jaworski and Thurlow (2010: 7) explain, nationalism is closely related to 'the nation's collective gaze at the physical attributes of landscape', and digital media provides a nation with an insight into and experience of those attributes. The features of physical environments I analysed in the previous chapters spread through/across digital space and become easily accessible to both Bosnia-Herzegovina's citizens and diaspora who become a part of 'virtual community spaces' (i.e. online meeting points that bridge the 'virtual' and the physical) (King, 2017). In this sense, digital media, including cyberspace, where people actively build their identities (Jones, 2010), 'are seen as an extension of our physical selves' (Ivkovic and Lotherington, 2009: 17), and thus our physical space. Along these lines, this chapter aims to bring out an important section of Bosnia-Herzegovina's digital framework, suggesting that readers' comments open up the space of very specific narrativity and interaction in which citizens speak up about the demoralizing post-war trajectories. To address how the physical space extends into the virtual, I have found it useful to think in terms of Jones' (2005; 2010) and King's (2011; 2012; 2017) contributions to the study of virtual environments in which they demonstrate that cyberspaces depend on physical spaces, and vice versa. King's (2011) basic premise is that places are formed in cyberspace via online language use, and thus online chat rooms are places. As Jones (2010: 153) explains, places/spaces are constructed not only through the objects and boundaries, but also through 'interaction with others who are operating in the "same" space'. Therefore, digital media spaces in which active social interactions take place is 'folded into a wider semiotic field of human communication' (Thurlow and Jaworski, 2011: 220). In the context of linguistic landscapes, Shohamy and Gorter (2009: 315) have emphasized that cyberspace expands the linguistic landscape geography 'to include people who are not necessarily present physically but nevertheless become active participants in the linguistic landscape scenery in virtual ways'. Ivkovic and Lotherington (2009: 19) analysed the linguistic landscape of virtual spaces demonstrating that it 'functions as an identity marker, providing choice in textual access and expression'. However, in online spaces, similarly as in physical spaces, we do not 'simply talk' but, in King's (2012) terms, we own properties, cultivate identities, commit crimes and purchase things – we *do* things.

War online

The dataset for this chapter comes from a collection of online comments drawn from the online news site Klix.ba – one of the most visited internet news sites in Bosnia-Herzegovina, posting over 150 news articles daily. As claimed on its website, Klix.ba is an independent internet medium with *no political, NGO, or marketing agencies standing behind it*. As the Mandate of the Press Council in Bosnia-Herzegovina was extended to on-line media in 2011, Klix.ba was one of the first three online media portals joining the Press Council in Bosnia-Herzegovina and agreeing to adhere to the Press Code.[5] The dataset I analyse consists of three data subsets based on sixty reports:

1) 2,343 comments on graffiti appearing between 2015 and 2018 (54,73% of originally posted comments are not available)
2) 2,904 comments on memorial sites appearing between 2015 and 2018 appearing between 2015 and 2018) (52.87% of originally posted comments are not available)
3) 2,416 comments on commemorative events appearing between 2015 and 2018 (48.66% of originally posted comments are not available)

In articles prior to 2015, a large number of comments were deleted, and in 2013 Klix.ba had an overhaul of their user comments system resulting certain losses. Another practical reason for choosing the period from 2015 to 2018 was to keep the data somewhat consistent with the data analysed in previous chapters. The relatively high number of deleted comments is most likely due to Klix.ba joining the Press Council's campaign in fighting against intolerable online content (see the articles from the Press Code above) and removing a large number of comments. At this point, it should be mentioned that immediately below the comment section there is the following notice, essentially a disclaimer by Klix.ba: *Due to the large number of comments Klix.ba is not under obligation to delete all of the comments breaking the rules. As a reader you also accept the possibility that among the comments there can be content which is opposed to your religious, moral and other principles and convictions.* We can only suppose that the readers themselves are implicated in metalinguistic processes or the management of posted comments by evaluating what others write. A comment may have an overall negative (red) rating, meaning it has received more down arrows, but still remain visible. There appear to be two forms of 'punishment' for the reported comments. Some comments once reported and reviewed get deleted, while others are hidden behind a red box with the text *This comment has been hidden due to reports by other users* and the reader needs to click on the *Show comment* in order to reveal it. There are two ways of interpreting the standard disclaimer above through which the editors seem to be trying to absolve themselves of the responsibility for 'keeping the peace' in the comments section. A more sinister one would be that the editors leave the comments up in order to draw the audience to read, write and engage with the content. A less cynical one would be that they simply do not have the resources to monitor all of the comments for an extended period of time. One thing is clear, the digital space is monitored and regulated differently than the physical space. The graffiti, for example, often persist for a significant period of time, unless they are emplaced in important locations such as schools or religious structures. In the digital space, all comments end up on the same platform, in the same spot. Therefore, the actual words and their meaning, including the number of 'likes', become more important. In terms of the risk borne by the commenters, once the physical space extends into the digital domain there is much less to worry about. If one is caught drawing graffiti on a public building certain charges of vandalism can be brought, while in the digital sphere 'anything goes'. The punishment ranges from the most common – a comment being deleted, to a user being banned (of course, new user accounts are easily created). And in the worst-case scenario, if an explicit threat of physical violence is made and the authorities are convinced that it is serious then they might track down the commenter. Needless to say, authorities getting involved due to user comments on an online portal, is something that happens extremely rarely.

> Nationalism can be understood only when it is recognized as always part of the discursive articulation of particular social formations, always directed to the construction of a specific chain of discourse, the production of a specific notion of the specific nation and the national subject.
>
> (Finlayson, 1998: 103)

Drawing on the notion that discursive formation is the first dimension of nationalism, as Finlayson (1998) argues, the current study is organized and carried out along the methodological approach of Critical Discourse Analysis (CDA) (Kress and Hodge, 1979; Fairclough, 1992) which forms the basis for an analytical framework focused on discovering ideological and symbolic dimensions and meanings in discourse. More specifically, I will be incorporating some of the notions proposed by Wodak et al. (2009) in their Discourse-Historical Approach (DHA) to CDA, described as an adequate theory and methodology to analyse and understand 'the intricate complexities' such as national identity constructions, different kinds of discrimination, as well as discourses about Us and Them emerging in 'public, semi-public and quasi-private discursive contexts' (Wodak and Boukala, 2015: 89; Wodak, 2018). DHA distinguishes between three interrelated dimensions of analysis: the contents or topics of specific discourses, discursive strategies and the linguistic means that are drawn upon to realize both topics and strategies (Wodak, 2011). Defined as 'a more or less intentional plan of practices adopted to achieve a particular social, political, psychological or linguistic goal' (Reisigl and Wodak, 2001: 44), Wodak et al. (2009) propose different macro-strategies and sub-strategies achieved through a variety of linguistic devices. In the current study, I address constructive strategies (linguistic acts which constitute a national 'We-group' through particular acts of reference) and strategies of perpetuation and justification (primarily employed to defend and preserve a problematic narrative of national history) (de Cillia et al., 1999). Rhetorical schemes relevant to the current study are *topoi* and *narrative*. Topoi (Wodak and Boukala, 2015 after Keinpointner, 1996) are useful means for analysing argumentation strategies present in prejudiced and discriminatory discourses, and various forms of social exclusion and discrimination (Reisigl and Wodak, 2001). Narrative is defined as 'a specific micro-account, within an utterance or series of utterances, of a past series of events' (Kwon et al., 2014: 271). In the light of DHA, this analysis is carried out in two stages. The first stage includes identification and grouping of salient lexical selections. The second stage includes identification of discursive strategies to draw out the most salient topics (Wodak et al., 2009). Thus, my analysis is ordered as follows: first, I consider the discursive construction of the 'We vs They' rhetoric realized through labelling of social actors, the generalization of negative attributions and arguments justifying exclusion or inclusion (*Violent categorizations*) (Delanty et al., 2008). Here, I point to two interrelated systems of interactivity in readers' comments. Second, I highlight the most salient topics in the data realized through discursive strategies identified in the dataset: *From shaming to blaming* and *History in service of nationalistic ideology*.

Violent categorizations

Returning to one of the most pervasive axiomatic strategies in the discourse of nationalism – I start with the 'We vs They' rhetoric acknowledged as the key ingredient in constructing national collective, national identity and nationalistic sentiments. A preliminary overview of the sub-corpora expectedly resulted in high markings of We/They pronouns and their forms (i.e. *to you, yours, our, to us*) assigning to the commenters the roles of those who speak on behalf of Our group by mainly opposing the Other ethnic groups and self-proclaiming a sense of large-scale national collective. Although remaining mindful of the 'We vs They' rhetoric which plays a crucial role in the construction and representation of social relations (Fairclough, 1989; Hardt-Mautner, 1995) and has 'implications with regard to power, distance, formality, solidarity, and intimacy' (Costelloe, 2014: 320), in order to refine and supplement this output I look beyond these *unmemorable clichés*, as Billig (1995) calls them. In this sense, I focus on another pronominal contrast blended with the 'We vs They' rhetoric; namely, 'I vs You' particularly standing out and directly pointing to two interrelated systems of interactivity. The first system refers to the online conversation between members of different ethnic groups, filled with explicit provocations, insults and threats supporting, inter alia, distinction, devaluation of others and distancing. Here, readers primarily, if not exclusively, express opinions that do not simply come up in face-to-face conversations or when they do, they often result in physical confrontations (OSCE, 2012). In a number of *quasi-rational arguments* Wodak (2008: 64), it becomes apparent that the national We and the different They surfaces everywhere. Indeed, as de Cillia et al. (1999) observe, 'even those participants in the discussions who critically address nationally motivated generalizations cannot avoid its usage: sooner or later, every participant resorts to We'. Consequentially, reader discussions constantly go back and forth between I/We and You/They. The clearest example would be the following fairly long excerpt of quite a tense conversation between several members of different ethnic groups commenting a report on *The White Armbands Day*.

Extract 1 (Klix.ba: 31 May 2017)

Tume 31.05.2017.
The RS is a historical and civilizational error, allowing something to be formed on the grounds of genocide is proof of a major clouding of the mind, EU started to collapse the day it allowed this.

PopusioGaLaktasenkoO 31.05.2017.
OH POTURICE YOU ARE JUST BEING FUNNY HAHAHAHHAHAHAH YOU SHOULD START TO SHOOT EACH OTHER with SNIPERS AS A PART OF THE INSTALLATION HIHIHI

Admiral Sa 31.05.2017.
@PopusioGaLaktasenkoO You are a big looser... limited as a balcony. Put yourself in a position where someone yours was killed in this way... Act so

this never happens to anyone… because there is no more JNA… this time the outcome for the Serbs would be much worse, but it would still be a crime so NO TO CRIME!!!

hladjenjemuda 31.05.2017.
@PopusioGaLaktasenkoO ahahahahahaha, what does a crude forest pig know about performance, that's why you pushed people into concentration camps and corrals as you feel comfortable doing that by force, I will sniper your mother over her hairy smelly ass

BORDO DNK 31.05.2017.
That's what the United States decided, through the Dayton Agreement, they had prepared much earlier. The EU has no voice here, just like us. With the rest I agree, they have been rewarded for the genocide.

PopusioGaLaktasenkoO 31.05.2017.
@hladjenjemuda just cry and curse, you are feeding my soul

dubrava1929 31.05.2017.
The Basis of law and justice according to the International Court of Justice: EVERYTHING BASED ON GENOCIDE CANNOT EXIST AND ALL RESULTS OF GENOCIDE ARE CANCELLED!!! If this is not the case, what the UN and the International Courts serve anyway then as well as THE DECLARATION OF FREEDOM AND HUMAN RIGHTS AS A BASIS FOR FORMING THE UN in the first place? If this is not done, it can be claimed that the UN and International Court have died in B&H together with the victims of Genocide!

hladjenjemuda 31.05.2017.
@PopusioGaLaktasenkoO of course it feeds your soul because that's all cattle can understand. go roll Into the mud

noler 31.05.2017.
Poturice wanted a war and now they are masters at whining. Every day here they call for the death of serb children and everything that is serbian. As if the last war was not enough for them… we will never forgive you for the serb children and women. You turkified bastards.

PrivilegeEscalation 31.05.2017.
Since the dawn of time, one nation would attack others… taking their territory, women, property, etc. If Bosniaks want to survive sooner or later they will have to act. Everything else are just fairy tales. How to justify this, it is not a problem in the slightest.

Extract 1 is already very much indicative of the whole dataset, which was taken from a comments section on a report that consists of sixteen pictures taken on the site, a forty-eight seconds long video recording of the commemoration event, and a relatively short text describing one of the concentration camps formed in the area of Prijedor. In general, the comments section works as a space for an anonymous debate triggered by this particular event in the wake of contemporary memorializing activities in Bosnia-Herzegovina. However, the first comment posted on this report, just like many others which follow, does not allude to *The White Armbands Day*. Instead, the debate starts with the claim that the Serb Republic is *a historical and civilizational error* since the entity was established on the grounds of genocide (The Serb Republic is referred to as *the genocidal creation* as pointed in Chapter 2). The reader directly starts questioning the legitimacy of the Serb Republic entity and articulates a common opinion among all ethnic groups that the final peace deal to stop the war is a poor solution (i.e. the division of Bosnia-Herzegovina into entities) due to the lack of a mindful response of the European Community (EC) to a four years long bloodshed. Such claims are also set in the context of globally mediated discourses where the war is referred to as 'one of Europe's most shameful chapters of atrocity and bloodletting since World War II'.[6] However, Europe (as indicated in the comment) which quite expectedly, and for Bosnian Muslims primarily, lost its integrity, is not the only one responsible for the unacceptable territorial divisions in Bosnia-Herzegovina. Consider the comments soon to follow – *That's what the United States decided… The EU has no voice here, just like us; the UN and the International Court have died in Bosnia-Herzegovina together with the victims of Genocide*. As it will be pointed out later in the analysis, online comments eagerly produce what Bishop and Jaworski (2003) call *a discourse of blame*, placing responsibility both on those who (are believed to have) committed and ordered atrocities, as well as on the world's leading organizations and countries as the only ones with the power to both stop the war and broker a peace deal which would satisfy all parties and result in prosperity for all. Nowadays, especially in the Bosnian Muslim community, these 'peacekeepers' (e.g. UN, NATO) are seen as mere bystanders and know-it-alls with a reputation for sounding smart but useless: *And Europe and the world were only watching. It is a shame that the worst concentration camps at the end of the twentieth century could exist. I will vote NO to enter the EU. Fuck their fascist mothers. I will not give my pride away after they silently watched while everything was happening, they disgust me* (Klix. ba: 26 May 2017). The first comment in Extract 1 provokes a series of posts and the discussion immediately progresses into a verbal confrontation forcefully accomplished through ridiculing and insults. Note how You/I becomes exclusive in the sense of attacks on personality based on belonging to a certain ethnic group

(Erjavec and Poler Kovačić, 2013). Observable in Extract 1 is also an instance of appeal to empathy followed by a capitalized call to act, yet not violently by committing a crime – *NO TO CRIME*. Interestingly, the reader firstly indicates in case this would be an act of violence, Serbs would face retaliation without the support of the JNA which no longer exists. Ridicule and insults (e.g. *masters of weeping, Poturice*[7]) are the typical responses to appeals to civic victimhood and vulnerability, often seen as a weakness of one ethnic group. Indeed, there is almost never a recognition of the victims on the other side. Comments clearly and explicitly refer to the past (a) and speculated future conflicts, realizing the *topoi of threat* (Wodak and Boukala, 2015) (b):

a) *You pushed people into concentration camps and corrals as you feel comfortable doing that by force.*
b) *If Bosniaks want to survive sooner or later they will have to act. Everything else are just fairy tales. How to justify this, it is not a problem in the slightest.*

Bishop and Jaworski (2003: 250) explain that the war-related vocabulary invokes nationalistic sentiments especially if it is interlinked with another key ingredient – that of temporality since

> the way the nation is discursively brought into being and how a sense of shared national present is articulated through references to the past and speculation about the future, both near and distant. Specifically, the nation is imagined in terms of its past through the invocation of a variety of [...] military references.

Frequent references to bloodshed accomplish multiple rhetorical moments. Firstly, as Baruh and Popescau (2008: 86) explain, 'blood shed from fighting for the country is one of the most powerful metaphors that give meaning to patriotic feelings' and it teaches people about the value of their homelands. It seems that *knowledge* of the history of conflicts on Bosnia-Herzegovina's lands (even during the Ottoman occupation in the sixteenth century, as well as the fascist 1940s period) also gives the readers a sense of when to call for vigilance, sometimes in an explicitly violent or/and insulting way. Secondly, the repetition of these unforgettable ethno-national tragedies further establishes the category of conditional utterances 'constructed as warrants as "if p, then q follows"' (Kwon et al., 2014), identified as topoi and exemplified in the comment (b) above. Since topoi are primarily treated as 'a salient part of argumentation' based on presupposed knowledge of participants in specific contexts (Kwon et al., 2014), they are useful for the analysis of various statements, including both valid and fallacious arguments 'orators or opponents (use) to persuade their audience of the validity of their opinions' (Wodak and Boukala, 2015: 94). More specifically, topoi illustrate complex schemes in the discursive construction of nationalism. It is precisely comments such as the example (a) above that have the quality of premises justifying comments such as the example (b). Ethno-national stereotypes invoking the memories of suffering of the most vulnerable ones – children and women position the readers to project opposed ethnic groups and their members into the future, remaining still very much threatening entities whose hateful sentiments did not and will not change, and hence must not be taken for granted. The second system of interactivity refers to relatively short exchanges moving in a quicker pace between the members of the same ethnic group. These are usually accomplished through comments carrying either agreement and support, or dissent and condemnation. Unlike the examples above, such comments illustrate complex dimensions of interethnic inclusion and exclusion. Comments in which readers merely indicate that they read a comment and agree with it by replying with a short post, humorous reference or chant littered with sarcasm are not meaningful or critical even though they are based on shared ideological views and strengthen and reinforce the ethnic We. Hence, these powerfully promote unification and convey a strong sense of togetherness. The role of *micro-messaging* (Baron, 2010) in simulating speech conventions is apparent in such sections where the comments are much shorter than the maximum allowed (500 characters). As Herring and Androutsopoulos (2015: 132) explain, writing messages in 'short bursts can also be a strategy to approximate a faster, more "speech-like" pace and/or to hold the floor by not leaving time for another participant's message to intervene while one composes a complex utterance'. Hasty 'big likes' that these comments get construct small coalitions or teams (cf. Kwon et al., 2014) revealed through family references (e.g. brother) or the affirmations of friendships (e.g. *jaran* – of Turkish origin *yaran* for a close friend, equivalent to buddy, pal). Readers who most often get such kind of support are those claiming that *the malefactions should be reported about everyday so that the future generations do not forget* (Klix.ba: 31 May 2017). As Extract 2 indicates, readers also show their support by completing each other's comments through which, in this case, they acknowledge that there is a shared need for revenge:

Extract 2 (Klix.ba: 20 May 2017)

Ljutac 20.05.2017.
There will be vengeance.
Hercegovinaa 20.05.2017.
In due time serbs, in due time

lololol 20.05.2017.
we will free the occupied 18% in due time

As de Cillia et al. (1999: 160) explain, components generating a sense of mutual understanding and collective ethnic identity are 'persuasive linguistic devices which help invite identification and solidarity with the We-group, which, however, simultaneously implies distancing from and marginalization of Others'. On the other hand, intra-ethnic differences are pointed out in readers' claims as well as short scenarios based on opposed ideological views that attack any isolated positions of neutrality. Criticism goes so far that members of the same ethnic groups are being compared to the greatest enemies whose attitudes are strongly disapproved of and evaluated as the sole ground for all the evil that the other ethnic groups caused during the war – e.g. *With those such as yourself cleric-fascists and sick so-called believers with an IQ equal to your shoe size, this poor Bosnia will never exist. You are the same as the chetniks and ustashe you dumb goatfucker* (Klix: 20 August 2017). Pro multi-ethnic coexistence and neutrality is not an option here, either you're are fully in or you are out. When deviation from an expected manner of thinking is noticed, interethnic relationship is ipso facto jeopardized. And although the messages are not quite the same in the sense that these readers are not 'threatened' with violence since they belong to the in-group, the messages are still quite explicit and not neutral. In April 2015, Klix reported on the removal of graffiti *Serbs on the willows* discussed in Chapter 2. What we see in Extract 3 is how a reader criticizes a member of the same ethnic group, vigorously countering undesirable attitudes towards the removal of this graffiti. The comment *This should be done with all nationalistic graffiti not only in Sarajevo but all over the country* is replied to in the following way:

Extract 3 (Klix.ba: 23 April 2015)

Delavesta 23.04.2015.
And you are some multi-culty bosnian licking serbian assholes.... In the rs there are antibosniak graffiti at every step, and nobody paints them over nor condemns them, apart from Bosniaks of course, but you hurried up to lick chetniks' assholes... Because of those like you 92' happened, concluding with 95'... Take a look blind man, whatever humane action you take, serbs will hate you again and wait for an opportunity to slaughter you... A serb can be a good man, but serbs will never be good people... narrow-minded blind man

Despite the moderation policies of Klix.ba, the vocabulary used by the readers is mostly similar and, in some instances, identical to the intense lexical quality found in graffiti, e.g. *A dead Serb, the best Serb*. Although it might seem that the content of the reported graffiti effectively triggers the re-articulation of the same pejorative terms from the first dataset, adjective and noun collocates which are used as indicators of ethnicity in all three corpora, point to non-euphemistic choices used as a means for homogenization of the enemies: e.g. Bosniaks – *Balias, hybrid, genetic waste of Serbs, toothless poor, Poturice*; Serbs – *Chetniks, stink, monsters, genocide-men, Nazi mites, criminals, animals*; Croats – *Ustashe, minority, nationalists, fascists, quasi-Croats*. Throughout the three datasets, pejorative ethnic markers – *Balijas, Chetniks* and *Ustashe*, offer constant reminders of who the enemy is. Just like subtle We/They pronouns, these terms are endlessly repeated, and not just in the digital sphere but in/through a number of different modes (just like the usage of *Chetniks* on the official monument raised in the memory of a young boy in a rural Bosnian Croat municipality Usora I visited in 2016 reading: *On this place by a Chetnik's grenade as a civil victim of war was killed*). Such lexical choices are effective in intensifying nationalistic sentiments (Reisigl and Wodak, 2009) precisely because they 'offer constant, barely conscious, reminders' (Billig, 1995: 93) not just of national identities but of more the dangerous, war period synonyms to war criminals and killers. As Del Ponte (2006: 553) argues, these derogatory terms need to be understood 'both in their historical context and in the context in which they were used during the conflict'. To follow Tirrell (2012), we nowadays find harm in these historically embedded terms since they are publicly repeated in the amount that they become appropriated and normalized. In the analysed sample specifically, whether the goal is ethnic exclusion, public humiliation or accusation, readers mostly refer to Bosnian Croats simply as Ustashe, to Bosnian Muslims as Balijas, and to Bosnian Serbs as Chetniks. These terms are especially significant since they denote all of which what nationalism in the country is based on: ethnicity and nationality, war crimes and distrust. To label ethnic groups with these pejorative terms is so important that the readers resort to use the following neologisms or online jargon:

Republika Srpska (Serb Republic) – *Republika Svrbska* (closed compound of Scabies + Serb)*Srpski* (Serbian) – *Smrdski* (closed compound of Stink + Serbian)
Federacija (Federation of Bosnia-Herzegovina) – *Pederacija* (closed compound of Faggot + Federation)
Bošnjaci (Bosniaks) – *Mošnjaci* (closed compound of Scrotum + Bosniaks)

This strategy of *renaming* (Erjavec and Poler Kovačić, 2012) is precisely what might prevent the editors from easily noticing and removing potentially controversial comments. However, I am not arguing that readers use such jargon exclusively in attempts to avoid the removal of their posts. This is indicated by the numerous examples where the terms are not modified in order to be 'hidden', but rather to explicitly ridicule ethnic groups. The discursive strategy of *negative other-presentation* (van Dijk, 1993) is taken further in the next examples. One of the predominant forms of categorizing ethnic groups/nations is accomplished through references to mental deficiency (Reisigl and Wodak, 2001) where the readers point to the shared features of mental illness using quite a limited but straightforward lexical set, as Extract 4 shows:

Extract 4 (Klix.ba: 2016/2017)

ferrachi 06.11.2017.
Serbs = ETERNAL PSYCHOPATHS
albicilla 31.05.2017.
Peace to all souls harmed or killed by the hand of a genocidal tribe which makes the Balkans primitive, the only tribe which is in conflict with everyone.
To all Serbs gathering here:
PSYCHIATRIC HOSPITAL OF THE SARAJEVO CANTON
Nahorevska 248
+387(0)33 206-732
albicilla 31.05.2017.
It has to be remembered, children must know how sick the Serbs are. There are honourable exceptions, however as a collective they are the sickest group on the planet, shoulder to shoulder with cannibals from the most backward tribes of the world.

Here, the reference to *being sick* seems to be closely related to the concept of the outgroup as a biological threat or what Savage (2007) identifies as *partial dehumanization* (after Bernard et al., 1971). By pointing to mental disease, the readers confirm the status of humanness since mental illness affects human beings, just like cancer or any other disease. However, the comments above are in fact the reactions to what the readers understand as nonhuman, animalistic behaviour and ultimately not in accordance with what is regarded 'normal'. In the words of Susan Sontag (1990: 74), 'disease, which could be considered as much a part of nature as is health, [is] the synonym of whatever [is] "unnatural"'. In this sense, comments almost exclusively sent to Bosnian Serbs, denying them mental faculties, work as a way of communicating rancour towards all Serbian people equally responsible of unspeakable carnage. Thus, war crimes committed against non-Serbs are understood as the product of collective disease developed in the parent-body Serbia – e.g. *Serbia is an enemy to its own people first, then to all the peoples around it. Serbia needs a Doctor to treat it, she is sick. Sick of Nationalism and hate* (Klix.ba: 31 May 2017). Such rhetoric also enacts 'moral exclusion and delegitimization' (Bar-Tal, 1990; Tileaga, 2007: 720) defined as specific cases of categorization based on 'moral values, rules and consideration of fairness'. When moral boundaries are crossed and things that humans simply should not do are done, they are denied the status of humans and their national integrity is deconstructed. In simple terms, taking away a groups' humanness means, at least to some degree, erasing their nationhood. *Moral evaluation* (van Leeuwen and Wodak, 1999; van Leeuwen, 2018) produces seemingly legitimized forms of extreme hostility and exclusion which are rationalized and appropriated by, for instance, arguing that coexistence with *psychopaths* is simply not possible. Note how in Extract 5 there is a shift from a general intellectual disability to a more extreme form of dehumanization connected to the semantic fields Bishop and Jaworski (2003) identify as 'waste matter' and 'animals/non-humans':

Extract 5 (Klix.ba: 2015/2017)

marijanb14 30.11.2017.
@bosnjakislambosanski.. muslims are shit… You again and always prove it. Muslims are shit… The best description of muslims in b&h. Muslims are shit!!!!!

DISTANCERO 06.08.2017.
Muslims – so-called balijas are the genetic waste of the Serbian people!!!

PasjalukPasjaluk 31.05.2017.
a bloodthirsty people, sick to their core
imagine being fulfilled by slaughtering raping butchering abusing someone

posao1000 03.08.2015.
Orthodox rats on klix in large quantities. I must call for sanitation to perform deratization
There are no worse people than orthodox rats.
Bosniak orthodox are special rats which we will use for all kinds of research haha

zemljanin1973 02.08.2015.
In the Balkans it is valid: "What a smart person is ashamed of, a fool is proud of". I do not know how anyone can glorify varmints, who displayed their heroism by torturing and killing civilians and children. These are not people, nor animals, they are the lowest forms of life.

Such lexical choices construct others as 'unwanted waste, residue and dirt' (i.e. *shit, rats, varmints*), categorizing groups as non-humans which is 'the ultimate strategy of bringing offence to others' (Bishop and Jaworski, 2003: 263) and a part of a much broader discursive strategy of pejoration (Coupland, 1999). However, in Tirrell's (2012: 186) terms, 'a deadly language game' is not a simple question of insults and the casual 'repetitions of hollow speech acts'. What is especially troublesome is the readers' understanding of the concept unwanted waste. Certainly, the representation of Serbs as rats denies their humanness, but more importantly, the Serbs are associated with impurity and danger that needs to be 'removed from civilized society' (Tileaga, 2006). Both the use of dehumanizing terms and even something as simple and 'neutral' as *cleansing* are all equally historically embedded for the citizens. Reminiscent of the anti-Semitic trope during the Nazi period when Jews and other enemies most of whom were seen as having a Jewish connection were categorized as outsiders, liars, cheats, physically degenerate and dirty, these create images of a dangerous enemy and place distrust towards the other ethnic groups.[8] In the context of war-period Bosnia-Herzegovina, Norman Cigar (1995: 71) argues:

> Perhaps nowhere was the power of language to categorize and destroy as evident as the choice of the term 'cleansing', used freely in unofficial discourse to describe the violent removal of Muslims. Logically, a procedure with such a name could only be viewed as positive and desirable, the implicit antithesis and correction of an assumed impure, unnatural, and demeaning state.

After the war, the Serbs' existence is in the same way a precondition for some of the Bosniaks' 'threat, engendering fear and hatred, while at the same time no moral reproach, or indeed question, need be considered in relation to their destruction' (Tileaga, 2006: 429). As every impurity and disease has to be defeated, the reader comments, and especially those posted on reports about the annual commemorations to murdered civilians, naturalize/normalize the 'everyday' aggressive sentiments against those who murdered their people, evidenced in explicit references to a future conflict – *I sincerely hope that we too will kill 8000 svrbs (Scabies+Serbs) in the future; BURN ALL CHETNIKS AT THE STAKE AND SAVE THE WORLD FROM EVIL* (Klix.ba: 2017/2015).

To sum up, it is quite clear that derogatory and violent categorizations are not used only to spread fear and disgust, but to empower one ethnic group while weakening the other(s) (Tirrell, 2012). As Tirrell (2012) goes on to argue, the use of deeply derogatory terms specifically might have a double effect where at the same time the extremists of one ethnic group build their confidence and power, while the other ethnic group is being denied its humanity. The strategy of pejoration that allows collective blame and punishment (Savage, 2007) is compounded with the destruction of one group's nationhood and further reinforced in explicit calls to violence. It is precisely the derogatory/violent syntactic structures and their use in context that clearly provide strong initial indications regarding the main themes in the dataset, alluding that 'evaluative meanings are not merely personal and idiosyncratic but widely shared in a community' (Stubbs, 2001: 75). Now that I established two interactive chains of online communication, I highlight the most salient topics of these conversations: *From shaming to blaming* and *History in service of nationalistic ideology*.

From shaming to blaming

To start with, the theme of shaming and blaming opposing ethnic groups works as a part of the broader 'We vs They' rhetoric. The dominating 'moral agents fighting evil' (Vanderford, 1989) here are Bosniaks, reminding mostly Bosnian Serbs (and only occasionally Bosnian Croats) about the atrocities the Serbs committed. Quite expectedly, the principal reasons for shaming are specifically the Srebrenica Genocide, killings of children and the raping of women, serving primarily as 'an invitation to self/national reflection' (Every, 2013). By this token, shaming is essentially about *What THEY did*. Here, again, we see categorization of others 'excluded from the realm of acceptable norms and/or values' (Bar-Tal, 1990: 65). Consider Extract 6:

> **Extract 6** (Klix.ba: 2017)
> djecko 31.05.2017.
> Shame on you chetniks
> SamoZajedno 26.05.2017.
> Serbs, are you ashamed? If you are not and if you do not experience catharsis and admit to the evil deeds, your children will have to. Are you not ashamed of transmitting the disgrace to them, what kind of people are you?
>
> Posljedni Samuraj 09.02.2017.
> Every Serb who feels any emotion for human life should watch this or should shut up forever this is a great disgrace for the serb people and serbia which allowed this what happened in SREBRENICA to happen.

Linguistic means for shaming are straightforward; mostly direct questions like *Aren't you ashamed?* or claims *You should be ashamed*. The readers shaming the enemies seem to be attempting 'to construct them as existing outside of normal human society' while presenting themselves as 'morally appropriate, sensitive and socially aware' (Every, 2013: 677, 679). Less commonly, the readers give more detailed descriptions of the committed crimes an ethnic group is accused of, adopting the victim identity only for their own group. Such comments work as a means to legitimize the previously seen explicit calls to violence. Regardless of the readers' aims, to emphasize their group's victimhood or/and to invite a form of national reflection, the comments analysed indicate that shaming does not seem to be very effective:

> When people shame us in a degrading way, this poses a threat to our identity. One way we can deal with threat is to reject our rejecters. Once I have labelled them as dirt, does it matter that they regard me as dirt?... Disrespect begets disrespect.
>
> (Braithwaite, 2000: 287–8)

Although ethnic groups, Bosnian Serbs specifically, are not always shamed in the most degrading ways, they are nonetheless previously constructed extremely negatively through derogatory and dehumanizing terms. Following Braithwaite's (2000) observations, Every (2013: 672) explains that shaming can actually strengthen the bonds between the members of the accused group which 'does not take on the identity of the "ashamed", but rather re-constitutes the frame from "shameful" to "oppressed"' and angry. Taking back the role of 'true victims' for their own group, the readers respond back mostly through ridicule, sarcasm and 'attacking back' (Every, 2013) as outlined in Extract 7:

Extract 7 (Klix.ba: 2017/2016)

TM0 31.05.2017.
Just how many Prijedor children were killed in 1941–45 by muslims and croats

lalalal 26.05.2017.
What did poturice think? That they could walk freely and slaughter serb children? Well it shall not pass. We will free the rest of B&H from you wahhabis, poturice, occupiers eventually
...

Vonj 26.05.2017.
What kind of ice-cream one cannot find in Srebrenica?
weeeell, family pack;D;D;D

Pretorian 09.07.2016.
@bajro1980 Oh fuck it, it is still nothing compared to how much we owe you for Jasenovac, ‚ndh, austro-hungary, turks… we forgave you everything only for you to stab us in the back again every time, well its enough!!!

kupo 09.07.2016.
@pelevratimifriz… truly, truly these bh. muslimhood are perishable goods… I am not a nationalist or anything alike, but brother they stink… with their whining eternal victims, disingenuous, duplicitous, general weeknes, inadequacy… they should all be sent to Turkey where their spiritual homeland is!

The discourse of blame works in a similar way and fosters the construction 'We vs They'. In a dataset of over 7,000 comments, the discourse of blame is primarily achieved through more or less explicit predication. However, consider the equally frequent case of blaming realized through the comparison of the war in Bosnia-Herzegovina, especially the killings of civilians, with the Fascist period in Germany and the Nazi mass murder of Jews (Extract 8).

Extract 8 (Klix.ba: 2017/2016/2015)
Nocna Straza 31.05.2017.The Serbs are the most genocidal people in the history of the world, not even the nazi Germany can compete with them. However their fascist propaganda and lies have convinced the dim-witted Serbs that they are the eternal victims that just so happens nobody likes.
pro et contra 06.08.2017.the terrorizing, torturing and killings in this and in other camps were worthy of Hitler's camps, they also clearly showed their true face the bearded nazi terrorists
Bess93 23.05.2017.Such hate displayed by Serbs towards Bosniaks and Croats as was the case in Prijedor is hard to imagine for a normal person. Omarska and Keraterm will be remembered as places where man has shown his darkest side. The nazis killed masses of people quickly and effectively, the serb criminals in Prijedor took pleasure in killing people slowly for days. Apart from the butcher of Omarska and Keraterm there are also the two reporters of K. Vjesnik, Zivko Ecim and Mile Mutic, true criminals who were never convicted.
vodenicar2 12.04.2016.To live with Serbs and Croats is similar to how the jews lived with nazis
Noting however that nazis are gentlemen compared to the afore mentioned
Zmaj1967 08.07.2015.Why didnt you simply keep people in prison as prisoners of war as is done normally in wars. It is only if the intention is GENOCIDE that in so few days so many people are killed in this way. That is how Hitler exterminated the jews during the world war 2.

Invoking and mediating Germany's past in order to 'unveil' Serbs' cruelty and inhumanness is certainly not a new phenomenon. In the context of the war in Bosnia-Herzegovina, Holocaust analogies appeared frequently in public discourse and media, primarily to pressure those who had the power to act. As Steinweis (2005: 281) explains, particularly American newspaper columnists 'compared the methods of Serbian leader Slobodan Milošević to those of Adolf Hitler'. Roy Gutman's *Like Auschwitz* (1992), Ed Vulliamy's *The shame of camp Omarska* (1992), Mark Danner's *America and the Bosnian Genocide* (1997), are just a few pieces drawing parallels with the horrific images from the Holocaust period. Comments shaped by Holocaust references integrate *topoi of comparison* (Wodak et al., 2009) and fulfil 'a persuasive function' (Reisigl and Wodak, 2001) about Serbs utilizing Hitlerized methods for eliminating non-Serbs during the war. Equalizing local war crimes with the Nazi Fascist ideology serves to overemphasize the portrayal of Serbs as inhuman. The torture and the killings in concentration camps are seen as the most inhumane acts that have the Nazi ideological meanings as the background. Although the readers mostly claim that the Serbian acts are equally paradigmatic of the worst crimes against humanity, it is not uncommon to find various attempts to portray Serbs and their crimes even worse than the Nazis'. With this analogy the readers discursively construct a *community of victims* (Wodak et al., 2009), in some cases through the national solidarity with Croats, while in others Bosniaks are a closed group of victims and objects of both the Serbs' and Croats' cruelty and hatred since *to live with them is like Jews living with Nazis*. In the analysed sample, Bosnian Serbs specifically continue to be portrayed as ultimate non-humans, dangerous and sick, yearning for Great Serbia, following Fascist ideology, and betraying and killing their neighbours. Just like with the examples of shaming, when a Fascist-Nazi comparison is invoked, the responses shift towards denial, avoidance or attacking back: In this sense, both discourses of shame and blame do not succeed in constructing any meaningful debates. On the other hand, comments are probably not meant as contributions to the debate in the first place, but function as expressions of anger and distrust. Such comments mostly appear in the sections of reports on memorializing activities in the Prijedor region (and they would probably appear in the comments sections of the reports about Srebrenica as well, but comments on those reports are almost exclusively disabled). Again, despite the ICTY's ruling that ethnic cleansing in Prijedor was not committed with genocidal intent, readers repeatedly invoke the scale of the inhumane acts (torture, rape, murder) as premises for the claims that follow. The readers also specify the guilty ones and the number of victims through the *topos of numbers* (Reisigl and Wodak, 2001) legitimizing their right to remember and express deep-seated anger, as well as to make bold appeals to ethno-national unity as Extract 9 shows:

Extract 9 (Klix.ba: 2017)

Djiksoni 26.05.2017.
SERBS KILLED 3372 CHILDREN IN B&H, WOUNDED HEAVILY OVER 14.000 CHILDREN, RAPED 756 CHILDREN, RAPED 50.000 WOMEN, 53 CHILDREN BELOW AGE 7 WERE SHOT BY A SNIPER IN THE HEAD.. THAT'S WHAT SERBS AND THE RS ARE

munja123 31.05.2017.
In Prijedor the serbs killed:
-102 children
-256 women
-3.173 civilians
-31.000 civilians went through the camps
-53.000 expelled
No man is greater than you, Bosniak, to have the right to inflict injustice upon you, and you Bosniak are no lesser than any other man to endure anyone's injustice, nor to give up on any right to respond with righteous anger to every injustice! Remember that for yourself and for your people!

In alignment with Hoskins' (2014: 662) observation that 'the glut of media is also a glut of memory', Loke (2012) notes how online comments accommodate controversial topics containing emotionally loaded elements that attract a large number of responses and receive validation. Thus, online comments do not only provide an easily accessible site for analysing contemporary networked narratives of attachment and belonging (White, 2015), but an everyday affective *opinion pipeline* (Santana, 2011) that hinges greatly on the emergent media-memory relationship. What we know from Hoskins (2014: 662) is that media and memory 'share locus in their categorical instantiation in the everyday'. Indeed, an inevitable part of Bosnia-Herzegovina's everyday life is the war memory, as the past is simply everywhere and always. As Baruh and Popescu (2008) explain, nationalist discourse is not simply a discussion about a nation, nationhood or nationality, but rather, dialogues involving one's country are marked by the emotional etiquettes they had been given. What the examples above show is that online platforms serve as 'unique expressions of contemporary culture' (Pauwels, 2012) and have very real and important content to convey. Online comments are often about a mediatization of war memory even when they strongly and strategically express nationalistic sentiments. To follow Finlayson (1998: 108), nationalism is not just about 'asserting the primacy or significance of the national'. At this point, it is worth mentioning that online comments I analyse here are posted along very specific reports, all related to the war memory in one way or another. Consequently, they render different mechanisms of memory and memorialization practices that are still vigorously insisted on by the citizens, and inextricably forged through a new *network memory* that transforms 'the temporality, spatiality, and indeed the mobility' of Bosnia-Herzegovina's past (Hoskins, 2009: 92–3). It is along these lines that we also see the emergence of a new space for post-war *digital memory mediation* (Garde-Hansen et al., 2009) encouraging specific kinds of affect and providing 'a peek into society's temperament' (Loke, 2012).

History in service of nationalistic ideology

The second topic which emerges from online conversations about the elements of Bosnia-Herzegovina's physical space is related to the discursive construction of the country's national past produced through readers' interpretations of historical events. For readers, the importance of starting discussions about historical events can hardly be overstated. Although the comments seem to be the readers' reactions to the elements of semiotic landscapes that Klix.ba reports about, quite literally, an article regarding a commemoration for example, only occasionally invokes discussions about that event per se. Instead, often without any reference to the reported event, readers engage in discussions about historical heritage and territorial rights that seem to be at the heart of turbulent conflicts in Bosnia-Herzegovina. Generally speaking, comments on Klix.ba work as verbal confrontations accomplished through insults, ridiculing, provocations, threats, etc., based on belonging to a certain ethnic group. However, ethnic groups also tend to define others not only with reference to their characteristics and personal beliefs about their evilness, but through the construction of Bosnia-Herzegovina's political history and *national body* (de Cillia et al., 1999) (i.e. the national territory with its boundaries). Historical heritage, as well as 'spatial and territorial dimensions are likewise significant in this discursive construction of national identity' (Wodak et al., 2009: 26). Comments across three sub-corpora render interpretations of a problematic narrative of *historical truths* which refer to controversial acts or events of the past (de Cillia et al., 1999: 161). Janićko's (2015: 48–50) study of printed newspapers shows that the discourse of nationalism is projected through different ideological references, e.g. Bosniak nationalism claiming the right of the Bosniaks to a nation-state within the current Bosnian borders, inherited directly from the Yugoslavian Socialist Republic of Bosnia and Herzegovina, and assuming the marginalization of Serbs and Croats into minorities, or Serb nationalism defending the territorial autonomy of Bosnian Serbs and demanding separation from Bosnia-Herzegovina and possibly unification with Serbia. Similarly, reader comments illustrate that they achieve a rhetorical construction of ethno-nationalism through competing primordial rights to territory and national legacy. Such sentiments we find in the comments section of the most commented report in the dataset about the sixteen meters high monument erected to commemorate the members of the Army of Bosnia-Herzegovina (where the majority of soldiers were Bosniaks, however there were Croats and some Serbs as well) and a local brigade of a small municipality of Gradačac in the north-eastern part of Bosnia-Herzegovina with majority Bosniak population. Here we also see that provoking discussions occur between all three ethnic groups, and not only Bosnian Muslims and Serbs as most of the comments in previous sections illustrate. The report shows an opening picture of military members saluting. Bishop and Jaworski (2003: 254) explain that the militaristic visual images serve to 'multimodally generate and explicitly evoke a militaristic framework'. By this token, the series of eighteen images showing the activities during this event in an evocative way are very important in reinforcing reader comments and forming their attitudes towards the monument. Below the images, the report text reads *This monument was forged in the heroism and blood of the bravest sons of Bosnia-Herzegovina, Bosnian lilies who almost barehanded stood on the defence line of Bosnia-Herzegovina. The lily is a symbol of the resistance, courage and immense love for our homeland* (Klix.ba, August 2017). However, it seems that the readers strongly disagree with the symbolism presented in the report text and renew ancient nationalism. The most salient discussion in this comments section refers to the symbol of lily, specifically to whom does the national marker belong to? Duijzings' (2007: 153) observation that 'myths, memories of distant historical events and remembrances of more recent events blend together' is encapsulated in Extract 10:

Extract 10 (Klix.ba: 20 August 2017)

hrhbZDS 20.08.2017.
old Croatian crest used by the hrvatinićs, štubićs, kotromanićs etc... since the bosniaks don't have a history of their own they have to appropriate other's history. The good thing is they are slowly returning to their previous faith.

hrhbZDS 20.08.2017.

again using croatian heraldry and hymn starting with the thousand year old country. poturice, it is easier for you to return to the Croatian faith which you sold for a handful of turkish flour:)))

Banovenjive80 20.08.2017.
That exact lily is held by St. Anto in his hand. You appropriated everything you don't have anything of your own.

strateg 20.08.2017.
Nothing without Croats…….. and the lily is a symbol of catholics, Christians, our Kotromanic, Tomasevic, Katarina… nice…

hrhbZDS 20.08.2017.
@katoni… nobody is fuming, we are only pointing out that you are using our old croatian crest. It would be more logical if you used some two crossed scimitars with a crescent moon and star background.:))

tigarbengalski25 20.08.2017.
@EXM https://hr.wikipedia.org/wiki/Heraldi%C4%8Dki_ljiljan… a little Wiki education my Bosniak… if nothing else… catholics, Christians CROATS.. Bosnians don't even exist as a nation let alone the Bosniaks..that is some sort of Turkish waste, always labourers always servants..as I see even today that is what you are

Extract 10 illustrates how the readers interpret history differently and use it to emphasize their national legacy and attachment to the territory. The way readers understand their national symbol is specifically through its relation to larger past contexts. Regardless of the time when one people, as part of the Kingdom of Bosnia (from 1154 to 1377) with its different intra-national religions shared the land and tradition, the contemporary citizens try hard to state clearly that they had never been members of one people, rather that they always had different national identities. Indeed, commenters go as far back in history as it suits their ideological narrative. In the extract above, we see comments posted by Bosnian Croats who claim that Bosniaks use the national symbol of the lily which was stolen/appropriated from Croats, in order to commemorate their national heroes and fallen soldiers. The rhetorical strategy used by the readers is the invocation of emblematic figures of the past (Baruh and Popescu, 2008) and appeals to ancestors who provided and established nationhood and national identity, as well as the socio-cultural character of today's ethnic groups. For example, the readers mention Kotromanić, the king of late medieval Bosnian royal dynasty (before losing the territory to the Ottomans/Turks), as well as Katarina Kotromanić, Tomašević, Tvrtko, etc. The invocation of these names, by both Bosnian Croats and Serbs, takes place in the context of minorization of Bosniak people portrayed as those who *have no history, have nothing of their own, appropriate Croatian and Catholic symbols*, and should use symbols originating from the Middle East and Turkey (scimitars, a star and crescent moon) more recently connected to the Islamist terrorist organizations. Historical claims about this 'controversial' symbol progress into discussions in which readers emphasize the unworthiness of Bosniak national identity, delegitimizing their right to the territory. Here, it is not the territory of any ethnic group that is minorized, rather it is extremely prominent and appropriated, while the ethnic groups living in or sharing these territories are minorized and described as illegitimate and without an ethnic-based claim to the land. This is mainly accomplished through identifying people as originating from each other – Bosnian Croats and Muslims as *tribes which claim explicitly that they are not Serbs*, Bosnian Serbs and Muslims *come from Croats*, Bosnian Croats *are not real Croats*, Bosniaks are not even a nation but merely *Turkish servants and waste*. Unlike the strategy of dehumanization, claims about which nation is primordial and which one is out of place is how nationhood is taken away. Ultimately, the comments about ethnic groups identified as having no nationhood and homeland indicate that national consciousness emerges through ancient past. Generally speaking, the readers support memorializing activities which honour the victims and the heroes of their ethnic group. However, monuments are obviously not only about remembering and honouring the victims but rather about competition since they 'reshape space and time along ethno-national lines' (Bougarel et al., 2007: 26). Just as memorializing activities, reader comments 're-appropriate both time (history) and space (territory)' and as Duijzings (2007: 153) further argues, should be understood as 'a part of a much wider effort to inscribe the new political order into the landscape'. As there can be no nationality without a country, and no country without a territory, establishing the true owners of the territory is extremely important. The narratives about territoriality create and affirm 'discursive togetherness' (Wodak and de Cillia, 2007) of the in-group, while also producing and sustaining hatred towards the out-groups. The actual monuments and the victims they are supposed to honour are secondary at best, mentioned in passing or not at all in many cases. The only thing that matters is the politicization of the narrative. Equally secondary are the semiotic resources whether they are graffiti, monuments, museums or events, it matters not – anything will do to get the wheel of hate rolling.

Conclusion

This chapter looked at online comments which reveal how physical spaces are transformed into online formats enabling people to actively participate in the war (memory) discourse. Although online comments give us a broad sense of how citizens represent and understand their physical environment, generally speaking, they do not directly reflect their attitudes towards the elements of public space reported on the Klix.ba website. Instead, the comments even redirect attention from the content of the reports. Often, without any reference to reported events, readers engage in discussions about ancient and more recent violent history, as well as national legacy and attachment to the territory. In this sense, it is clear that the citizens focus mainly on the violent history of the country. Although not commented on directly, as would have been expected, the physical spaces do work as extremely effective triggers for expressing deeper ethno-nationalistic sentiments. It is clear that 'internet nationalism' in Bosnia-Herzegovina is fabricated through the homogenization of the enemy accomplished via (a) pejoration and/or dehumanization; (b) evaluative attributions of negative traits; (c) neologisms or post-war jargon that delivers public humiliation; and (d) micro-messaging mimicking a faster speech-like pace following the heated and violent We/They and I/You rhetoric. The invocation of the war and the use of war time vocabulary are prominent, lexical choices are often non-euphemistic and are in fact direct accusations and produce the discourse of shame and blame. Ethnic groups are mostly described as dangerous, evil or those who cannot be trusted, recognized and imagined in terms of their respective pasts and their involvement in violent actions. In this vein, the issue of distrust and speculation about the future are explicitly presented as emanating from an ethnic group's evil 'nature'. Additionally, in order to emphasize their supremacy and distinctiveness, readers interpret history differently and use it to claim their national legacy and rights to the territory. Just like in any other genre, through the portrayals of victimhood and explicit categorizations of victims and perpetrators, online comments try to establish definitions of justice, responsibilities for vengeance, and 'historical truth'. As Baruh and Popescu (2008) explain, everyday nationalism is set precisely in people's habits of speech, and although extremely 'hot', they are normalized. In this sense, the comments resemble graffiti. In spite of being deleted frequently, user profiles banned or comment sections closed, they keep coming back and they are literally everywhere. They create the *third space* (Hughey and Daniels,

2013) between physical and virtual landscapes, and allow for everyday public construction of imagined, evil nations/ethnic groups. Although the commenters work in a relatively anonymous and constrained space and we do not know their exact identities, the people participating in these discussions and flagging certain terms and ideas by reusing and reposting them, create a massive virtual body that supports nationalistic sentiments. Although the most popular websites in Bosnia-Herzegovina 'emphasize sensationalist news [...] often supporting their stories with shocking videos and provocative photos' (Open Society Foundations, 2012: 28) and the 'publication of a news article online is a first step that triggers conversation with and among readers on the comment boards' (Nielsen, 2012: 87), the investigation of the content of the reports (e.g. images, headlines) was beyond the scope of this study. Nonetheless, it should be emphasized that online comments certainly do not exist in isolation, rather in a sense they are often reflective of the reports which influence them through a complex interplay between linguistic and visual elements, especially through headlines. Together, reports and comments are playing out against the backdrop of Bosnia-Herzegovina's realities – the bizarre political situation and social disputes. In this sense, they are a part of a much larger narrative about Bosnia-Herzegovina's socio-political woes. Throughout the analysed data, constructive discussions are not present and there is an insignificant number of comments calling for reconciliation and criticizing explicitly violent commenters. What is particularly interesting here is that the online comments are, for many people in Bosnia-Herzegovina, perhaps the only possible means of inter-ethnic communication since such discussions 'in real life' are often avoided. When comparing physical and virtual spaces, Ivkovic and Lotherington (2009) say that in physical spaces signage explicitly targets the (local) population, while in virtual landscapes this is not the case as the entrance to cyberspace like Klix.ba is not controlled or restricted. The comments presented in this study managed to 'fly under the radar', and we can only imagine the troublesome nature of those that were actually deleted. However, it should be pointed out that most of the visitors on Klix.ba are Bosnian Muslims since the website originated in Sarajevo (previously named *Sarajevo-x*). Although, I have not found any hard data on the ethnic distribution of the visitors, it would be logical to assume that Bosnian Serbs and Croats prefer other news portals (i.e. originating in Herzegovina and the Serb Republic, Croatia and Serbia). It is more than obvious that the readers mostly emphasize how Bosnian Serbs' criminal past must not be forgiven nor forgotten, and it cannot be known how the 52 per cent of the deleted comments are distributed among the members of different ethnic groups, and whether or not any bias exists. All this implies that virtual landscapes, although not controlled and restricted in the sense Ivkovic and Lotherington (2009) talk about, they are in fact contested and claimed just as physical spaces are. It seems that not only are the readers 'unknown' but so are those who regulate and control the virtual landscape. A question then arises: Have the comments posted by Bosnian Serbs and Croats perhaps been deleted in order for the Bosnian Muslims to have free passage in claiming the virtual space, or are the visible comments simply the result of assumed visitor distribution between the ethnic groups? Now that I have demonstrated how physical landscapes extend to virtual spaces, in the next chapter I turn to the ways people actually talk about the war and how traumascapes move intergenerationally and to the dispersed diasporic geographies of Bosnia-Herzegovina.

5

(Un)Realities of War in Second-Generation Oral Narratives

Beyond Bosnia-Herzegovina

Along with the destruction of physical space, socio-economic hardship, torture and mass killings, the displacement of over two million people is another significant consequence of the war in Bosnia-Herzegovina.[1] In the year prior to the war and after the war started in April 1992, a million citizens emigrated to Western European countries, Canada, the USA and Australia (Kupiszewski, 2009). Some refugees were sent back to Bosnia-Herzegovina once peace had been officially restored, yet half a million people scattered around the world retained the status of permanently displaced people (Valenta and Ramet, 2011). As the Human Rights Watch reports: 'lack of economic opportunities and inadequate housing remain the main impediments to returns, but the political crisis and related ethnic division makes the climate for returns even less favourable'.[2] In 2004, the UNHCR confirmed that one million war refugees had returned to Bosnia-Herzegovina. However, many soon applied for emigration visas and moved to other countries. At the very same time, many returnees are considered internally displaced as they did not go back to their homes. They rather settled in ethnically homogeneous areas in order to avoid the status of ethnic minorities (Valenta and Ramet, 2011) – the status Bosniak returnees, for example, have in the Serb Republic municipalities. As of June 2009, more than 117,451 Bosnians were registered as internally displaced: 66,215 in the Serb Republic (almost all ethnic Serbs), 50,468 in the Federation (90 per cent Bosniaks and 10 per cent Croats) and 768 in the Brčko District.[3] The Union for Sustainable Return and Integration in Bosnia-Herzegovina reports that those who decided or had no choice but to stay in the country find themselves in a precarious position: only 1 per cent of the returnees are employed, 47,000 families have no homes and security, 2,550 families live in collective centres, 2,700 households are without electricity. In this sense, returnees come to be viewed as socially handicapped – just another social burden alongside poverty and unemployment. And this is precisely why, as a result of the on-going socio-political dysfunctions in the country and political elites devouring the economy through rampant corruption, the current trend of emigration is constantly rising. In this sense, the Bosnian diaspora remains quite large after the war with people carrying their stories and *moving memories* forward and beyond. It has been estimated that around one-third of the total population of Bosnia-Herzegovina or 1,727,173 emigrants who were born in Bosnia-Herzegovina live in fifty-one countries around the world, with 60 per cent living in twenty-eight EU countries (Ministry of Security Bosnia-Herzegovina, 2019). The Ministry of Security has only partial data on the number of their descendants (i.e. host-country-born second generation), thus we can only speak accurately of the number of those who were born in Bosnia-Herzegovina and who have been settled in European countries. The countries with the largest number of these people are Germany, Austria, Slovenia, Sweden and Switzerland. As one example of the rather large Bosnian diaspora in Europe, I focus on their descendants living in Switzerland. Although most of people arrived to Switzerland at the time of the war, the Federal Office for Migration (FOM) (2014) states that the demographic of Bosnia-Herzegovina should not only be equated with war refugees and asylum seekers since it also stems from two previous waves of economic migration:

1960s: migration primarily economic in nature as Switzerland needed foreign labour;
1980s: workers leaving Yugoslavia in the midst of economic crisis and high unemployment.

According to official statistics, the diaspora of Bosnia-Herzegovina in Switzerland represents around 2 per cent of the foreign population in the country, but a precise number cannot be given because the official data do not include naturalised people and it is affected by a person's national identification, where a significant number of people from Bosnia-Herzegovina are actually included in the statistics as Croats or Serbs since they have dual citizenship (FOM, 2014). More than 65 per cent of people from Bosnia-Herzegovina are located in seven cantons: St. Gallen, Aargau, Zurich, Vaud, Lucerne, Bern and Ticino, and most of them come from Prijedor, Bratunac and Srebrenica (FOM, 2014). Just to be clear, it is precisely these Bosnian places that saw the most horrific violence during the war. Bratunac, for example, a municipality in eastern Bosnia-Herzegovina, 'was forcefully taken by Bosnian Serbs where expulsions were accompanied by killings, sexual assaults and rapes. Between 1992 and 1993, properties of Bosnian Serb villagers in this area were burnt and destroyed by Bosnian Muslims where thousands of Serbs fled, while some were put into detention, were tortured, abused and killed.'[4] Confronted by such traumas, a significant proportion of immigrants in Switzerland (violence refugees or *Gewaltflüchtlinge*) who experienced the war directly (e.g. people who were held in concentration camps, witnessed scenes of extreme violence, and/or lost family members) face somatic disorders, depression and post-traumatic stress disorder – consequences which have affected new generations as well, as stated by the FMO (2014: 77):

> Mental suffering that had such a dramatic effect on B&H refugees in Switzerland has also left its mark to a certain extent on their children. For many years the children grew up in an atmosphere of 'family depression', undermining their self-confidence. In search of role models, these children were faced with exiled parents, overwhelmed by their traumatic experiences following a failed attempt at socio-professional transition in Switzerland.

It is thus not an arbitrary choice that survivors and witnesses frame their psychological conditions narratively since they are 'certainly beyond words, and yet, dispossessed of everything, words are all they have left' (Wieviorka, 1994: 25). After all, traumatic experiences, possessed in one way or another, often constitute 'the core of the life stories' (Leydesdorff et al., 2002) which people share as they try to explain what happened not only to themselves but to the groups they belong to (Alexander, 2004). Along these lines, the processes of adopting the memories of war through different forms of continued participation in Bosnia-Herzegovina's society are reflected in the inter-ethnic social relations, which are inevitably situating and extending arenas of the same political conflicts we find in Bosnia-Herzegovina. In this respect, the FOM (2014) clearly emphasizes that the diaspora in Switzerland should be in fact identified as three separate diasporas – Bosniak, Croat and Serb. These divisions are defined by transnational cultural production structured on the basis of ethnic and religious affiliations which maintain strict ethnic boundaries reflecting the promotion of nationalism and the ambiguity of post-war atmospheres in Bosnia-Herzegovina (Eastmond, 1998). In this chapter, I aim to show that the post-war politics of Bosnia-Herzegovina observable in diasporic settings is framed through collective suffering and reminders of unresolved trauma that discursively emerge in everyday social anxieties. In what follows, I set theoretical aspects grounded in trauma theory and discourse studies which frame this analysis and explain the leap between the snapshots of war memories and diasporic contexts.

Historical trauma

Though potentially taking on a mythical quality for new generations to come, it has been accepted in discourse studies that life stories primarily serve a therapeutic role. In Schiffrin's (2003: 539) terms, 'narrative templates and narrative language can enable survivors to confront, cope with, and possibly overcome, the pain of their past'. Such narratives extensively emerged when people from Bosnia-Herzegovina, attempting to get on with their lives and formalize their status in host countries, needed to provide evidence of trauma. Dimova (2006: 51) observes in her examination of Bosnian refugees in Berlin how 'these people have been torn between required (and often exaggerated) remembering of their past war experiences, and the contemporary, real, but unrecognized trauma related to fear of detainment and deportation'. Indeed, displacement and its causes, which are bound up with trauma, continue to be told, retold and remembered in many different ways (Halilovich, 2013). Stories are ways we shape our identities – our sense of self. Of course, oral and written forms are most prevalent (Crawford, 2014). Quite understandably, it is mainly through narrating stories that the testimonies of suffering and transnational memory come to be produced and the legacies of trauma extended to new generations. Obviously, working through a difficult experience is not the only function of testimony (Felman and Laub, 1992; Langer, 1991). It is often said that trauma has to be preserved so that violent histories do not repeat themselves. Regardless, the processes of responding to trauma are not straightforward and cannot be assumed to be exclusively manifested though neat linguistic forms. Photography is another powerful reminder of past atrocities (Sontag, 2003), as well as something banal like walking past riddled facades. Furthermore, deep emotional silences are just as common as obsessive storytelling (Baranowski et al., 1998). Gabriele Schwab (2010) has demonstrated that people inherit violent histories not only through what they have been told but also through 'the traces of affect'. In this sense, those inheriting trauma

> become avid readers of silences and memory traces hidden in a face that is frozen in grief, a forced smile that does not feel quite right, an apparently unmotivated flare-up of rage, or chronic depression.
>
> (Schwab, 2010: 14)

The truth is, shared stories of war trauma often only confirm one's own personal observations of the already uneasy diasporic spaces. In one way or another, however, new generations are complexly implicated in sensing the 'pain of others' (Sontag, 2003) via the maintained and (publicly) shared post-war storytelling.

> There is for all of us a twilight zone of time, stretching back for a generation or two before we were born, which never quite belongs to the rest of history. Our elders have talked their memories into our memories until we come to possess some sense of a continuity exceeding and traversing our own individual being.
> (Conor Cruise O'Brien, 1948)

The observation by O'Brien (1948), who explored the historical inheritance of memory in intimate settings, opens up a space for rethinking how the signs of trauma persist across generations as narratively resituated in subsequent lives. In recent years, the trope of *historical trauma* has become quite fashionable for invoking the premise that people can transmit trauma experiences intergenerationally. Adopting the concept from psychoanalytic literature and Holocaust studies in the 1990s, Brave Heart (2003: 7) defines historical trauma as 'cumulative, emotional and psychological wounding, over the lifespan and across generations, emanating from massive group trauma experiences'. Although the concept was originally used to describe the torments of Aboriginal people subjected to colonialism (i.e. American Indian groups, Native Alaskan communities, Aboriginal peoples in Canada) and the children of Holocaust survivors (e.g. Duran et al., 1998; Kellermann, 2001; Kirmayer et al., 2014), in the past two decades the term has been used to describe the long-term impacts of the legacy of slavery and the cultural-historical elimination of other groups that share a history of oppression, victimization or massive group trauma exposure (e.g. Armenian refugees, Palestinian youth, the people of Cyprus, Israelis, Mexicans) (Mohatt et al., 2014).

Capturing the ways narratives become embedded into a group's consciousness (LaCapra, 2001), historical trauma specifically addresses the multigenerational aspect resulting from the complex relationship between the individual and the collective, and upends our firmly grasped definition of trauma as exclusively manifested through chronic depression, suicidal ideation, substance abuse or somatic symptoms. Explaining its complex nature, Crawford (2014) highlights two key features of historical trauma. Firstly, what defines historical trauma is the collective experience of a shared group identity which affects multiple aspects of the individual, family and community. Secondly, the nature of historical trauma is cumulative and passed intergenerationally to existing and future group members through various means which 'tear the social fabric' (Eyerman, 2001). The workings of historical trauma resemble the way an individual experiences trauma. In Arthur Neal's (1998) terms, just as individual trauma involves a range of maladaptive responses, historical trauma involves fear and feelings of vulnerability which are representable, communicable and shared with others. However, this does not necessarily need to be felt by everyone in a community, experienced directly by any or all (Eyerman, 2001), nor manifested dramatically in post-traumatic symptoms. In other words, historical trauma is not marked exclusively by psychological pain and disturbances – it is not always so acute and obvious. As Erikson (1976: 153) explains, 'it works its way slowly even insidiously into the awareness of those who suffer from it, so it does not have the quality of suddenness normally associated with trauma'. Lastly, it is entrenched only when 'sociological and psychological conditions are established by the systems and structures that triggered the original trauma in previous generations' (Atkinson, 2002: 81). Certainly, this is similar to what Marianne Hirsch (2008: 5) calls *post-memory* – 'the relationship that the "generation after" bears to the personal, collective, and cultural trauma of those who came before — to experiences they "remember" only by means of the stories, images, and behaviors among which they grew up'. The notion of post-memory does not seem to be fully applicable to this study chapter because it is defined as the relationship to a past mediated through imagination, projection and creation, but not by remembering. Thus, I privilege historical trauma arguing that inherited trauma is not forged and mediated exclusively by the act of storytelling (nor by the images or behaviours of victims) or imaginative projection. Rather, historical trauma emerges when different trauma reminders (e.g. shared stories) are combined with one's direct and lived-experience of the consequences of that trauma manifested through/in different forms and genres. As Weber (2015: 11) puts it, there is no doubt that language provides a skeleton for expressing the memories, but 'the meaning, the flesh filling out the structure within it, comes from something beyond the words themselves'. The quality of trauma (i.e. the way it exists in one's mindscape) seems to vary across narrative and experiential layers which help us to understand its affective impact. Notwithstanding all this, intergenerational narratives become trauma chains when new storytellers retell the narratives as new protagonists who enrich the narrative content with other features (Agha, 2007). The touchstone notion here for both trauma and language scholars goes back to Labov's (2006: 43) observation that 'in all narratives of personal experience, the listener learns of the event in the same way that the narrator did'. This is to say that the stories told cannot be set apart from the listeners who ultimately become speakers themselves (Bakhtin, 1986). In Bauman's (2004: 100) concrete terms, stories are inevitably 'reported, rehearsed, relayed, quoted, summarized'. In this regard, the narrative structure of trauma transmission can be described as belonging to a particular sub-genre of life stories that Georagakopolou (2007) calls *shared stories*. Although such stories and their meanings fully emerge within the family milieu, as Denham (2008) explains, it is the way in which such mechanisms are 'emplotted, framed and contextualized' in broader collective contexts that is of significance. A layering of narrative turns is the key (Mohatt et al., 2014) when systematizing how the personal/intimate translates into the shared/collective. For example, the first layer could be simply observing a parents' reaction to the news about a traumatic event; the second layer could refer to a conversation about it, while the third layer could include an interaction with the members of the groups which are directly implicated in that traumatic event and so on. To follow Hirsch (2004), historical trauma narratives are produced when we move from the notion of individual responses to traumatic events towards the notion of collective responses. They are realized as discursive assemblages of all the elements establishing historical trauma in the first place: complex cumulative losses; contemporary collective distress; shared by many; a temporal structure that causally links the suffering of the present to past events; emplotting a trajectory of trauma; loss from the past through to the present, and perhaps even to an imagined future (see Crawford, 2014). Thus, at a basic level, *historical trauma discourse* is situated in a complex interaction between people, past and present, especially in the context of new diasporic generations whose experiences relate to and shift constantly between here/there and now/then while they evoke other actors, places/spaces and temporalities in their stories. Their interconnectedness in historical trauma narratives is effectively captured by Bakhtin's notion of 'chronotope' (1981), which is useful when engaging with the life stories of social actors who reconcile their personal experiences with collective suffering and consciousness:

> Chronotopic representations enlarge the 'historical present' of their audiences by creating chronotopic displacements and cross-chronotope alignments between persons here-and-now and persons altogether elsewhere, transposing selves across discrete zones of cultural spacetime through communicative practices that have immediate consequences for how social actors in the public sphere are mobilized to think, feel and act.
>
> (Agha, 2007: 324)

One example is readily apparent in formal programmes in Switzerland promoting knowledge of language, history and culture of the parents' home country called *Heimatliche Sprachen und Kultur – HSK*. Quite expectedly, Bosnian Croats prefer the HSK-Croatia for their children, while Bosnian Serb children attend the classes of HSK-Serbia. One of the history lessons in the HSK-Croatia in Bern, for instance, was organized around the Croatian War of Independence or the Homeland War, specifically what happened in the town of Vukovar as the symbol of Serbo-Croatian conflict. Here, children construct the imagery of war after attending a history class and workshop *Remember Vukovar* through their drawings of ruins and tanks firing shells. And while Bosnian children and Croatian children of Vukovar who grew up in the war attempt to find meaning and healing through similar non-verbal modalities (Kollontai, 2010), diaspora children imagine the war, perhaps for the very first time, precisely through non-linguistic forms. Such learning processes potentially connect children to their ancestral homeland, preparing them for the 'serious' stories most often shared in the family circles as they get older. Another example shows that just as in Bosnia-Herzegovina, albeit far more rarely, physical space in Switzerland is marked with the unofficial semiosis produced by diasporic groups. It concerns the strategically emplaced graffiti which appeared on the façade of the Embassy of Bosnia-Herzegovina in December 2017 during the period when six Bosnian Croat political and military leaders, convicted of persecuting, expelling and murdering Bosnian Muslims during the war, were making an appeal to the ICTY. The graffiti read: *Six of Herzeg Bosnia, Heroes, Praljak* (with the sign of Ustashe). Slobodan Praljak was a celebrated general who committed suicide inside the ICTY courtroom in 2017 after hearing he had lost his appeal against a twenty-year-prison sentence. The label *Herzeg Bosnia* is also quite provocative here because it makes a claim to what is currently the territory of the Federation of Bosnia-Herzegovina, an entity which both Bosniaks and Croats share, although some Croats would prefer to have an independent entity. The narratives of territorial contestation are circulating in diasporic spaces as well and serve to express nationalistic tendencies of diaspora members/communities. That is why the flagpole on the balcony of the Embassy was destroyed and the flag of Bosnia-Herzegovina was missing. What we ultimately see is that, just like in the unsettled instances of Bosnia-Herzegovina's graffscape (in Chapter 2), these disruptive moments also sustain the affective trajectories of diasporic spaces. This is precisely how diaspora *does* war-legacy practices. The critical point made by the examples above is that the meanings and consequences of the war in Bosnia-Herzegovina also emerge beyond its geographical boundaries. Re-enacted discursively (and rendered semiotically), the sentiment and politics of *Never forget* is literally brought to the host country. Keeping all of the above in mind, I organize this chapter around the FMO's report regarding the effects of war trauma on diaspora descendants, addressing the ways they were ingrained through oral narratives received from parents and/or family members and their own personal experience of diasporic atmospheres. My analysis of these second-generation stories asks how do second-generation people of B&H heritage living in Switzerland learn and talk about the war. More specifically, how do they discursively (re)construct and make sense of the inherited violent past the inherit?

Stories of war

In this chapter, I focus on the second-generation for two reasons. Firstly, there is an obvious gap in discourse studies regarding the transmissibility of trauma, especially concerning the second-generation of a diaspora. The narrative features of historical trauma and the role which personal experiences play outside of a violent conflict tend to be overlooked. It is also rather surprising that trauma itself has not been the subject of more attention since the discursive approach brilliantly contradicts convictions which assert that traumatic experiences cannot ever be captured by language or are extra-discursive, indescribable and utterly unspeakable. This being said, there is some research regarding the survivors of the war in Bosnia-Herzegovina (both citizens and diaspora members) with their first-hand war experiences (e.g. Halilovich, 2010; Ten Bensel and Sample, 2014; Bašić, 2015; Simic, 2017 – mostly with wartime rape victims). Secondly, it can be expected that the second-generation is more capable of integrating their experiences into coherent stories unlike victims and witnesses whose narratives are often marked by chaos or distortion (Leydesdorff et al., 2002). Altogether, I interviewed fifteen second-generation people who were either born in or who now live in Switzerland (fictitious names appear in this chapter). Most of the informants were born in Switzerland (cantons of Luzern, Bern, Aargau, Aarau, Schwyz and Solothurn). Four informants were born in Bosnia-Herzegovina before the war – Doboj and Velika Kladuša. One informant was born in Slovenia. I interviewed six men and nine women between the ages of eighteen and thirty-seven (average age: twenty-five). One informant belonged to the third-generation, an eighteen-year-old girl (Ema). Her mother came to Switzerland as a twelve-year-old child, and her father during the war.

The concept of trauma was not mentioned to informants. As the interviews were of a semi directive structure, a set of questions was used, especially when it was necessary to stimulate the informants to talk, where I focused mostly on family war history and the transmission of knowledge about the war in Bosnia-Herzegovina. Other questions, which helped to close the interviews, concerned the reasons for the current reinforcement of ethnic divisions, the issues that damage social relationships and possibilities for post-war reconciliation. Most of the informants were brought up in a religious environment, but not all respondents consider themselves religious today. Their concept of identity and their true home is tied to their parents' background and the ethnic group they belong to. Thirteen respondents identified ethnically as: Bosnians, Bosniaks, Croats, Bosnian Serbs and Bosnian-Herzegovinians, yet their identities are fully interstitial:

> *I see myself as completely different from Swiss people in behaviour and way of life. I am not Swiss nor a typical Bosnian Serb but something in between.* Filip, 24
> *When I was in the USA I said that I am from Switzerland. I mean who can explain to them what Bosnia is. And here in Switzerland when someone asks me where am I from, I say, of course, Bosnia.* Mia, 23

Two of them did not declare themselves ethnically or nationally emphasizing that they do not feel at home in Switzerland nor in Bosnia-Herzegovina:

> *Here I am an alien, Yugo Scheiße. And there as well I am Swiss, a foreigner. I do not want to declare nationaly.* Dino, 28
> *I am not Swiss nor Bosnian. I do not feel at home either here nor in Bosnia.* Maja, 36

The informants' parents were all born in different parts of Bosnia-Herzegovina (then Yugoslavia), they had come to Switzerland either to escape the war or for economic reasons. Most of the informants confirmed that they had not lost family members during the war. All this greatly affected the informant's own perceptions of the war and current social trends in complex ways, especially the way they based their views on the past in general. It also created an important backdrop to the sense of national (ethnic) suffering. Methodologically speaking, I approach oral narratives as discursive practices and 'resources for the representation of self and other as they create "worlds" in their stories' (Schiffrin, 2002: 318). The analysis is organized around the two perspectives proposed by Shiffrin (2003) pointing to how a narrative schema (knowledge) is transformed into the language used to recount a story (action). A *competence-centred perspective* privileges narrative templates which serve as both individual archive for personal experience and cultural resources for collective memories, while a *code-centred perspective* focuses primarily on the language of narrative. These perspectives, as Schiffrin (2003) explains, are the two broad analytical domains which provide information not only on how stories are told, but also on how experience is organized. Since it is difficult to determine what exactly makes personal stories traumatic, my analysis is supplemented by different 'signals of trauma' proposed by BenEzer (2002) in his study on the narratives of young Ethiopian Jews migrating on foot to Israel. He suggests particular forms of expression which are not to be used as diagnostic criteria in the clinical sense, but as a way of detecting traumatic experiences within narratives. Ultimately, I have chosen to focus on five trauma signals (out of thirteen) and narrative manifestations because I am interested specifically in verbal communication and discursive 'content' (adapted from BenEzer, 2002: 34–6):

Self-report: reporting that a certain event was traumatic and emphasizing it as being extremely distressing or wounding or referring to its particularly negative (and/or long term) unsettling effect.

Hidden event: narrating an event which was not in the main story, accompanied by distressing emotions such as mourning, grief, shame or guilt which were also not previously expressed.

Emotional detachment or numbness: reporting events which seem to have had a horrifying quality or horrifying consequences for them but show no emotions during the narration and stay rigorously within the verbal mode of reporting.

Repetitive reporting: retelling an experience in its entirety or with an extraordinary reiteration of its minute details, time and time again, as if the narrator is unable to move on, which is in contrast to his or her style of narration in the rest of the account.

Forceful argumentation: narrators stress the reasons for their behaviour within a situation instead of relating the facts, as if the traumatic quality of the event is connected to their conduct in that situation which they feel they should justify.

The five signals provide a basis for assessing painful and disturbing memories, and thus a framework for indicating emotionally charged responses in the informants' accounts. In simple terms, the signals were applied first to detect traumatic experiences in life stories and organize them accordingly. Huyssen (2003) suggests that the narratives of memory should not be read only through the prism of trauma since they become marked exclusively by pain. Stories should be situated in socio-cultural contexts as well (Pickering and Keightley, 2009). In this sense, the application of trauma signals helped me to draw out the most salient tropes from my data which also focus on the social aspects of trauma, and not exclusively on the 'experiencing self'. 'Self-reporting' and 'hidden event', for example, give a better understanding of personal trauma because these signals involve an informant's evaluation of an event as traumatic. Whereas 'forceful argumentation', for instance, often points to experiences brought into a social context.

In this section, I present portions of stories told by several informants. My particular interest is in transcripts which are rich in detail and representative of thirteen hours of recorded interviews. Certainly, not all participants offered the same depth of insight in their stories, carefully avoiding the details I was most eager to learn about (e.g. *Do you think you will pass these stories on to your children one day? If so, what will you say to them?*). During the interviews, there were moments of silence or strategically 'skipping' what exactly was told or who said what. However, the interviews generated rich data in relation to the 1992–5 Bosnian war as a common topic of B&H diaspora discourse. Clearly, not all informants talked in an orderly or coherent manner. Since recalling certain traumatic events often results in *emotional disorientation* (e.g. the concentration camp experience of an informant's father) where feelings of anger, sadness or humiliation rise up, the stories of some informants were incomplete, containing inconsistencies and gaps as they kept switching quickly to another distressing experience or coming back to the same stories. The trope of a traumatized child/adult was never explicitly raised in the questions during the interviews. The only question which potentially supported a reconstruction of emotional injury was: *Have you ever had any concerns or fears related to the war? If so, would you describe them? How often have you experienced this?* The sections I present in this chapter are not always parts of long or 'big stories', as Bamberg (2006) calls them, but are kinds of 'mini-tellin' or 'small stories' (Georgakopolou, 2007; Bamberg and Georgakopolou, 2008) which nonetheless are equally powerful in constructing the relationship between informants and 'small incidents', thus unveiling what those big stories are actually about. In the next section, I show how informants located their own experiences in the war memories and trauma they inherited and how they structured their lives around this. The portions of stories I present here are brought together on the basis of a thematic coherence. The analysis is organized around the two interconnected rhetorical tropes of communicating war memories: *Remembering the feeling*, *Naming the enemy* and *Encountering the enemy*. It is through these salient tropes that I want to rethink how people give their memories and traumatic experiences an expressive form, assimilating them into conventional narratives (Pickering and Keightley, 2009).

Remembering the feeling

The opening question was strategically designed to start the conversation about the war – *How did you find out about the war in Bosnia-Herzegovina? Who told you about it and what exactly have you been told? What happened?* However, this is an open-ended question which does not set any kind of limit or specification on the type of narrative that is perhaps expected (De Fina, 2003). The ways in which informants were introduced to the war in Bosnia-Herzegovina vary in accordance with their family histories related to the war period. Two important factors concern the nature of their parents' settlement in Switzerland – whether one or both of them came to the country as refugees/displaced persons or whether they came before the war for economic reasons. The second, perhaps even more important factor, regards the loss of family members during the war. In cases where the parents came to Switzerland in order to 'escape the war', leaving family members behind, emotional investment is evident in stories produced as neat narrative formats. Informants whose parents did not 'transition' in such ways, offered brief accounts in which it is obvious that there was a process of receiving the stories of war, although it remains hidden. This is clearly evident in the first short passage taken from Ines' story (Extract 1) who was born in 1995, the year when the war in Bosnia-Herzegovina officially ended. Her parents, originally from Tuzla, *explained* to Ines what happened, referring specifically to the biggest collective loss, the Srebrenica Genocide. Interestingly, in her brief account, Ines mentions how she learnt about the war through people's refugee status thinking that the word *refugee* was one's surname (lines 5–8).

Extract 1: Ines, 21	
1 Ovdje nisi to mogao ni vidjeti ni osjetiti	Here you couldn't see it nor feel it
2 ali išli bi često dole onda.	but we would go there often then.
3 kao dijete sam pitala na primjer šta su minska polja	as a child I asked for example what are mine fields
4 'Hej tata šta je ovo ili šta je RS'?	'Hey dad what is this or what is RS?'
5 onda.. slušala bi da ljudi druge nazivaju imenom i onda izbjeglica	then... I would hear people calling each other by name and then refugee
6 na primjer Amela izbjeglica.	for example Amela refugee.
7 ja nisam uopće znala šta to znači jer sam mislila da je to prezime	I never even knew what that meant because I thought it was a surname
8 ali roditelji su mi onda objasnili šta je to	but then my parents explained to me what that was

9 zašto je to bilo	why that was
10 pogotovo ljudi iz Srebrenice šta je bilo.	especially the people from Srebrenica and what it was.

Ines describes war as something that one *sees and feels*, experiences directly. She, however, saw its traces, mediated and negotiated through material-visual frames providing a certain post-war context (*mine fields*, the Serb Republic entity) (lines 3–4). Ines avoids retelling the information she received from her father about the small incidents of encountering mine fields, or (most probably) border signs of the Serb Republic. Going to Bosnia-Herzegovina (mostly when visiting family) seems to be one of the key tropes for creating and re-experiencing war memories precisely because of the interaction with the post-war environment, especially the material remains of the destruction and violation – the ruins of war, and spaces which are construed as the *enemy's* or *stolen*. That such environments create a picture of what happened to those who lived and suffered there during the war is something Navaro-Yashin (2009) demonstrates through her pensive notion of *spatial melancholia*. Navaro-Yashin claims that the post-war environment (made of ruination, subjectivities and residual affects) discharges its energy upon people and generates an affect which creates a kind of melancholia. This happens especially when people literally trace the ruins around them to a certain traumatic time and space. Navaro illustrates how affective materialities such as bullet holes are symbolized, politicized and interpreted by people. Indeed, when informants discuss the post-war environment of Bosnia-Herzegovina, they try to understand and remember it while reflecting on the pre-war nature of their parents' homeland. They talk about seeing flags in strange, unexpected places, scripts on public signs, riddled facades, monuments, graveyards, abandoned properties, destroyed objects and divided schools. In this regard, Dino recalls how he felt when visiting his mother's and father's birth places:

Extract 2: Dino, 28	
1 Osjećam da sam u RS-u	I feel like I am in RS
2 po čemu?	in what way?
3 pogotovo kad idemo za Sanski Most kroz Prijedor	Well especially when we go to Sanski Most through Prijedor
4 odkad sam bio dijete bio mi je trn u oku	It has been a thorn in my eye since I was a child

5 SRPSKI SANSKI MOST	SERB SANSKI MOST
6 ima table i onda ide Sanski Most	there is a sign and then comes 'Sanski Most'
7 to me peklo	that hurt me
8 kakav srpski Sanski Most?	what Serbian Sanski Most?
9 o čemu pričaš?	what are they talking about?
10 Odeš u sela oko Prijedora	And when you go to villages around Prijedor
11 vidiš isključivo pravoslavne crkve	all you see are Orthodox churches
12 sve drugo srušeno.	everything else is destroyed.

In the same vein, describing the post-war atmospheres of Bosnia-Herzegovina, Sanja remembers Trnopolje, the location of a concentration camp operated by Bosnian Serbs:

Extract 3: Sanja, 37	
1 Kod škole krst ispred Trnopolja	At the school outside Trnopolje
2 stavljen je tamo krst sa nekim pustim imenima	there is a cross with numerous names
3 a znaju da su Muslimani tamo ubijeni	and they know that it was the muslims who were killed there
4 TA OBILJEŽJA SU LAŽNA	THOSE MEMORIALS ARE FALSE.

That stories told by parents and family members are not the primary medium of transmitting the memory of the war is shown in another passage taken from Adi's story (Extract 4). Adi was born in Luzern, three years before the war. His parents came to Switzerland in the 1980s for economic reasons. They did not lose family members during the war. Adi explains there is no point in denying that he was explicitly told who the aggressors were. However, the stories of war he received from his parents were transmitted to him not as *an imperative to hate, but as a crash course for kids*, he recalls. Since he strongly identifies as a Bosniak, Adi was always interested in the history of his parents' homeland and its peoples. Importantly, he recalls many personal experiences in diaspora settings that I present later in the analysis. What is interesting in Adi's accounts are the sources of war memory which he found in different discursive forms investigated thoroughly, as emphasized several times throughout the interview (e.g. books, documentaries, visuals). The following transcript in Extrcat 4 shows Adi's reliance on photography evaluated as a valid medium of war memory (cf. Sontag, 2003; Hirsch, 2008).

Extract 4: Adi, 27	
1 Zato što sam stotine sati proveo u pričama o tome	Because I spent hundreds of hours in stories about it?
2 u dokumentarcima o tome.	in documentaries about it.
3 bila je jedna knjiga	there was one book
4 ne sjećam se imena autora niti imena te knjige	I can't remember the name of the author or the book
5 ali je ta knjiga vizualno žrtve rata pokazivala.	but the book showed the victims visually.
6 znači knjiga je kao album slika mrtvih ljudi	so the book was like **an album of pictures of dead people**
7 jednostavno full u detalje	**simply fully detailed**
8 vidiš jednostavno glavu raznešenu od granata	you see simply **a head blown away by a shell**
9 vidiš komadići ljudi leže litre i litre krvi prosute svugdje	you see **pieces of people lying, litres and litres of blood spilled everywhere**
10 vidiš kako se granatiraju bolnice kako se kolju ljudi masovne grobnice	you see how **hospitals are shelled, how people are slaughtered, mass graves**
11 ali ne samo činjenice tih zločina već i mehanizme van toga.	but not just the facts of these crimes, but also the mechanisims outside of that.
12 ekonomija u tom ratu.	economy in that war.
13 šta znači priča curice od nekih sedamnaest godina u jednoj noći gdje ju je dvadeset ljudi silovalo?	what does a story of a little girl of some seventeen years old in one night when twenty men raped her?
14 i takvih ima od sedam osam godina	and there are those of seven or eight years
15 pa do ne znam koje godine.	up to I don't know how many years.

Previously in his story, Adi told me how in comparison to ordinary Swiss people, he actually knows what war is: *I know what it means to run, what war means for civilians, launching shells on cites – that is not a military operation but real places being burnt and destroyed.* I asked him why he thought so and the above passage was a part of his answer. The brutality of war is narrated emphatically as if he witnessed it himself. This is quite understandable since these are 'the facts' fully integrated into his own war story. For him, a testimony of a raped girl cannot be non-factual. Yet, *emotional detachment* (BenEzer, 2009) is evident as Adi remains within a reporting mode. In his story, the actors committing these crimes are not identified, yet whoever is held responsible is, of course, *the enemy*, as later explained.

I turn now to clearly the most emphatic of the passages that I am presenting here (Extract 5). The notion of trauma is axiomatic within a short story told by Ema, the youngest informant in this study (eighteen years old). She was born in the Canton of Aarau but now she lives with her parents in the Canton of Schwyz. Her mother, Sanja, whose story I also address, came to Switzerland at the age of twelve, which makes Ema a sort of third generation B&H descendant. The war story of Ema's family is a complex one – burdensome and painful. Although her mother came to Switzerland in 1991 to escape the war with her parents, Ema's father was imprisoned in one of Prijedor's concentration camps mentioned in Chapter 3. After he was released, he came to Switzerland and got the status of a displaced person. Her father's experience marked this family significantly, yet it is still treated as practically a forbidden topic. The reason for this is quite simple. Her parents still struggle to decide what exactly she and her younger brother should be told. She knows that her father was imprisoned in the camp, she remembers his teeth falling out when she was a small child, she knows about the Srebrenica Genocide, but she was also 'spared' details. This is why Ema talks to her grandfather about the war when she visits him in Kozarac (near Prijedor) and looks for documents and video materials online so she can learn about the war.

Ema's short story about how she understands the war was almost immediately interrupted when she explained the war in one word – *genocide*. She started to cry, and the interview was stopped for a couple of minutes. Shook up and sobbing, Ema emphatically continued telling me that she could not understand how people simply disappeared, her father's family members specifically. Ema finds the meaning of the war in silence and the visual representation of absences, which she feels intensely.

Extract 5: Ema, 18	
1 Meni roditelji nisu odmah pričali o ratu i sad mi još uvijek govore tako	My parents didn't talk to me about the war at the time and they still do not to this day
2 na nivou škole sa šest godina smo prvi put pričali o tome	at the school level when I was six we mentioned the war for the first time
....	....
3 za mene je taj rat....	for me that war is
4 GENOCID....	A GENOCIDE....
((crying))	((crying))
....	....
5 () Jednostavno.... nije mi bilo jasno gdje su ti ljudi nestali	() I just couldn't understand how these people vanished
6 pričali su mi za neke osobe kojih nema koje ja nikad nisam upoznala	I was told about some people that were not there, that I never met
7 nisam mogla skontati ko su oni iako je jedna od tih osoba bio stric mog oca.	I couldn't understand who they were even though one of these people was my father's uncle.
8 tamo u Kozarcu - kod nas ima neki spomenik i sva su imena ispisana	there in Kozarac - there is a monument and all the names are written
9 i onda sam vidjela da su svi u Kozarcu pobijeni i skontala šta znači rat.	and there I saw that everyone in Kozarac was killed and I understood what war meant.

Extract 5, too, points to an affective learning accomplished also through an interaction with the post-war environment – in this instance, a monument to the civilians killed in her father's birth place is preserved memory (Figure 19). It is this particular part of Kozarac's visual landscape that has a strong effect on Ema. This is the point where a mythological place becomes concrete and understood on a new level. Felman and Laub (1992) explain that visits to sites of trauma are an important step in the establishment of new idioms for talking about past violence. That thousands were killed in the Prijedor municipality is something Ema was already familiar with. But it was only when she confronted hundreds of names and familiar surnames inscribed on the stone that she re-established the meanings of the war and faced its impact on this already small community she enjoys visiting.

Figure 19 Monument to the innocent killed citizens of Kozarac 1992–5 © Maida Kosatica 2017

Later in her story, Ema explains who the enemies are, confirming that she does not socialize with Serbs or Croats in Switzerland. She finishes her story in the following manner:

Extract 6: Ema, 18	
1 Naučila sam iz rata da im ne vjerujem	I learned from the war not to trust them
2 i da ih mrzim	and to hate them
3 kako da vjeruješ nekome ko ti je pobio pola familije?	how can you trust someone who killed half of your family?
4 nije lako preći preko toga.	it is not easy to get over that.

This evaluative account serves as a forceful argumentation (BenEzer, 2002) which justifies her feelings of resentment towards other ethnic groups and is analogous to Ema's mother's story, thus allowing us a glimpse into their family narratives and indicating that the stories of war memory told in family contexts are co-constructed (Extract 7):

Extract 7: Sanja, 37	
1 Prva stvar kroz rat koju sam tako reći naučila	The first thing that I so to say learned through war
2 jer ipak ja u ratu nisam bila, ali ipak indirektno naučila	because I wasn't really in the war, but I indirectly learned was
3 prvo pitanje zašto tačno je nedužan narod stradao i zašto smo napadnuti uopće?	first question why exactly were innocent people killed and why were we attacked in the first place?
4 i uvijek je to i želim istaknuti pitanje	and it is always that, I want to emphasize this question
5 **zašto smo?**	**why we were attacked?**
6 nisam ja bila u ratu ali to je moj narod i suosjećala sam sa svojim narodom.	I wasn't in the war but it is my people and I emphatized with my people.
7 imali smo strah i strepili smo samo da tijekom rata ovdje nekako čujemo ima li preživjelih	we were afraid and were nervous during the war just to hear somehow if there are survivors
8 hoće li nas crveni krst nazvati da nam kaže ima li ko preživjeo	will the Red Cross call us to tell us if anyone survived
9 hoće li doći kakva vijest	will any news arrive
10 sve smo moguće kanale koristili	we used all possible channels
11 provodili vrijeme uz radio i TV	spent time with the radio and TV
12 hoće li doći kakva vijest	will any news arrive
13 zar je moralo preko takvog nasilja i ubijanja da se dođe do svijesti na kraju?	did through such violence and killing some sense have to be arrived at in the end?
14 u biti su živjeli sa krvoločnim komšijama	in reality they lived with **bloodthirsty neighbours**

15 i da ti komšija kojem vjeruješ može takvo nešto napraviti?	and that this neighbour who you trust could do such a thing to you?
16 ja to ne mogu nikako razumijeti i kroz to nastaje ovo nepovjerenje prema Hrvatima i Srbima	I cannot understand that at all, and through that the distrust towards Croats and Serbs comes to be
17 vlasima u Bosni	**Vlachs in Bosnia**
18 ne kršćanima nego njima	not Christians **but them**
19 nakon svega ne želim tračiti vrijeme i tražiti dobrog Srbina i Hrvata	after all that I do not want to waste time looking for a good Serb and Croat
20 toga nema nemam vremena niti to želim.	there is no such thing, I don't have time, nor the will.

Co-narrating how she experienced the war in Bosnia-Herzegovina, Sanja biographically points out the consequences of the violence on the diaspora. She discursively constructs her family's diasporic lives during the war period as collectively extended through constant fear and feelings of powerlessness. Living in despair, anticipating the news of missing loved ones through different broadcasts is telling of the emotional costs of war on the diaspora which evidently live on to this day. She expresses feelings of betrayal, particularly in relation to the incomprehensible violence aimed against innocent civilians by *bloodthirsty neighbours* (line 14). Her distrust towards Croatian and Serbian Vlachs in Bosnia bears a resemblance to her daughter's attitude (in Extract 6), as the account ends with certainty that there is no point in giving a second chance to any of them. Such attitudes seem to be deep-seated in her husband's first-hand traumatic experience as we can see in Sanja's next account of self-reporting (BenEzer, 2002), explicitly constructing this family as deeply traumatized. Answering the question about whether the war affected her life directly, Sanja says (Extract 8):

Extract 8: Sanja, 37	
1 Da, u svakom slučaju mogu reći s tim šta je Adem direktno bio povezan.	Yes, in any case I can say with what Adem was directly connected to.
2 on je bio u koncentracionom logoru i to što je preživo traume	he was in a concentration camp and the fact he lived through this trauma
3 a one su se ispoljavale u našem zajedničkom životu.	and they were reflected in our lives together.
4 prvo njegovom a onda kad smo se upoznali i vjenčali.	at first in his life and then after we met and got married.
5 prošli smo zajedno kroz tuge u smislu te traume i razmišljanja	we went through sorrow together in the sense of this trauma and reflections
6 šta reći našoj djeci šta trebaju znati	what should we tell our children what should they know
7 upravo te odluke kada i šta tačno im reći?	exactly these decisions when and what exactly we should tell them?

8 mi smo se savjetovali sa psihologom šta i koliko kad da kažem svojoj djeci o ratu	we asked a psychologist about what and how much we should tell our children about the war.
9 išli smo na familijarno savjetovanje zbog trauma.	we went to family counselling because of the trauma.

That parents' psychological conditions in families shattered by war agony affect new generations is also evident in Dino's story, who grew up in a closed, intimate, diasporic setting in which trauma emerged as a part of everyday family discourse. Dino was born in Slovenia. Before he was born, his parents moved to Slovenia for economic reasons. With his parents, he arrived in Switzerland when he was two years old. As we shall see briefly, in his story, it is possible to identify several trauma signals. The content he retells winds around a series of events associated with his mother and his own experiences in both Switzerland and Bosnia-Herzegovina. In Dino's story there is no clear distinction between switching from his direct experiences to what he learned from his mother and other people. All parts seem to be fully integrated. Simultaneously, he links his experiences, transmitted stories and observed behaviours into a 'tidy narrative package' (Ochs and Capps, 2001) projecting his own war memories. These discursive events, experienced on a daily basis for years, have been completely assimilated into Dino's life, eventually becoming his life story (Extract 10).

Extract 10: Dino, 28	
1 Teško mi se sjetiti ali mislim da je to sve bilo i na TV-u i roditelji su pričali o ratu.	It is hard for me to remember but I think it was all on TV and my parents were talking about the war.
2 moj otac nije u ratu nikoga izgubio a mama je 80% bliže rodbine	my father didn't lose anyone in the war but my mother lost 80% of her close relatives
3 mamu, brata, sestriće, bratiće, mog kuma.	**mother, brother, sisters in law, brothers in law, my godfather.**
4 mi smo gledali na TV-u *Dead or Alive* emisiju i njenog brata smo vidjeli na TV-u	we were watching on TV the *Dead or Alive* show and saw her brother on TV
5 moja mama se bojala imala je sestru što je ostala u ratu	my mother was scared she had a sister that stayed back during the war
6 znači rat kad je počeo počeli su i problemi u našoj kući	when the war started that is when problems in our house also started
7 moja mama je POLUDJELA	my mother went CRAZY
8 ne zna kako su joj sestra mama braća gdje joj je rodbina	**she does not know anything about her sister mother brothers where her relatives are**

9 telefoni rade slanje para hrane humanitarne pomoći	the phones were on all the time money was sent food humanitarian aid
10 ona je tamo i išla pred kraj rata.	she went there before the end of the war.
11 Na početku rata to sve so se događalo za moju mamu je bilo neshvatljivo	At the beginning of the war all that was happening was incomprehensible to my mother
12 nije se mogla smiriti tri-četiri godine	she could not calm down for three-four years
13 tad je bio agressor bila je protiv Srba i tad je govorila protiv njih	there was an aggressor then she was against the Serbs and spoke out against them
25 Ona se pokušala i ubiti tabletama šaku-dvije je uzela moj brat se probudio	She tried to kill herself with pills took a handful or two of them and my brother woke up
26 izašla je u tri ujutro iz spavaće i nije više mogla i htjela se ubiti.	she came out of the bedroom at 3 a.m. she could not take it anymore and wanted to kill herself.
27 moj mali brat je primjetio ustao i probudio oca imao je tad četiri-pet godina	my little brother noticed got up and woke my father up he was four-five at the time
28 i onda smo ju spasili.	and then we saved her.
32 ona je bila u Bosni i kad je rat stao	and she was in Bosnia when the war stopped
33 ona je otišla tamo da traži brata	she went there to look for her brother
34 znala je da je ubijen ali je htjela naći njegovo tijelo	she knew he was killed but wanted to find his body
35 i davala je pare da se njegovo tijelo nađe	and she gave money for his body to be found
36 na kraju je iskopala dvjesta ljudi tražeći njega našli su donji dio njegovog tijela bez glave.	in the end she dug up **200 people** looking for him they found the lower part of his body without the head.

Dino's mother's trauma and psychological struggles are evidently central in his life story. Here as well, we see that Dino does not prioritize what he was told about the war but what he observed and experienced himself. From the account that the war was learned through television and parents' stories, Dino almost impatiently switches to the great loss his mother experienced, emphasizing that *80 per cent of her family was killed*. Then he returns to the popular TV show *Dead or Alive* informing the diaspora about civilians who managed to escape death. Line 6 in Extract 10 is especially important here, seeming to be both introducing and summarizing how tremendously this family was affected by the war. Dino emphatically recalls how his mother *went crazy*, supporting this with a glimpse into their household chaos. As later indicated in Extract 11, his family relived the war torment on a daily basis. In line 13 (Extract 10), we see one fragmentary verbal reference to the aggressors where Dino confirms that the enemies were explicitly named and talked *against*. Suddenly, Dino switches to one of his own experiences that I present in the next section. He then reveals what seems to be a hidden event of this story, since he never comes back to it again – the atmosphere of family depression reached the point of a suicide attempt prevented when his younger brother woke up their father. Yet, emotional detachment is evident here as well as throughout lines 33–8 (Extract 10). Obviously, when I met Dino in Emmenbrücke he was twenty-eight years old and he certainly had had many years to reflect on these events (his mother's attempted suicide and the exhumation of family members in episodes). Nonetheless, this should not be interpreted as complete emotional numbness because trauma can be identified by the presence of either too much or too little emotion since we cannot know what constitutes enough in the context of trauma (BenEzer, 2009). Lines 26–43 in Extract 10 show that the main protagonist of Dino's story is his mother who he constantly returns to. Structurally speaking, this passage is indistinguishable from the rest of his narrative (see repetition in lines 7–17 in Extract 11). Although Dino often jumps between different episodes, his story contains repetitive reporting (BenEzer, 2002) indicating his inability to move on from what might be the strongest link to the war memory – his mother's trauma and mental health. This is quite an expected trauma signal as repetition is a key characteristic of trauma narratives. Organizationally speaking, through all references to his mother, Dino ultimately creates tidy narrative chains which work chronotopically as he tries to distance himself and set temporal limits around his mother's emotional breakdown (Pickering and Keightley, 2009). Within his whole story, Dino employs spatio-temporal deixis and linguistic resources to frame the narratives as there-and-then as opposed to here-and-now, just like separate chronotopes which nonetheless go hand in hand. These chronotopic narratives are, in Blommaert's (2015: 11) terms, 'historically configured tropes pointing that "how-it-was" is invoked as relevant context' in trauma discourse. The sections in Extract 11 are self-reports since Dino himself says he was traumatized.

Dino says his mother eventually found closure and *does not hate* those who killed their family *anymore*, but trauma surely left its marks on her physical and mental health as she still takes medicines. Although Dino situates himself within his story as an observer narrating what happens to others around him, he does not seem to fully digest the family trauma which is embedded not only into his memory, but his interstitial identity. Dino is utterly disappointed in people, the people of Bosnia-Herzegovina specifically. He rarely goes to his parents'

Extract 11: Dino, 28	
1 Kao dijete sam se osjećao zakinutim	As a child I felt left out
2 jer svako je imao kuma a ja nisam jer je moj ubijen	because everyone had a godfather but I didn't because mine was killed
3 pogotovo kako je umro i šta su s njim radili.	especially the way he died and what they did to him.
4 traumatiziran sam zbog načina kako je umro	I am traumatized because of the way he died
5 ali više sam traumu osjećao i vidio preko mame.	but I felt and saw the trauma more through my mother.
6 ja sam gledao kao dijete kako je ona osjećala šta joj fali i šta joj je oduzeto	as a child I was watching how she felt it all what she was missing and what was taken from her
7 ona je obolila od toga, dobila je čir prije je bila zdrava	she got sick from it she got a stomach ulcer she was healthy before
8 ona i dan danas uzima medikamente zbog preživljenog stresa	and to this day she takes medicine because of **the stress she went through**
9 plus mi smo trebali imati sestru ali nemamo jer ju je mama rodila mrtvu	on top of it all we were supposed to have a sister but we don't have her now because she was a stillborn
10 rođena je mrtva zbog tog stresa	she was born dead because of all that stress
11 ona nije spavala radila je svaki dan bila pored TVa da čuje jel jos živ brat sestra familija	she didn't sleep she worked spent all day in front of the TV to hear if her brother sister family was alive
12 mi smo na TV gledali ko je u logorima	we were watching on TV who was in the concentration camps
13 malo malo eno mog rođaka a ovo je onaj ovo je komšija ovaj onaj	every once in a while there was my cousin and this is that person, this is a neighbour, this one or that one
14 svaki dan TV slati pare zovi u Bosnu došlo pismo	**every day TV, sending money, calling to Bosnia, receiving letters**
15 to tako je godinama bilo SVAKI BOŽJI DAN	**it was like that for years, EVERY GOD GIVEN DAY**
16 ona je izgubila kvalitet života to sam gledao	she lost her quality of life I watched that
17 izgubila je volju za životom	she lost the will to live
18 tad to nisam ni skužio odmah	at the time I did not even realize it
19 konto sam neke stvari ali nisam razumio tad sve	I understood some things but I didn't understand everything
20 da ja povežem sve... rat bolest njeno ponašanje.	to connect it all.. the war, illness, her behaviour.

homeland, and he mentions his own social exclusion in both Switzerland and Bosnia-Herzegovina. Self-reportedly, Dino finally refers to his own trauma which he inherited primarily through his mother who gave birth to a stillborn, as well as through the loss of his sister and of a godfather who was killed by *Them*. However, Dino avoids talking about the depiction of violent and brutal death which he did not witness first-hand but was told about. Such gaps in language are precisely the 'ambivalent attempts to conceal and express trauma otherwise shrouded in secrecy or relegated to the unconscious' (Schwab, 2010: 4). It is more than understandable how feeling and watching such a burdensome familial atmosphere day by day is traumatic and emotionally exhausting for anybody, let alone a child.

Naming the enemy

Another prevalent source of diasporic war memories is the rhetoric of identifying the enemy which is important primarily in the maintenance of hostility between social groups (Staub, 1992). Resulting in the continuity of ethnic divisions, this rhetoric is necessary for the establishment and reinforcement of prejudicial attitudes and beliefs in one's life. Terms, labels and categories used for naming the enemy emerge as one of the most important parts of nationalist discourse and discourse of violence in general (e.g. in the language of those who speak about crimes they witnessed and violent incidents they went through (O'Connor, 1995)). What naming does for ethnic groups in Bosnia-Herzegovina is something already demonstrated in Chapter 4, whereas this chapter is more concerned with illustrating the transition from imaginary to 'real'. In her study with Croatian and Bosnian children, Povrzanovic (1997) shows that the violent context and the parents are the primary source for establishing clear, negative and hostile images of the enemy. Although a peaceful setting cannot be compared to the conditions in which the citizens of Bosnia-Herzegovina lived during the war, the notion of dangerous enemies is equally mediated in Bosnia-Herzegovina itself and in the diaspora, especially because diasporic spaces are shared by the same ethnic groups. During the 1990s, parents in the diaspora believed that it was necessary to solidify the picture of the enemy in their children's imagination. This was a way to cement a sense of distrust and constant caution as an imperative and reasonable response. However, naming strategies are not always so simple, and receiving the warnings is not straightforward, especially in case of informants who come from mixed marriages. This is evident in Maja's story transcribed in Extract 12. Maja was born in Luzern to a Bosnian Muslim mother and a Bosnian Serb father. They did not lose family members during the war. She was raised an Orthodox

Christian and she practised her faith religiously until the age of eighteen. After she married a Bosnian Muslim, she converted to Islam. She says that *he was not Muslim enough* which led to irreconcilable differences in their marriage and a few years ago Maja divorced him. Today, she works and lives with her sons in Luzern.

Extract 12: Maja, 36	
1 Kod kuće jer sam vidjela da majka prati vijesti ali nije me to nešto nasekiralo ni ništa	At home I saw that my mother was following the news but it didn't particularly bother me or anything
2 ali sam vidjela da ona prati to i onda sam skontala da se nešto dešava	but I saw that she was following that and then I realized that something was going on
3 i čula sam da je rat ali ja nisam mogla zamisliti šta je rat.	and I heard there was a war but I couldn't imagine what war was.
4 tek kasnije nekako - znači nakon možda jedno četiri godine	somehow later – so after perhaps four years
5 kad je nena i dajdža i tetka moji morali izbjeći	when grandma and uncle and aunt of mine had to flee
6 oni su iz Brčkog	they are from Brčko
7 e onda sam u tom smislu analizirala	it was then that I analysed it in that way
8 tu se pričalo da je	it was said that
9 - naravno majka je bila nasekirana jer nena rahmetli je pobjegla na jednu stranu, dajdža na drugu, tetka na treću	- of course my mother was worried because grandma god rest her soul ran away to one side, uncle to the second, and aunt to the third side
10 i onda se pričalo – onda se otvoreno reklo da Srbi napadaju Muslimane	and it was said then – it was openly said that the Serbs were attacking the Muslims
11 e to je bilo konkretno	that was concrete
12 i na kraju kad je nena došla ona je nama pričala šta se dešavalo, šta je ona doživjela ustvari	and in the end when grandma came she told us what had happened, what she experienced actually
13 pogađalo me to zbog nje, bilo mi je žao	I was affected by it because of her, I felt sorry
14 s druge strane sam zastranila jer sam se ja tad smatrala pravoslavnom	on the other hand I went astray because at that time I considered myself orthodox Christian
15 znači bilo mi je to	that's what I experienced
16 – nije da sam se osjećala krivom ali sam proživljavala to	– it isn't that I felt guilty but I lived through it
17 zato što je moj narod uradio to nešto a i ovi drugi su moj narod	because my people did that something and these others are my people as well
18 znači to je s osjećajima bilo malo teže.	therefore emotionally it was a bit harder.
19 nikad nisam pričala s članovima familije o ratu, uvijek sam izbjegavala	I never talked about war with members of my family, I always avoided it

20 slušala sam šta drugi pričaju ali ja nikad nisam rekla šta ja mislim	I listened what others were saying but I never said what I thought
21 bilo me strah govoriti da ja to možda ne vidim tako kako ovi drugi vide.	I was afraid to speak that I perhaps don't see it the way the others saw it.

Maja starts her story by recalling how the war was introduced to their household with her mother following the news. As in Ines' story (see Extract 1), Maja too remembers learning about the war through family's refugee statuses and a constant concern about where they ended up. She remembers being told that *Serbs attacked Muslims* (line 10). In this family's context, the stories of the enemy's violent intentions were supported by narrations of her grandmother who managed to flee. Maja confirms that these stories affected her since her mother's family suffered, but she was also confused because those who attacked them were the ethnic group her other family belonged to (lines 13–18). Maja's narrative accounts indicate what Schwab (2010) and LaCapra (2010) point to when arguing that the descendants of both victims and perpetrators inherit a burden for which they may go through different emotions. In Maja's case, the perpetrators were her family, and this left her with unanswerable questions at the time. Emotional disorientation is emphasized through silence and fear, especially prominent in the family setting (lines 19–21). Maja recalls later in her story that she felt ashamed during the period of adolescence when her school friends would ask about the war and Serbs attacking her mother's ethnic group. This could be the reason why she often suffered from loneliness and alienation. After she converted to Islam, she started to declare herself Muslim and she calls Bosniaks her people now. Today, she sees her father's ethnic group as the enemies arguing that she realizes why they were named so in the first place (Instances of forceful argumentation are found in the accounts of Maja's negative experiences when visiting her father's family in the Serb Republic – such passages are however situated within the next sub-section). Spillmann and Spillmann (1997) explained that viewing other groups as enemies is accomplished through different rhetorical tactics:

Negative anticipation: All acts of the enemy, in the past, present, and future become attributed to destructive intentions toward one's own group.

Putting blame on the enemy: The enemy is thought to be the source of any stress on a group.

Identification with evil: The enemy is intent on destroying a group's dominant value system

Zero-sum thinking: What is good for the enemy is bad for us and vice versa

Stereotyping and de-individualization: Anyone who belongs to the enemy group is ipso facto our enemy.

Refusal to show empathy: Consideration for anyone in the enemy group is repressed due to the perceived threat and feelings of opposition.

Similarly, Lasswell (1995: 18) argues that 'for mobilization of national hatred the enemy must be represented as a menacing, murderous aggressor, a satanic violator of the moral and conventional standards, an obstacle to the cherished aims and ideals of the nation as a whole and of each constituent part'. However, it does not seem that the acts of naming the enemy in diasporic spaces aims towards national hatred per se. Informants in this study never employ such a strong rhetoric. This, of course, does not mean that they have not heard the words *bloodthirsty neighbours* as Sanja mentions in one of her accounts above (Extract 7, line 14). But even if such explicit terms were used, it is still questionable how young children understand the concept of enemy and whether the emergence of enemy images in diasporic spaces leads to national hatred. Such considerations are however beyond the scope of this study. The following passage indicates that the discursive construction of enemies served primarily to ensure the caution, the notion of betrayal and the all too familiar distinction between Us – innocent victims and Them – who cannot be trusted. What Extract 13 shows is how children of the diaspora must not only learn the feelings of war but must also learn to identify and name the enemy.

Extract 13: Alma, 21	
7 Sa prijateljicom Slađanom se i danas družim i nju sam upoznala u prvom razredu	To this day I still get together with my friend Slađana who I met her in the first grade
8 i tad se uvijek pričalo 'nemoj ići od nje ne volimo mi to'	and then it was always said to me 'do not go to her place, we don't like that'
9 dijete sam bila i nisam razumijela zašto ja nju nebi trebala voliti	I was a child and I did not understand why I should not like her
10 govorili su svi su Srbi () i ni jednom ne treba vjerovati	they told me that all Serbs are () and that none of them can be trusted
11 druži se ali nemoj previše	hang out with them but not too much
12 budi oprezna pogotovo kad si u grupi	be careful especially when you are in their group
13 njihovoj mogu ti zabiti nož u leđa.	they could stab you in the back.

Alma, born in Aargau the year the war ended, does not tend to stay away from the members of other ethnic groups in Switzerland. Besides Slađana, Ines, a Bosnian Croat descendant, is one of her best friends. Yet, she was always told 'not to hang out with' the other ethnic group (line 11), who were portrayed through long-standing stereotypes and de-individualization. Alma now understands why her parents were giving her these *warning orders*, but when she was a young child, she did not comprehend their instructions. Similarly, Ema recalls her father's warnings in Extract 14.

Extract 14: Ema, 18	
1 U petom razredu	In the fifth and sixth grade
8 Srpkinja mi je bila najbolja prijateljica	a Serb was my best friend
9 ali tata je uvijek govorio pazi se	but my dad always told me to watch out
10 smjela sam ići kod nje kući	I was allowed to go to her house
11 ali tačno na sat	but I had to be on the dot
12 kad je isto njen otac kod kuće	and when her father was home as well
13 ali nisam nikad smjela ići noćiti	but I was never allowed to spend the night at her place
14 iako joj nikad nisam rekla zašto.	even though I never told her why.

The rhetoric of naming the enemy provides a framework for the diasporic jumps from 'intimate and imagined' to 'public and experienced'. In the next subsection, we see that the realization of the enemy – both mental and physical – is primarily affected by the social environment in which children grow up (Oppenheimer, 2005: 658). Once more, we see that the inheritance of trauma unfolds against the backdrop of everyday family narratives. It seems that the violent past is fully appropriated when family discourses fuse with personal experiences of inter-ethnic spaces. To understand the shared stories about the enemy means to see one and hear one – discursive embodiment is the key.

Encountering the enemy

I now turn to the final rhetorical sub-trope identified across my interviews pointing to the ways inheritance of war memory hinges on and is strongly implicated in tiny moments and little memories turning into big ones through complex second-generation but first-hand encounters with the enemies. I introduce the last part of my analysis with Adi's story about his early school days spent in the small village where he lived (Extract 15). The elementary school in this small place near Luzern was attended mostly by children of ex-Yugoslavia diasporas since they were settled precisely in this area. Adi says that in his classroom there were more children who spoke his language than Swiss. Consequently, children of three ethnic groups shared the interactional space, learned about and confronted each other. Adi tells the story of friends supposed to be enemies in Extract 15.

Extract 15: Adi, 27	
1 Ja sam se družio sa tim Draganom	I was friends with this Dragan
2 i on se mnogo volio hvaliti kako je njegov narod uspješan	and he liked to brag about how his people were **successful**
3 jak..	**strong**..
4 a pogotovo je spominjao vojnu jačinu kako su oni moćni i *whatnot*	he especially mentioned the military strength how powerful they are and whatnot
5 i šta je meni intersantno tu je to što sam ja na to odgovara 'i kod nas je tako'	and what was interesting to me here was that I was answering to it with 'It's like that with us as well'
6 ne zato što sam htio umanjiti to što on hvali nešto svoje	not because I wanted to diminish his praises of something of his own
7 nego sam htio spomenuti da imaju i drugi	but I wanted to mention that there were others too
8 nikad nisam imenovao tu stranu nego je on rekao 'moje i naše'	I never named that side but he said 'mine and ours'
9 a ja sam rekao 'moje i drugo naše'.	and I said 'mine and another ours'.
10 I sjećam se nakon dugo vremena i puno takvih komentara	And I remember after a long time and after many such comments
11 on je stao jednom isped mene i pitao me 'a koji su to mi' o kojima ti govoriš?	he once stood in front of me and he asked me 'and who are these we you are talking about'?
12 od tada nikad više nije pričao o tome	from that moment onward he never talked about it again
13 jer je znao tačno šta to znači	because **he knew exactly what it all meant**
14 on je znao šta se radi i ko je protiv koga	**he knew what was being done and who was against whom**
15 i znao je to isto od kuće	and he knew all that from his home
16 samo što je on to gledao na jedan herojski način i bio je ponosan na to	only he was looking at it in a heroic way and was proud of it
17 a ja nisam	and I was not
18 meni je to bilo kao..	to me it was like..
19 'zašto mi to uopće govoriš'?	'**why are you even telling me this**'?
20 primjetio sam da ga je bilo sramota što je to govorio prije	I noticed that he was ashamed about all that he had said before
21 jer tek u tom trenutku kad sam mu ja rekao s koje sam strane	because **only at that moment when I told him which side I belong to**
22 on je shvatio da je cijelo vrijeme govorio ustvari protiv mene.	he realized that **he had been speaking against me the whole time.**

What becomes evident in the above passage is that the two boys were not fully aware of their 'differences' at first. Adi opens this story by explaining how his friend was making war-related comments until Adi himself replied with statements indicating that they are in fact *not of the same group* (lines 8–12). Adi says that his friend assumed that if people share the same language, then they must belong to the same group. We can only suppose that at this age children themselves would not be able to *brag about the military strength* of a nation/ethnic group – this is surely something narrated and adopted in the family context. Adi himself confirms this in line 15. In line 19, Adi seems to be evaluating Dragan's pride in war heroes as a direct provocation as he emphatically reports his own question *Why are you even telling me this?* What exactly they told each other remains hidden, but Adi recalls explaining to Dragan which side he belonged to. This is the point when the boy realized that he had been *speaking against* his friend. If Adi interpreted Dragan's affective response to this verbal exchange correctly, then this passage re-illustrates that the children of those portrayed as perpetrators are also experiencing different emotions related to trauma such as guilt and shame (lines 20–3) (compare to Extract 12). At the same time, Adi seems to be rediscovering his enemies; an enemy imagined through shared stories was suddenly revived, becoming a real one, a new one. The truth is, the two boys were never real enemies to begin with, or perhaps not yet enemies, but simply the children of enemies. Adi says that after this event he stayed in a collegial relationship with Dragan, but they stopped being close friends. I briefly turn to more complex inter-ethnic second-generation encounters that illustrate that confrontations are not always 'peaceful' and not always verbal. The first one is described in Dino's account where he recalls getting into a fight because he was named a *Balija* (Extract 16).

Extract 16: Dino, 28	
14 ali ona se nakon toga smirila u smislu da me učila nakon toga da ne mrzim druge.	but she calmed down after that in the sense that she taught me not to hate others.
15 a nisu svi tako djecu učili	but not all children were taught that way
16 i to znam jer ja sam bio u drugom razredu kad sam se potukao ovdje s jednim Srbinom	I know that because when I was in second grade I got into a fight with a Serb here
17 jer me nazvao Balijom	because he called me a Balija
18 on je imao sedam godina	he was seven years old
19 od kud njemu u Švicarskoj ta riječ?	where could he get that word in Switzerland?

20 da ga roditelji ne pitaju s tim riječima	without his parents feeding him such words
21 jer ne možeš ti znati riječ Balija ili Ustaša a biti dijete od 7 godina	because you can't know the word Balija or Ustasha as a seven-year-old kid
22 od kud je on to naučio nego od roditelja	where could he have learned it if not from his parents
23 to je kao dresiranje pasa a moji roditelji nisu to radili nego su civilizirani	that is like dog training but my parents did not do that because they are civilized
24 iako je naš narod.. seljaci generalno.	although our people.. are peasants in general.

Just like Adi, Dino thinks nationalistic name-calling is mediated through parents' war narratives. Disappointed in 'his people' (all ex-Yugoslavia ethnic groups), he likens them to dog trainers and ignorant provincials with simplistic thinking (the pejorative meaning of the term peasant – *seljak*). This example shows how the act of naming the enemy is perceived so strongly, producing the kind of harmful rhetoric through which children ensure that the image of the enemy stays locked in memory. Sanja also retells another shared-diasporic family story containing bullying in the classroom, albeit one which is not a part of her personal experience. Rather, the story concerns her cousin's experience of being attacked by a classmate belonging to the enemy ethnic group (Extract 17).

Extract 17: Sanja, 38	
1 Od strica kćerka ona je druga generacija kad je bila sedmi osmi razred	The daughter of my uncle she's the second generation when she was in the 7th or 8th grade
2 išla je u školu s vršnjacima Srbima	she went to school with her peers Serbs
3 i baca je jedan na pod	and one of them threw her on the floor
4 i stavlja lenijar pod vrat i kaže	putting a ruler on her neck and said
5 'hoćeš da te sad zakoljem meni je dedo rekao kako se kolju Balije'?	'you want me to cut your throat my grandpa told me how to slaughter Balijas'?
6 upravo ti izrazi druge generacije su šokantni.	such expressions coming from the second generation are the truly shocking ones.

What is especially troublesome in this encounter is the embodied form of what was a common method of killing Bosniak civilians, and thus odiously hurtful and traumatizing as it revives the memory of the Srebrenica genocide (also referred to as *the Srebrenica slaughter*). Sanja nonetheless metalinguistically evaluates it as an example of shocking second-generation expressions. For some reason, the verbal seems to be dominant for Sanja. Certainly, as Thurlow (2001) argues, abusive language (e.g. pejorative slang) internalized in the school environment compromises the psychological health of young adolescents. Such threats and name-calling, most probably, become quickly adopted by other children listening to their peers verbalizing them. However, the imitation and performance of the slaughtering act in Sanja's account is also of crucial importance because it shows how strongly hatred can be implanted in and acquired by young minds. How the same threat is produced and responded to, we see in another example of traumatic adult-child encounter described in one of Adi's narratives (Extract 18).

Extract 18: Adi, 27	
26 Jednom sam imao – cura iz razreda	I once had – a girl from my class
27 problem sa mnom.. ona me napala iz čista mira	had a problem with me.. she attacked me for no reason
28 imao sam 10 godina	I was 10 years old
29 znači 5 godina poslije rata	so that was 5 years after the war
30 ona nije bila iz Bosne nego Srbije	she was not from Bosnia but from Serbia
31 i ne iz grada nego sa sela i imali su *advanced level* odnosa prema drugim narodima	and not from a city but from a village and they had an 'advanced level' of attitudes towards other peoples
32 odnosno prema muslimanima	primarily Muslims
33 ona je meni nešto uradila ali mi nije bilo jasno zašto je to uradila	she did something to me but it was not clear to me why
34 jer ja s njom nisam imao nikakve veze pa sam ju pratio kući da ju pitam	because I had nothing to do with her so I followed her home to ask her
35 i njen otac je izašao sav napuhan i kaže – dere se na mene da će me zaklati	her father **came out fuming and says – screams at me that he will cut my throat**
36 u tom trenutku sam mislio znam da kod njega na svakoj strani u autu i u bašti su 4S	I thought at the moment knowing that everywhere in his car and garden is the 4C sign
37 i u tom trenutku sam pomislio hoće on mene baš zaklati jer u ulici toj nema nikog nego isti takvi ljudi	I thought **he really will cut my throat** because in this street there is no one else apart from people like him
38 u tom trenutku sam se prepao i jedva disao	I was scared at that moment and could barely breathe

39 na kraju te ulice su bile dvije kuće gdje su živjeli Albanci s Kosova	at the end of this street there were two houses where Albanians from Kosovo lived
40 i jedan od tih ljudi	and one of these people
41 jedan stariji čovjek je došao i njega smirio da me pusti	an older man came and calmed him down to let me go
42 mislio sam da će me vratiti u tu devedeset drugu ratnu godinu.	I thought he would put me back to the war year of 92.

This passage illustrates one of the ways in which B&H diasporas become part of the 'authentic' war discourse, especially how the second-generation children may be implicated in trauma discourse, which is evidently a prominent feature of the everyday life of the diaspora. Adi starts his narrative with self-interruptions which most likely occurred due to his second-language insecurities. As he recalls, this encounter happened five years after the war, when he was ten, with a girl raised in a family having *an advanced level* of hateful sentiments (lines 31–2). What exactly led to this confrontation Adi seems not to remember clearly, claiming that she got angry with him without any particular reason. Finding himself alone in the enemy's environment, Adi recalls a harm-threat which made the war real and very much present. Making the effort to correct himself (*came out fuming and says – screams at me*) and reorder the threat (*slaughter* into *cut my throat*) as to self-explain it, Adi mostly remembers the exact feeling when the old fear (what Walton (1978) calls *quasi-fear*) met a real one – *being scared and barely breathing*. It is precisely this feeling that plays a crucial role in making this experience traumatic for a child, later turning into a traumatic memory for an adult. By definition, trauma occurs in cases where 'the person experienced, witnessed, or was confronted with an event or events that involve actual or threatened death or serious injury; or a threat to the physical integrity of himself or herself or others' (American Psychiatric Association, 1994: 427). Accordingly, a person responds to trauma with 'intense, fear, helplessness, or horror' (American Psychiatric Association, 1994: 428). As explained by psychiatrists, following a traumatic event, fear experienced by an individual is stored in a cognitive network with the information about the sources of the threat (Foa et al., 1989). As a result, Adi avoids any contact with people showing the nationalistic signs he remembers being emplaced in the enemy's environment (line 36). In his answer to my question *How do you know about the 4S sign?*, Adi says he was already familiar with such symbols and their meanings, thus treating them as warning signs. Other stories, too, contain references to the representation of nationalistic signs flagged in diasporic settings which informants interpret as provoking. What Adi's story ultimately shows is that the second-generation creates the war memory through a complex interplay of shared stories and affective experiences. Previously learning that people were slaughtered in the Bosnian war and having a new experience of being threatened with the same kind of violence, Adi revives the enemy and the war itself – *I thought he would put me back to the war year of 92.*

Conclusion

Through a discourse analysis of oral narratives, this chapter explored the dynamics between the received stories and personal experiences of the second-generation B&H diaspora which ultimately reflect the migration of war remembering and the discursive nature of historical trauma. Whether organized as tiny moments or big narratives, the stories of the second-generation also include references to other people, places/spaces and temporalities (Schiffrin, 2002) as 'dimensions' that play a significant role in the way descendants construe the inherited past. Creating a complex repertoire of historical trauma discourse, informants use different strategies to narrate themselves/their personal experiences, while taking on the roles of main protagonists or/and observers situated in/between the diasporic space and their parents' homeland. The discursive analysis of fifteen interviews indicates that the ways of narrating trauma hinge principally on the loss of family members and the burdensome family atmospheres created by the war. However, it is also clear that the informants who did not suffer such consequences are still complexly invested in the inherited war memory. The family evidently serves as a space for memory transmission and the mediation of war and trauma discourses. In family contexts, B&H descendants engage with the narratives transmitted by the first-generation (i.e. shared stories) produced principally through the rhetorics of learning about the war and defining enemies. For example, we saw that certain examples of name-calling utilize the kind of hurtful language which ensures that the image of the enemy stays locked in memory. In stories told by informants who grew up in families shattered by war agony, it is possible to identify certain trauma signals (BenEzer, 2002). These are particularly evident in the stories of informants whose parents or close relatives have suffered from violent war events (e.g. the abuse experienced in concentration camps). Their stories are composed mainly of reports on the emotionally exhausting process of growing up in depressing family atmospheres.

They discursively construct the loss of loved ones, emotional breakdowns of parents or feelings of despair and powerlessness. Some of them initially position themselves almost exclusively as observers of their family settings, narrating the experiences of traumatized protagonists as they try to turn the suffering into a learning experience and set temporal limits around the family trauma (Pickering and Keightley, 2009). However, they eventually come to organize their narratives around self-reporting and acknowledging their own trauma as they seem to fully embrace their inherited family histories. The second-generation seems to prioritize not what they were told about the war, nor the warnings given about enemies, but what they have observed and experienced themselves. They 'gain knowledge' and create their own memories through, for example, the notion of displacement and people's refugee statuses, or through visual media such as war photography or documentaries. The meanings of war are also re-established through the elements of post-war Bosnia-Herzegovina's semiotic landscape (e.g. monuments, mine fields, ruins, graffiti) which lead to *spatial melancholia* (Navaro-Yashin, 2009). Indeed, the fact that these people do not live in Bosnia-Herzegovina does not mean they are not implicated in the affective learning processes of war memory. That the second-generation is fully invested in trauma discourse has also been illustrated through examples of inter-ethnic encounters which generate emotions that are carefully reported in oral narratives, and central in framing experiences as traumatic. When it comes to the ways that war becomes real for the second generation, discursive embodiment is key – the enemy must be seen and heard. Experiences of receiving verbal threats, for example, show that even those who did not lose any family members and did not grow up in uneasy family settings, are not liberated from resentment, fear and trauma. By putting the discourse and trauma studies into a dialogue, this chapter demonstrates that war trauma extends to new generations and diasporic spaces as descendants continue to be implicated in a fusion where they recount their personal experiences and retell inherited stories. Understandings of war by those who did not experience it directly need not to be confused with war 'fictions'. They have deep roots in diasporic spaces and realities. The meaning of violence which produces collective suffering is not a matter of receiving the right story about it, but of how people navigate their own experiences in alignment with the war narratives transmitted to them. Indeed, historical trauma is discursively constructed through the complex interplay of shared stories and affective experiences that are 'emplotted, framed and contextualized' in broader collective contexts (Denham, 2008). Historical trauma discourse is situated in an affective interaction between people, past and present (temporalities), places and spaces (spatialities) (cf. Schiffrin, 2003), especially in the context of new diasporic generations whose experiences relate to and shift constantly between here-there and now-then. Although all sorts of traumas can be interpreted and treated primarily as autobiographical discourses, they do not obey the boundaries of the intimate, time or space. They are inevitably systematized as powerful social discourse. In the context of Bosnia-Herzegovina, this happens when the personal trauma of war victims becomes communicated in/through institutionalized discourses and co-constructed as collective memory (Felman, 2002). Richards (2016: 42) offers a notorious example of the communication of trauma by the ICTY through the process of making an argument about the meaning of the consequences of war for the nation-state: 'this requires concerted, purposeful translation of private, individual instances of trauma into collective traumas that must be collectively assimilated by not just the former Yugoslavian countries, but by an international audience as well'. Hence, trauma does not only endure in the spaces materially affected by violence and the lives of those living there, nor is it simply brought to the homes, schools or communities of diaspora settings. It exists in wider cultural contexts as it circulates across broader discursive terrains.

In this sense, I close the final analytical chapter with one of the quotes opening this book – 'trauma is never simply one's own because we are implicated in each other's trauma' (Caruth, 1991: 192). Consequently, trauma seems to resonate not only in contemporary Bosnia-Herzegovina's *structure of feeling* (Williams, 1977), but also in the spaces beyond its borders, as it continues to haunt new generations, their present and future – trauma travels. Life stories serve as valuable moments of reflection which give researchers an opportunity to further explore not only the language of trauma, violence or remembering (i.e. How people talk about/remember the war), but the place for provoking profound questions such as *When do the ghosts hunting us become our teachers?*

Conclusion

Symbolically, I end writing this book in July, the Srebrenica genocide anniversary. Ending this book does not get easier from starting it. Julys bring irremediable sorrow for many people. This is a month of grief and inconsolability. The very notion of happiness is practically seen as inappropriate and even shameful. Emotional exhaustion is almost required and considered a moral achievement. But the reality is that to endure the indefinable emptiness at these times is an almost impossible struggle. Julys do not only echo with Bosnia-Herzegovina's 'emotional regime' – the mode of emotional expression and thought dominant in the particular temporalities and cultural context (Reddy, 2001). They also bring the complex interplays between language (written and spoken), visuals, spatial practices and affect to spaces beyond the country itself. To illustrate this better, let me go back five months before the war officially ended. Not long before the so-called *Scorpion operation in Trnovo*, a large number of Bosnian Muslim civilians were brutally abused, beaten to death and systematically executed in/around the small place of Potočari in Srebrenica. In August 2001, the International Criminal Tribunal for the former Yugoslavia determined that the numerous massacres committed in this small area constituted genocide. In brief, since April 1993, the Srebrenica enclave was declared a zone under the protection of United Nations. In July 1995, this safe zone protected by a detachment of peacekeepers from the Netherlands (Dutchbat) was overrun by Bosnian Serb forces. Thousands of unarmed civilians started to walk from Srebrenica to Tuzla in an attempt to escape the Bosnian Serb soldiers, but on their way most of them were killed and their lifeless bodies thrown into mass graves. To prevent their discovery, the graves were dug up in September and October 1995 and the victims' remains, dismembered with the use of heavy machinery, were scattered into a number of secondary and tertiary graves in more remote locations of the so-called *Death Road* (Jugo and Wastell, 2015). Since then, between 8 and 10 July, thousands of people walk the reverse route every year until they reach the Potočari cemetery, where on the fourth day they attend a burial service for the genocide victims who were previously exhumed from the many mass graves found in/around the area. Activities performed over these four days do not only change the actual site of violence, but other dimensions of the country's landscape are complexly re-shaped by those who dwell in it. The discursive, embodied and spatial production of this commemoration hinges on a particular layering of the discourses of remembering encapsulated nicely, but inadequately in the snapshot of annual narratives. While the 'supporters' walk the *March of Peace*, coffins with the victims' remains are trucked through the country until they reach the massive cemetery. The coffins are then passed down from hand to hand and then lined up in the memorial hall – *Memory Room* – where they are mourned over before the collective burial starts (Figure 20). The *Peace March* represents an ethical/moral struggle for a global value-system taking the shape of a massive *living memorial* made of thousands of bodies acknowledging the site of trauma. The route is not marked with any official monuments; however, placards with arrows pointing in the direction of the discovered nearby mass graves allow people to note the rise in number and density of crime sites as they approach Potočari, subtly drawing attention to the kinds of sites selected for hiding the human remains throughout the region (Cyr, 2014).

As Cyr (2014) explains from the point of view of scientific discourse and visual culture, the march mediates the experiences of both memorialization and

Figure 20 Memorial room in Potočari © Maida Kosatica 2017

investigation of a 'forensic landscape' as a contested site of violence.[1] Essentially, a criminal case is being presented, the evidence brought forth in order to establish the validity of the charges and to counter the narratives of denial. In 2018, thirty-five victims' remains were buried. A relatively 'small' number, primarily resulting from the previously mentioned reburials in secondary and tertiary mass grave sites which hampers the discovery and identification of over a thousand still missing bodies. Yet the 'shock news' and the disturbance of memory have not failed to mark the 23rd annual commemoration as well. One of the exhumed body remains belongs to a twenty-year-old woman who was six months pregnant. This was not just a mediatized snippet of information, but now a painful reminder of the youngest and oldest genocide victims, both females – a new-born baby girl and a ninety-four-year-old woman, both exhumed in 2012. Multiple references in the media to the coffin number seventeen also compelled the public to affectively and morally engage with the commemoration. This coffin carries a single bone from a man whose mother approved the burial, afraid of dying before finding some sense of closure. What makes annual commemorations even more traumatic, especially for the victims' families, is the re-burial of victims whose only recently discovered remains are added every year to the already buried ones. In 2018, there were eighty of them. At the same time, the international media and countries world-wide send messages of support and empathy, examples include Croatia projecting another *Srebrenica Flower*, Sweden by throwing white lilies into the water of Stockholm's Nybroviken, or Great Britain with the official receptions organized in the Manchester Cathedral and East London Mosque. Diasporic spaces remain especially involved in the circulation of linguistic and embodied practices contributing to the expansion of a traumascape. Trauma distributed beyond Bosnia-Herzegovina's ethno-national boundaries shapes such ephemeral transformations of diasporic public spaces. Even the bodies of mourners become a media for remembrance, they also represent the transnational political action contributing to the country's own fight against the denial of violence (Martin Rojo, 2014). Starting yet another cycle of reliving the trauma, Julys cannot pass without precisely this rhetoric of denial. The readily apparent examples are dynamically configured in/through the 2018 digital as well as spoken discourse. A Serbian television host joined by Serbian politicians, and by those convicted of war crimes but nonetheless glorified military leaders, commented: *Every year when TV broadcasts the commemoration, when foreign statesmen come, they bring dead bodies from who knows where and bury them in Srebrenica*, mediatizing the rhetoric of denial through accusations that the numbers of killed civilians are falsely increased.

Back in Bosnia-Herzegovina, a Serb Republic politician tweeted: *I mean, if you love the genocide that much, wait for the next opportunity*, which was immediately reported and classified as a direct threat. The US Embassy in Sarajevo together with the Office of the High Representative in the country strongly condemned the posted comment. As if the opinions and actions of foreign powers somehow matter. Later that day, 11 July 2018, the local media released a video showing that even the youngest generation continues to be implicated in deeply rooted ethno-national divisions and the indoctrination of hate. The video shows a young boy in Mostar celebrating Croatia's qualification to the finals of the 2018 football World Cup and chanting loudly 'Knife, Wire, Srebrenica'. The boy's disturbing chant raised an equal level of anger expressed through public meta-discursive responses promoting inflammatory nationalistic sentiments. It was in this way that the cycle of harm and suffering was furthered. And not much is different today. In 2021, mourners went to the Potočari Memorial Centre for a commemoration of the 26th anniversary of the Srebrenica Genocide and the burial of nineteen more victims. While many people commemorated the victims and remembered the genocide, others have denied it. Coincidentally, the law colloquially known as 'genocide denial ban' was imposed by the former High Representative for Bosnia-Herzegovina on 23 July 2021. One wonders if enforcing this law directly leads to another armed conflict since it would undoubtedly involve arresting some of the members of Bosnian Serb political elites. In the meantime, in Serbia, a country directly involved in Bosnia-Herzegovina's trauma, murals of war criminals jailed for life for the genocide in Srebrenica are being painted. Examples like these continue to feed the kind of nationalism that stems from violence which produced collective trauma in the first place. The Srebrenica Genocide in particular continues to be trivialized by those who deny it; it is a despicable way of ridiculing the victims. The genocide in the country where it happened sadly remains shrouded in ignorance, the misinformation is deliberately propagated by some, and inadvertently sustained by others simply through a lack of interest. Moll (2013) explains that the nature of Bosnia-Herzegovina's contemporary landscapes is defined by the fact that neither ethnic group truly dominates the public memory on its own, rather they control it together while at the same time disputing each other's right to the shared space. In this sense, being implicated in the practice of post-war ethnonationalism, such landscapes provide an important theoretical framework on their own. The story about the Srebrenica Genocide commemoration illustrates, of course, just a small piece of the complexity of remembering in post-war contexts. Nonetheless, I invoke it here because it speaks to each of the chapters in my book which work together to reveal a range of layered, interconnected discourses of remembering. Caught between the past war and ongoing tensions, these discourses are a precondition to the traumascapes as complex communicative semiotic systems and phenomena that need to be studied precisely as such. Remembering is only one socio-discursive aspect people are left with after violence, but it is almost certainly the most dominant one. It is a psychological truism that remembering is not simply monolithic, rather it comes in different 'flavours' (Sapolsky, 2004). In this sense, I have sought to argue that a range of linguistic and other semiotic practices are deployed in the construction of trauma memory and remembering. And it is precisely these practices that allow us to understand the very mechanisms through which people construct and express their own traumas. With this, however, I do not mean to imply that to understand remembering simply means to search for the ways of talking or writing about trauma, building monuments or exhibiting war artefacts. Discourses of remembering, whether manifesting in the physical environment, virtual spaces or personal stories, stem simultaneously from individual and collective needs to abide by the moral norms and responsibilities, as well as from political, pedagogical and even economic demands (e.g. the flourishing war tourism sites of Sarajevo). As a matter of fact, I too have my own moral and ideological stances vis-à-vis the war in Bosnia-Herzegovina and a desire to 'take the side' of those who have suffered and continue to suffer, regardless of which ethnic group they belong to. In simple terms, discourses of remembering do not come exclusively from emotions, chaos of trauma and grief, or the social order.

Through the identification of the discursive practices of remembering we inevitably see how all social structures (e.g. individuals, social groups, institutions, the media) construct ideologies, maintain or reject power and dominance, position themselves in regard to history, blame and subjectivities. For these reasons, memory is a truly rich subject for critical research because it is implicated in the discursive strategies which directly point to the legitimation of control, naturalization of the social order and relations of inequality (Fairclough, 1989). In the context of post-war Bosnia-Herzegovina, this is easily highlighted because the underpinning ideological frameworks are glaringly obvious. It is quite clear why parents in the Serb Republic are not allowed to have a monument for their killed children. There is no level of obfuscation or misleading narrative that can hide the true motives. Here, the ideological forces affecting post-war nation building, abuse of power and dominance, and the politics of silencing are more than visible. As Palmberger (2006: 525) writes, 'it is a question of power who is able to lead the public discourse and decides which memories to ban and which to promote'. Thus, I argue that discourses of remembering also constitute a language of resistance to power abuse and dominance. Methodologically speaking then, and in certain contexts, CDA becomes useful not only in exposing what is 'wrong' but also for reminding and warning about what binds people to suffering. Ultimately, I hope that my book addresses precisely the memory of suffering that Johann Metz (1999: 230) holds central in contemporary Bosnia-Herzegovina:

> [T]he memory of suffering became a shroud for the whole nation and a stranglehold on any attempt at interethnic rapprochement. Here a particular people have remembered only their own suffering, and so this purely self-regarding *memoria passionis* became not an organ of understanding and peace, but a source of hostility, hatred and violence.

Let me sum up, chapter by chapter, how I have tried to make this case. Aiming to point out that the past still has a firm grasp on the present, my first analytical chapter sought to explore graffiti as a special dimension of visually materialized discourse of remembering that works as a contributor to 'affective regimes' which underpin a complex disruption and appropriation of Bosnia-Herzegovina's contested spaces. Employing a combination of social semiotic and multimodal critical discourse analysis, I analysed the visual and discursive construction of 'linguistic violence', demonstrating how this concept's application as a semiotically broad one opens up new ways of analysing and interpreting the post-war graffscapes. What I argued was that 'linguistic violence' sustains its symbolic power through/in the intersection of language and space, ultimately becoming inculturated into the contemporary traumascape. Following Wee's (2016) and Stroud's (2016) recent contributions which call for the analytical attention to the discursive construction of affect as a somewhat neglected aspect of the field, I argued that graffiti contribute to the country's 'affective regimes' as they render the landscape particularly 'turbulent'. Ultimately, my first analysis showed how the graffscapes sustain – in both symbolic and material ways – a popular regime of mutual hatred, distrust, fear, anger and disgust, which cause people to (re)experience, (re)imagine and even (re)desire violence.

Continuing my exploration of Bosnia-Herzegovina's semiosis of remembering, in the next case study, I offered a close reading of commemorative initiatives and public art commemoration. Following Waksman and Shohamy's (2016) path to the moral dimension of the public spaces and spatial performances which primarily raise awareness of important social issues, this analytical chapter sought to map the discourses of remembering accomplished through 'living memorials'. Carrying a strong message of anti-violence and producing commemorative performances, living memorials show that the experiencing and affective body is key in the production of a more-than-visual/verbal, highly fluid discourses of remembering. What they ultimately point to is the dynamic entanglement of place/space, body and semiosis, as well as their transitory nature, introducing us delicately to the material implication of traumascapes in 'distant' spatialities. I argue that post-war remembering, especially remembrance that is strategically silenced and controlled, is discursively and semiotically transformed into global movements, achieved through affective, monolithic, 'massive body' and its experiences. It is precisely the united body of mourners and supporters that confronts the issues of repression and denial of atrocities more loudly and powerfully than any static memorials ever could. In places like Prijedor where one ethnic group dominates and makes all the decisions regarding the materialization of remembrance in public spaces, commemorative performances serve as a means to legitimize the status and claims of a minority group (Shohamy and Waksman, 2010). In simple terms, they are an answer to exclusion from the space. Indeed, semiotic landscapes of commemoration are not simply spatial texts that need to be read out, but they are deeply implicated in the processes of countering marginalization and silencing, pointing at those who maintain the space 'empty'.

In the next chapter, I sought to consider how embodied and spatial performances of remembering are manifested and extended in/through online space. Exploring the online comments, as most possibly one of the very few inter-ethnic 'relational spaces' (Jones, 2005), offered me a broader sense of how citizens actually understand the physical space they inhabit. Examining the most problematic user-generated content allowed me to control for the risks associated with simply presuming the social meanings and effects of the physical environment explored in previous chapters. Stepping away from the material manifestations of traumascapes and adopting the concept of 'internet nationalism' (Skey, 2009), the analysis set out to show how online meta-discursive practices create a kind of 'third space' (Hughey and Daniels, 2013) between physical space and mediascapes. The virtual landscapes, contested and controlled just as physical spaces are, enable the everyday public formulation of an imagined evil other (Anderson, 1983) as well as an active engagement in the production of extreme ethno-nationalism. When it comes to the readers' comments, it seems that 'hot' nationalism is embedded in people's daily lives, but certainly not subtly nor unnoticeably as banal nationalism is. War memory appears to serve as a trigger and result in extreme nationalism, hateful and violent language – a discursive behaviour that is habitual, normalized and mediated daily as thousands of people who visit one of the most popular news portal in the country, constantly write and read the same dangerous words. As pointed out by Higgins (2004), media promulgate nationalism, nationhood and national identity in all sorts of ways – through a mixture of 'small' words, 'big' words (in Billig's terms), explicit remarks or emotional appeals that lead to the universal spread of different nationalist sentiments. Comments sections or the nationalistic readings of public space introduce us to complex digital landscapes where users communicate about another form of communication (e.g. graffiti) and challenge the ways discourse analysts and sociolinguists think about discourse and the nature of language itself (Jones et al., 2015). As Jaworski and Thurlow (2010: 5) remind us, digital media have 'opened up new ways of representing, accessing and theorizing space/place', quite literally providing informational landscapes through online comments giving us an insight into how people experience (physical) space and discover deeper meanings behind it. Like graffiti, only materialized in/through a different kind of space, online comments occur just as threatening and oppressive 'verbal attacks' carrying messages of social fragmentation, and therefore should be approached just as attentively.

Finally, in my last substantive chapter I focused on experiential consequences of traumascapes, demonstrating yet another way they are produced, circulated and experienced. In this analytical chapter, I explored the dynamics between the received stories and personal experiences of the second-generation B&H diaspora living in Switzerland. This spoken dimension of war remembering ultimately reflects the discursive nature of 'historical trauma' which hinges principally on the loss of family members and the burdensome family atmospheres created by the war (memory). The family context evidently serves as a space for memory transmission and thus, the mediation of war. But quite surprisingly, the second-generation's knowledge and memories of the war are not exclusively based in 'hateful stories' about the enemies. They seem to prioritize not what they were told, but what they have themselves observed and experienced. The meanings of war are, for example, re-established through the elements of post-war semiotic landscape (e.g. monuments, mine fields, ruins, graffiti in Bosnia-Herzegovina) which lead to strong feelings of 'spatial melancholia' (after Navaro-Yashin, 2009). Such experiential consequences of traumascapes, resting on the collective war memory (and different for all ethnic groups), are thereby transmitted to diasporic spaces. In that way, the post-war semiotic landscape is mobilized anew. The second-generation's wholehearted engagement in trauma (discourse) has also been illustrated through examples of inter-ethnic encounters which generate emotions that are reported tentatively in oral narratives, and central in framing experiences as traumatic. Indeed, trauma does not only endure in the spaces materially affected by violence and the lives of those living there, but it propagates in wider cultural contexts across broader discursive terrains.

In the wake of this summary, I want to briefly revisit Tumarkin's (2005) notion of traumascapes. My central objective in this book has been to unpack some of the mechanisms and strategies used to produce and sustain war memory and trauma. More specifically, at the heart of my work has been an intention to tackle the ways discourses of remembering and the war persist. What becomes evident is that traumascapes are produced through intricate forms of social interaction, communication and discourse. They are sustained and animated in various forms and practices, through people, semiotic resources, across time and space. Tumarkin (2005) asserts that places or sites of trauma are physical, containing affective power exclusively through their locations. However, what my work here indicates is that traumascapes cannot be exclusively understood as material and geographically delimited. Rather, due to their complex vibrancy produced through the meanings people ascribe to them, they come to be understood as much more than material sites of violence confined to a single place. As Jaworski and Thurlow (2010) argue, space should not be understood as purely physical or neatly bound, especially since it is created through deliberate human intervention and meaning making. Indeed, remembering is inextricably connected to the movement of people and spaces. Phillips and Reyes (2011: 2) also point out, discourses of remembering 'travel across national boundaries and facilitate the emergence of new, transnational social structures ranging from international non-governmental organizations to transnational religious communities to broad cultural movements that are not bound by national borders or identities across a complex and varied global landscape'. In this regard, I refer to Violi (2017) to argue that the sites of trauma are traumatic precisely because they have been recognized and constructed as such with the values inscribed into them, which are then conserved and transmitted over time. I also argue against Tumarkin's claim that traumascapes persist and wield affective powers whether we take note of them or not. It is precisely our attention that gives them power. People engage with trauma in multiple ways – physically, cognitively, affectively, morally or politically. Consequently, the sites of trauma do not exclusively 'evoke only legacies of violence, suffering and loss' (Tumarkin, 2005: 12), nor are they primarily spaces for remembering and honouring. These sites are highly contested, abused and even desecrated. Sites of concentration camps that were literally flooded with blood remain without monuments or massive genocide graveyards with protesters displaying words of hatred are only some of the examples from my analytical chapters that point to this. In this way, I argue that the discourses of remembering, deeply rooted in collective trauma, tend to be easily converted to extreme rhetoric of nationalism and semiotic violence. Yet, becoming the official and recognizable idiom of public communication, these semiotic practices seem to be the unavoidable consequences of violence. At the same time, by putting the concept of traumascapes in relation to discourse studies and sociolinguistics scholarship, and by combining critical-semiotic-multimodal approaches, the book investigates broad but carefully defined collective forms of remembering and trauma. More importantly, however, I hope it will help to make Bosnia-Herzegovina and other traumascapes imbued with meanings more visible to the field and, in the process, to 'visibilize' the life of its citizens. And so to conclude, I refer to Abousnnouga (2012: 359–60) and his remarks in the research on commemorative war monuments, where he says:

> Even in this age of modern warfare, the horrific consequences of war are undeniable. Lives of innocent civilians lost or ruined through injury, hunger and bereavement, the lives of soldiers brought to an early end or changed forever by the physical or mental scars inflicted by battle, homes and other buildings reduced to heaps of rubble, these are the real consequences of war.

Although all of the above is true, what Abousnnouga's remark is missing is that both people (civilians) and the spaces affected by violence stay marked and particularly fragile. In countries such as Bosnia-Herzegovina, this instability and the prejudice of 'a barbaric, violent people with a "Balkan identity" who had hated each other for at least 500 years' (Hansen, 2006) lasts long after the war is ostensibly over. Such consequences should be enough to make these sites vital objects of academic study, regardless of the approach or methodology adopted. However, what is even more important at this moment is the fact that this particular post-war society has become a geopolitical battlefield of world powers, and local and international political elites. The spheres of influence of both Russia and the Western powers collide in Bosnia-Herzegovina. What has started in Ukraine in 2014 and escalated in 2022 appears to be spreading to the Balkans; this is exemplified in the 2016 coup attempt in Montenegro, a year before it joined NATO. And as Bosnia-Herzegovina's nervous calls for joining the EU have dwindled, tensions have risen anew in a society so utterly divided and conflicted. When we follow the recent reports to their logical outcomes, if Bosnia-Herzegovina tries joining NATO, is it really so hard to imagine such a fragile country crumbling into war once more? The weapons are there, the hatred is there, the desire for secession in both the Serb Republic and parts of Herzegovina is there. The only ingredient that appears to be missing is the spark inevitably provided or suppressed by the world powers. It appears that Bosnia-Herzegovina's instability is an ace up Russia's sleeve in its negotiations with the West. And as things stand, all symptoms of trauma and discourses of remembering seem to not be enough of a warning against the new violence that is coming.

Notes

Introduction

1. Available at http://www.icty.org/x/cases/stanisic_simatovic/tjug/en/130530_judgement_p1.pdf icty 2014
2. Available at https://www.theguardian.com/world/2005/jun/05/balkans.warcrimes
3. Available at https://www.bbc.com/news/uk-scotland-44396872
4. Available at https://faktor.ba/vijest/majka-zrtve-skorpiona-uzela-sam-i-ljubila-sinove-kosti-tada-mi-je-bilo-lakse-273078#6
5. Available at https://www.icty.org/x/cases/mico_stanisic/ind/en/sta-ii050225e.htm
6. Available at https://www.theguardian.com/world/2016/jul/01/bosnia-herzegovina-has-lost-a-fifth-of-its-pre-war-population-census-shows

Chapter 2

1. Available at http://www.nytimes.com/2015/08/02/fashion/a-kiss-deferred-by-bosnia-and-herzegovina-civil-war.html?_r=0
2. Available at https://www.osce.org/bih/107255?download=true
3. Council of Europe, Committee of Ministers (1997), Recommendation No. R (97)20
4. Criminal Code of Bih Article 145a – Inciting National, Racial and Religious Hatred, Discord or Hostility (1) Whoever publicly incites or inflames national, racial or religious hatred, discord or hostility among the constituent peoples and others who live in Bosnia and Herzegovina shall be punished by imprisonment for a term between three months and three years; (2) Whoever perpetrates the criminal offence referred to in paragraph (1) by abuse of office or authority shall be punished by imprisonment for a term between one and ten years.
5. ... *pa vi bombardujte, ubijte jednog Srbina, mi ćemo stotinu Muslimana, pa da vidimo sme li Međunarodna Zajednica ili bilo ko drugi da udari na srpske položaje, može li se tako ponašati sa srpskim narodom* (so you bomb, kill one Serb, we will kill one hundred Muslims, then we shall see if the international community, or anyone else, dare to strike against Serbian (military) positions, and can the Serbian people be treated in such a way). Available at https://www.youtube.com/watch?v=rDmwnfx3Ab4
6. The 'Serbs on the willows' quote is from West (1993).

Chapter 3

1. Available at https://www.icty.org/en/outreach/bridging-the-gap-with-local-communities/prijedor
2. Available at https://www.icty.org/x/cases/mejakic_old/ind/en/mea-ai010718e.htm
3. Stanišić and Župljanin Trial Judgement (n9) vol 1 para 597; Tadić Trial Judgement (n125) para 155; Kvočka Trial Judgement (n125) para 98. Slobodan Milošević 98bis Decision (n11) para 93 (finding that women held in Omarska camp were routinely called out of their rooms and raped, noting evidence that one woman was taken out five times and raped, and after each rape she was beaten). Available at http://www.icty.org/case/zupljanin_stanisicm/4
4. Available at https://www.theguardian.com/world/2004/sep/01/warcrimes.balkans
5. In 2019, the regional Association of Detainees brought a memorial plaque and placed it in front of the White House.
6. Available at https://www.theguardian.com/world/2004/sep/01/warcrimes.balkans
7. Available at https://www.newyorker.com/news/news-desk/bosnias-unending-war
8. See https://www.amnesty.org/en/latest/news/2012/12/banning-human-rights-marchrepublika-srpska-unacceptable/
9. Available at https://www.nytimes.com/2015/10/04/travel/sarajevo-tourism-history.html
10. https://www.nytimes.com/2015/10/04/travel/sarajevo-tourism-history.html
11. Available at https://www.dailymail.co.uk/news/article-2126117/Bosnia-remembers-11-541-chairs-laid-Sarajevo-memory-dead-20-years-bloody-conflict-began.html
12. Available at https://www.nytimes.com/2015/10/04/travel/sarajevo-tourism-history.html
13. Available at https://www.independent.co.uk/news/world/europe/twenty-years-on-from-its-siege-sarajevo-still-feels-the-emptiness-7624775.html

Chapter 4

1. *Nationalism is primarily a political principle that holds that the political and the national unit should be congruent* (Gellner, 1983).
2. Available at https://www.nytimes.com/2017/08/18/science/space/nyteclipsewatch-terms-of-service.html
3. Available at http://www.media.ba/bs/magazin-novinarstvo/bh-online-mediji-kako-zaustaviti-govor-mrznje-u-komentarima
4. Available at http://www.osce.org/bih/281906?download=true
5. An appeal by the Press Council in Bosnia-Herzegovina states that it is the editors' duty to remove comments containing *hate speech, discrimination, threats and*

    incitement, and to ban the ones posting them for a certain time or to completely revoke their right to post comments about articles… such matters as incitement to, representation of and portrayal of violence and ethnic, national or religious intolerance and violence, as the prevention of such activity is vital to the well-being of the people of Bosnia and Herzegovina (VZS, 1998) available at http://english.vzs.ba/

6. Available at https://www.nytimes.com/2017/11/22/world/europe/ratko-mladic-conviction-yugoslavia-bosnia.html
7. Poturice or 'Turkish offspring' (*Turkified*), a pejorative term related to the Ottoman Empire era of rule in the Bosnia-Herzegovina region (1463/1482 – 1878).
8. See http://www.hitler.org/writings/Mein_Kampf/

Chapter 5

1. Available at http://www.unhcr.org/afr/news/briefing/2004/9/414ffeb44/returns-bosnia-herzegovina-reach-1-million.html
2. Available at https://www.hrw.org/world-report/2010/country-chapters/bosnia-and-herzegovina
3. Available at http://www.uzopibih.com.ba/index.html
4. Available at http://www.icty.org/en/cases/interactive-map

Conclusion

1. Forensic landscape is a technical term recently proposed by archaeologists to describe the sites that await inspection or 'execution sites or body processing sites and evidence of the movement of the deceased to the grave or their deposition into the grave' (paraphrased by Margaret Cox et al., xxxx: 15 in Cyr, 2014: 85).

References

Abousnnouga, N. G. and D. Machin (2010), 'War monuments and the changing discourses of nation and soldiery', in A. Jaworski and C. Thurlow (eds), *Semiotic Landscapes: Language, Image, Space*, London: Continuum, pp. 219–40.

Abousnnouga, N. G. (2012), 'Visual and written discourses of British commemorative war monuments' PhD Thesis, Cardiff University.

Abousnnouga, N. G. and D. Machin (2013), *The Language of War Monuments*, London: Bloomsbury.

Achugar, M. (2008), *What We Remember: The Construction of Memory in Military Discourse*, Amsterdam: John Benjamins.

Agger, I. (1994), *The Blue Room: Trauma and Testimony among Refugee Women: A Psycho-Social Exploration*, London and New Jersey: Zed Books.

Agha, A. (2007), 'Recombinant selves in mass mediated spacetime', *Language and Communication*, 27: 320–35.

Alexander, J. C. (2004), 'Toward a theory of cultural trauma', in J. C. Alexander, R. Eyerman, B. Giesen, N. J. Smelser, and P. Sztompka (eds), *Cultural Trauma and Collective Identity*, Berkeley: University of California Press, pp. 1–31.

Alexander, R. (2006), *Bosnian, Croatian, Serbian, a Grammar: With Sociolinguistic Commentary*, Madison: University of Wisconsin Press.

Allen, M. J. and S. D. Brown (2011), 'Embodiment and living memorials: The affective labour of remembering the 2005 London bombings', *Memory Studies*, 4(3): 312–27.

American Psychiatric Association (1994), *Diagnostic and Statistical Manual of Mental Disorders*, Washington: American Psychiatric Association.

Anderson, B. (1983), *Imagined Communities*, London: SAGE.

Anderson, B. (1992), *Long-distance Nationalism: World Capitalism and the Rise of Identity Politics*, Amsterdam: Centre for Asian Studies.

Androutsopoulos, A. (2006), 'Multilingualism, diaspora, and the Internet: Codes and identities on German-based diaspora websites', *Journal of Sociolinguistics*, 10(4): 520–47.

Anthonissen, C. (2006), 'The language of remembering and forgetting', *Journal of Language and Politics*, 5(1): 1–12.

Anthonissen, C. and J. Blommaert (2006), 'Discourse and human rights violations', *Journal of Language and Politics*, 5(1): 1–142.

Appadurai, A. (1996), *Modernity at Large: Cultural Dimensions of Globalization*, Minneapolis: University of Minnesota Press.

Appadurai, A. (2001), 'Grassroots globalization and the research imagination', in A. Appadurai (ed), *Globalization*, Durham: Duke University Press, pp. 1–21.

Argenti, N. and K. Schramm (eds) (2010), *Remembering Violence: Anthropological Perspectives on Intergenerational Transmission*, New York: Berghahn Books.

Atkinson, J. (2002), *Trauma Trails, Recreating Song Lines: The Transgenerational Effects of Trauma in Indigenous Australia*, North Melbourne: Spinifex Press.

Baker, P., C. Gabrielatos and T. McEnery (2013), *Discourse Analysis and Media Attitudes: The Representation of Islam in the British Press*, Cambridge: Cambridge University Press.

Bakhtin, M. (1981), *The Dialogic Imagination. Four Essays by MM Bakhtin*, Austin: University of Texas Press.

Bakhtin, M. (1986), *Speech Genres and Other Late Essays*. (V. W. McGee, Trans.), Austin: University of Texas.

Bamberg, M. (2006), 'Stories: Big or small? Why do we care?', *Narrative Inquiry*, 16: 147–55.

Bamberg, M. and A. Georgakopolou (2008), 'Small stories as a new perspective in narrative and identity analysis', *Text and Talk*, 28: 377–96.

Baranowski, A. B., M. Young, S. Johnson-Douglas, L. Williams-Keeler and M. Mccarrey (1998), 'PTSD transmission: A review of secondary traumatization in Holocaust survivor families', *Canadian Psychology*, 39: 247–56.

Baron, N. S. (2010), 'Discourse structures in instant messaging: The case of utterance breaks', *Language@Internet*, 7.

Bar-Tal, D. (1990), 'Causes and consequences of delegitimization: Models of conflict and ethnocentrism', *Journal of Social Issues*, 46: 65–81.

Baruh, L. and M. Popescau (2008), 'Guiding metaphors of nationalism: The Cyprus issue and the construction of Turkish identity in online discussions', *Discourse & Communication*, 2(1): 79–96.

Bašić, G. (2015), 'Concentration Camp Rituals: Narratives of Former Bosnian Detainees'. *Humanity & Society*, 1–22.

Bauman, R. (2004), *A World of Others' Worlds: Cross-cultural Perspectives on Intertextuality*, Oxford: Blackwell.

Bauman, R. (2011), 'Commentary: Foundations in performance', *Journal of Sociolinguistics*, 15(5): 707–20.

Beeman, W. O. (1993), 'The anthropology of theatre and spectacle', *Annu. Rev. Anthropol*, 22: 369–93.

Bell, A. and A. Gibson (2011), 'Staging language: An introduction to the sociolinguistics of performance', *Journal of Sociolinguistics*, 15(5): 555–72.

BenEzer, G. (2002), 'Trauma signals in life stories', in K. L. Rogers, G. Dawson and S. Leydesdorff (eds), *Trauma and Life Stories: International Perspectives*, London: Routledge, pp. 29–44.

BenEzer, G. (2004), 'Trauma signals in life stories', in K. L. Rogers, G. Dawson and S. Leydesdorff (eds), *Trauma: Life Stories of Survivors*, New Brunswick and London: Transaction, pp. 29–44.

Bennett, C. (1995), *Yugoslavia's Bloody Collapse: Causes, Course and Consequences*, New York: NYU Press.

Ben-Rafael, E., E. Shohamy, M. H. Amara and N. Trumper-Hecht (2006), 'Linguistic landscape as symbolic construction of public space: The case of Israel', *International Journal of Multilingualism*, 31: 7–30.

Ben-Rafael, E. (2016), 'Introduction', *Linguistic Landscape*, 2(3): 207–10.

Bernard, V. W., P. Ottenberg and F. Redl (1971), 'Dehumanization', in N. Sandford and C. Comstock (eds), *Sanctions for Evil: Sources of Social Destructiveness*, San Francisco: Jossey-Bass, pp. 102–24.

Bezemer, J. and G. Kress (2014), 'Touch: A resource for making meaning', *Australian Journal of Language and Literacy*, 37(2): 77–85.

Bietti, L. (2010), 'Sharing memories, family conversation and interaction', *Discourse & Society*, 21(5): 499–523.

Bietti, L. (2011), 'Memory, discourse and interaction remembering in context and history', PhD Thesis, Universitad Pompeu Fabra.

Bietti, L. (2014), *Discursive Remembering: Individual and Collective Remembering as a Discursive, Cognitive and Historical Process*, Berlin and Boston: Walter de Gruyter.

Billig, M. (1995), *Banal Nationalism*, London: SAGE.

Birdsall, C. and D. Drozdzewski (2017), 'Capturing commemoration: Using mobile recordings within memory research', *Mobile Media Communication*, 6(2): 266–84.

Bishop, H. and A. Jaworski (2003), 'We beat 'em: Nationalism and the hegemony of homogeneity in the british press reportage of Germany versus England during Euro 2000', *Discourse & Society*, 14(3): 243–71.

Blackwood, R. and J. Macalister (eds) (2019), *Multilingual Memories: Monuments, Museums and the Linguistic Landscape*, London: Bloomsbury.

Blommaert, J. (2015), 'Dialogues with ethnography: Notes on classics and how I read them', *Tilburg Papers in Culture Studies*, 10(10): 138.

Boltanski, L. (1999), *Distant Suffering: Morality, Media and Politics*, Cambridge: Cambridge University Press.

Bolter, J. D. and R. Grusin (2003), *Remediation*, London: MIT Press.

Bougarel, X., E. Helms and G. Duijzings (2007), 'Introduction', in X. Bougarel, E. Helms and G. Duijzings (eds), *The New Bosnian Mosaic. Identities, Memories and Moral Claims in a Post-War Society*, London and New York: Routledge Ashgate, pp. 1–38.

Bourdieu, P. (1991), *Language and Symbolic Power*, Cambridge: Harvard University Press.

Brady, S. and F. Walsh (eds) (2009), *Crossroads: Performance Studies and Irish Culture*, New York: Palgrave Macmillan.

Braithwaite, J. (2000), 'Shame and criminal justice', *Canadian Journal of Criminology*, 42(3): 281–98.

Brave Heart, M. Y. H. and L. M. DeBruyn (1998), 'The American Indian Holocaust: Healing historical unresolved grief', *American Indian and Alaska Native Mental Health Research*, 8(2): 56–78.

Brave Heart, M. Y. H. (2003), 'The historical trauma response among Natives and its relationship with substance abuse: A Lakota illustration', *Journal of Psychoactive Drugs*, 35(1): 7–13.

Brown, S. D. (2012), 'Two minutes of silence: Social technologies of public commemoration', *Theory & Psychology*, 22(2): 234–52.

Brubaker, R. and F. Cooper (2000), 'Beyond "Identity"', *Theory & Society*, 29: 1–47.

Bucholtz, M. and K. Hall (2016), 'Embodied sociolinguistics', in N. Coupland (ed), *Sociolinguistics: Theoretical Debates*, Cambridge: Cambridge University Press, pp. 173–197.

Butler, J. (1997), *Excitable Speech: A Politics of the Performative*, New York and London: Routledge.

Butler, J. (2011), 'Bodies in alliance and the politics of the street', *European Institute for Progressive Cultural Policies*.

Butler, J. (2015), *Notes Toward a Performative Theory of Assembly*, Cambridge, MA and London, England: Harvard University Press.

Calhoun, C. (1997), *Nationalism*, Buckingham: Open University Press.

Carr, S. E. and B. Fisher (2016), 'Interscaling awe, de-escalating disaster', in E. S. Carr and M. Lempert (eds), *Scale Discourse and Dimensions of Social Life*, Oakland: University of California Press, pp. 133–56.

Caruth, C. (1991), 'Unclaimed experience: Trauma and the possibility of history', *Literature and the Ethical Question*, 79: 181–92.

Caruth, C. (ed) (1995), *Introduction to Trauma: Explorations in Memory*, Baltimore: Johns Hopkins University Press.

Caruth, C. (1996), *Unclaimed Experience: Trauma, Narrative, and History*, Baltimore: Johns Hopkins University Press.

Chiapello, E. and N. Fairclough (2002), 'Understanding the new management ideology: A transdisciplinary contribution from critical discourse analysis and new sociology of capitalism', *Discourse & Society*, 13(2): 185–208.

Chick, J. K. (1985), 'The interactional accomplishment of discrimination in South Africa', *Language in Society*, 14: 299–326.

Chomsky, N. (1965), *Aspects of the Theory of Syntax*, Cambridge: MIT Press.

Cigar, N. (1995), *Genocide in Bosnia: The Policy of 'Ethnic Cleansing'*, Texas: A & M University Press.

Clough, P. T. (2007), *The Affective Turn: Theorizing the Social*, Durham: Duke University Press.

Colaguori, C. (2010), 'Symbolic violence and the violation of human rights: Continuing the sociological critique of domination', *International Journal of Criminology and Sociological Theory*, 3(2): 388–400.

Collins, L. and B. Nelich (2014), 'Examining user comments for deliberative democracy: A corpus-driven analysis of the climate change debate online', *Environmental Communication*, 9: 189–207.

Connerton (1989), *How Societies Remember*, Cambridge: Cambridge University Press.

Connolly, A. (2011), 'Healing the wounds of our fathers: Intergenerational trauma, memory, symbolization and narrative', *Journal of Analytical Psychology*, 56: 607–26.

Conversi, D. (2012), 'Irresponsible radicalisation: Diasporas, globalisation and long-distance nationalism in the digital age', *Journal of Ethnic and Migration Studies*, 38(9): 1357–79.

Conway, B. (2008), 'Local conditions, global environment and transnational discourses in memory work: The case of Bloody Sunday (1972)', *Memory Studies*, 1(2): 187–209.

Conway, B. (2010), *Commemoration and Bloody Sunday: Pathways of Memory*, Basingstoke: Palgrave Macmillan.

Costelloe, L. (2014), 'Discourses of sameness: Expressions of nationalism in newspaper discourse on French urban violence in 2005', *Discourse & Society*, 25(3): 315–40.

Coupland, N. (1999), '"Other" representation', in J. Verschueren, J. O. Östman and C. Bulcean, C. (eds), *Handbook of Pragmatics*, Amsterdam: Benjamins, pp. 1–24.

Cranny-Francis, A. (2011), 'Semefulness: A social semiotics of touch', *Social Semiotics*, 21(4): 463–81.

Crawford, A. (2014), 'The trauma experienced by generations past having an effect in their descendants: Narrative and historical trauma among Inuit in Nunavut, Canada', *Transcultural Psychiatry*, 51(3): 339–69.

Cresswell, T. and C. Martin (2012), 'On turbulence: Entanglements of disorder and order on a Devon beach', *Tijdschrift Voor Economische En Sociale Geografie*, 103: 516–29.

Croegaert, A. (2011), 'Who has time for Cejf? Postsocialist migration and slowCoffee in neoliberal Chicago', *American Anthropologist*, 113(3): 463–77.

Cvitković, I. (2006), *Hrvatski identitet u Bosni i Hercegovini*, Zagreb and Sarajevo: Synopsis.

Cyr, R. (2014), 'The "forensic landscapes" of Srebrenica', *Культура/Culture*, 1(5): 81–92.

Daniels, S. and D. Cosgrove (1993), 'Spectacle and text: Landscape metaphors in cultural geography', in J. S. Duncan and D. Ley (eds), *Place/Culture/Representation*, London and New York: Routledge, pp. 57–77.

Danner, M. (1997), 'America and the Bosnia Genocide', *New York Review*, December 4.

Danner, M. (2009), *Stripping Bare the Body: Politics Violence War*. Hachette.

Dawson, G. (2016), 'Memoryscapes, spatial legacies of conflict, and the culture of historical reconciliation in "post-conflict" Belfast', in P. Gobodo-Madikizela (ed), *Breaking Intergenerational Cycles of Repetition: A Global Dialogue on Historical Trauma and Memory*, Opladen, Berlin and Toronto: Barbara Budrich Publishers, pp. 135–59.

Dayan, D. and E. Katz (1992), *Media Events: The Live Broadcasting of History*, Cambridge, MA: Harvard University Press.

De Cillia, R., M. Reisigl and R. Wodak (1999), 'The discursive construction of national identities', *Discourse and Society*, 10(2): 149–73.

De Fina, A. (2003), *Identity in Narrative: A Study of Immigrant Discourse*, Amsterdam and Philadelphia: John Benjamins.

De Ruiter, A. (2015), 'Imaging Egypt's political transition in (post-)revolutionary street art: On the interrelations between social media and graffiti as media of communication', *Media, Culture & Society*, 37(4): 581–601.

Debord, G. (1995), *Society of the Spectacle*, New York: Zone Books.

Del Ponte, C. (2006), 'Investigation and prosecution of large-scale crimes at the international level: The experience of the ICTY', *Journal of International Criminal Justice*, 4(3): 539–58.

Delanty, G., R. Wodak and P. Jones (eds) (2008), *Identity, Belonging and Migration*, Liverpool: Liverpool University Press.

Denham, A. R. (2008), 'Rethinking historical trauma: Narratives of resilience', *Transcultural Psychiatry*, 45(3): 391–414.

Di Nicola, V. (2018), 'Two trauma communities: A philosophical archaeology of cultural and clinical trauma theories', in E. Boynton and P. Capretto (eds), *Trauma and Transcendence: Suffering and the Limits of Theory*, New York: Fordham University Press, pp. 17–52.

Dimova, R. (2006), 'Duldung trauma Bosnian refugees in Berlin', in A. Szczepanikova, M. Canek and J. Grill (eds), *Migration Processes in Central and Eastern Europe: Unpacking the Diversity*, Prague: Multicultural Center Prague, pp. 47–53.

Douglas, M. (1966), *Purity and Danger: An Analysis of the Concepts of Pollution and Taboo*, New York: Routledge.

Duijzings, G. (2007), 'Commemorating Srebrenica: Histories of violence and the politics of memory in eastern Bosnia', in X. Bougarel, E. Helms and G. Duijzings (eds), *The New Bosnian Mosaic Identities, Memories and Moral Claims in a Post-War Society*, Ashgate, London and New York: Routledge, pp. 141–66.

Duncan, P. T. (2014), 'Remembering the future: Temporal tensions in the discursive construction and commemoration of Israel', *Critical Discourse Studies*, 11(4): 416–40.

Duran, E., B. Duran, M. Y. Brave Heart and S. J. Horse-Davis (1998), 'Healing the American Indian soul wound', in Y. Danieli (ed), *International Handbook of Multigenerational Legacies of Trauma*, Springer US, pp. 341–354.

Dwork, D. (1991), *Children with a Star: Jewish Youth in Nazi Europe*, New Haven and London: Yale University Press.

Eastmond, M. (1998), 'Nationalist discourses and the construction of difference: Bosnian Muslim refugees in Sweden', *Journal of Refugee Studies*, 11(2): 161–81.

ECRI (2011), 'Government comments on the report on Bosnia and Herzegovina'. Available online: file:///C:/Users/MAIDAK~1/AppData/Local/Temp/BIH-COM-IV-2011-002-ENG.pdf (Accessed 30 July 2018)

ECRI (2017), 'ECRI report on Bosnia and Herzegovina (fifth monitoring cycle)'. Available online: file:///C:/Users/MAIDAK~1/AppData/Local/Temp/BIH-CbC-V-2017-002-ENG.pdf (Accessed 30 July 2018).

Edwards, D. and D. Middleton (1986), 'Joint remembering: Constructing an account of shared experience through conversational discourse', *Discourse Processes*, 9(4): 423–59.

Edwards, D. and D. Middleton (1987), 'Conversation and remembering', *Applied Cognitive Psychology*, 1: 77–92.
Edwards, D. and J. Potter (1992), *Discursive Psychology*, London: SAGE.
Edwards, D. (1997), *Discourse and Cognition*, London: SAGE.
Eriksen, T. H. (2007), 'Nationalism and the internet', *Nations & Nationalism*, 13(1): 1–17.
Erikson, K. (1976), *Everything in Its Path*, New York: Simon & Schuster.
Erikson, K. (1994), *A New Species of Trouble: The Human Experience of Modern Disasters*, New York: Norton.
Erjavec, K. and M. Poler Kovačić (2012), 'You don't understand, this is a new war! Analysis of hate speech in news web sites' comments', *Mass Communication & Society*, 15(6): 899–920.
Erjavec, K. and M. Poler Kovačić (2013), 'Abuse of online participatory journalism in Slovenia: Offensive comments under news items', *Medij.istraz*, 19(2): 55–73.
Every, A. (2013), '"Shame on you": The language, practice and consequences of shame and shaming in asylum seeker advocacy', *Discourse & Society*, 24(6): 667–86.
Eyerman, R. (2001), *Cultural Trauma: Slavery and the Formation of African American Identity*, Cambridge: Cambridge University Press.
Eyerman, R. (2002), 'Music in movement: Cultural politics and old and new social movements', *Qualitative Sociology*, 25(3): 443–58.
Fairclough, N. (1989), *Language and Power*, London: Longman.
Fairclough, N. (1992), *Discourse and Social Change*, Cambridge: Polity Press.
Felman, S. and D. Laub (1992), *Testimony: Crises of Witnessing in Literature, Psychoanalysis, and History*, London and New York: Routledge.
Felman, S. (2002), *The Juridical Unconscious: Trials and Traumas in the Twentieth Century*, Cambridge: Harvard University Press.
Finlayson, A. (1998), 'Ideology, discourse and nationalism', *Journal of Political Ideologies*, 3(1): 99–118.
FitzGerald, E. M (2009), 'Commemoration and the performance of Irish famine memory', in S. Brady, and F. Walsh (eds), *Crossroads: Performance Studies and Irish Culture*, 86–99, New York: Palgrave Macmillan.
Foa, E. B., G. Steketee and B. O. Rothbaum (1989), 'Behavioral/cognitive conceptualization of posttraumatic stress disorder', *Behavior Therapy*, 20: 155–76.
FOM (2014), 'The population of Bosnia and Herzegovina in Switzerland'. Available online: file:///C:/Users/MAIDAK~1/AppData/Local/Temp/2C59E545D7371EE495A4A6B21623F42A.pdf (Accessed 30 July 2018).
Foucault, M. (1977), *Discipline and Punish: The Birth of the Prison*, London: Allan Lane.
Garde-Hansen, A., A. Hoskins and A. Reading (eds) (2009), *Save as . . . Digital Memories*, New York: Palgrave Macmillan.
Gellner, E. (1983), *Nations and Nationalism*, Ithaca: Cornell University Press.
Georgakopolou, A. (2007), *Small Stories, Interaction and Identities*, Amsterdam and Philadelphia: John Benjamins Publishing.

Giovannucci, K. E. (2013), 'Remembering the victims: The sarajevo red line memorial and the trauma art paradox', *Mediterranean Journal of Social Sciences*, 4(9): 449–52.

Glenny, M. (2000), *The Balkans: Nationalism, War, and the Great Powers, 1804–1999*, New York: Viking.

Goffman, E. (1959), *The Presentation of Self in Everyday Life*, New York: Doubleday.

Goh, R. B. H. (2016), 'Memorializing genocide: Embodied semiotics in concentration camp memorials', *Social Semiotics*, 28:1, 18–40.

Golańska, D. (2015), 'Affective spaces, sensuous engagements: In quest of a synaesthetic approach to "dark memorials"', *International Journal of Heritage Studies*, 21:8, 773–790.

Gutman, R. (1992), 'Like auschwitz', *Newsday*, July 21.

Halbwachs, M. (1980), *The Collective Memory*, New York: Harper & Row.

Halbwachs, M. (1992), *On Collective Memory*, Chicago: University of Chicago.

Halilovich, H. (2010), 'Beyond the sadness: Memories and homecomings among survivors of "ethnic cleansing" in a Bosnian village', *Memory Studies*, 4(1): 42–52.

Halilovich, H. (2013), *Places of Pain: Forced Displacement, Popular Memory and Translocal Identities in Bosnian War-Torn Communities*, New York: Berghahn Books.

Hall, S. (1988), *The Hard Road to Renewal: Thatcherism and the Crisis of the Hard Left*, London: Verso.

Halliday, M. (1978), *Language as Social Semiotic: The Social Interpretation of Language and Meaning*, London: Edward Arnold.

Halliday, M. (2001), 'New ways of meaning: The challenges to applied linguistics', in A. Fill and P. Mühlhäusler (eds), *The Ecolinguistics Reader: Language, Ecology and Environment*, New York: Continuum, pp. 175–202.

Hanauer, D. (2013), 'Transitory linguistic landscapes as political discourses: Signage at three political demonstrations in Pittsburgh, USA', in C. Hélot, M. Barni, R. Janssens and C. Bagna (eds), *Linguistic Landscapes, Multilingualism and Social Change*, Frankfurt: Peter Lang, pp. 139–154.

Hanauer, D. I. (2011), 'The discursive construction of the separation wall at Abu Dis Graffiti as political discourse', *Journal of Language and Politics*, 10(3): 301–21.

Hansen, L. (2006), *Security as Practice Discourse Analysis and the Bosnian War*, London and New York: Routledge.

Hardt-Mautner, G. (1995). 'Only Connect', *Critical Discourse Analysis and Corpus Linguistics*. https://www.researchgate.net/publication/238287338_%27Only_Connect%27_Critical_Discourse_Analysis_and_Corpus_Linguistics (31 December 2021).

Hayakawa, S. I. (1946), 'Poetry and advertising', *Poetry*, 67(4): 204–12.

Helbo, A. (2016), 'Semiotics and performing arts: Contemporary issues', *Social Semiotics*, 26(4): 341–50.

Hemon, A. (2013), *The Book of My Lives*, New York: Macmillan.

Herman, J. L. (1992), *Trauma and Recovery: From Domestic Abuse to Political Terror*, New York: Basic Books.

Herring, S. C. and J. Androutsopoulos (2015), 'Computer-mediated discourse 2.0', in D. Tannen, H. E. Hamilton and D. Schiffrin (eds), *The Handbook of Discourse Analysis*, Blackwell Publishing, pp. 127–51.

Higgins, M. (2004), 'Putting the nation in the news: The role of location formulation in a selection of Scottish newspapers', *Discourse & Society*, 15: 633–48.

Hinton, A. L. (2002), *Annihilating Difference: The Anthropology of Genocide*, Berkley, LA and London: University of California Press.

Hirsch, J. (2004), *After Image: Film, Trauma and the Holocaust*, Philadelphia: Temple University Press.

Hirsch, M. (1997), *Family Frames: Photography, Narrative, and Postmemory*, Cambridge, MA: Harvard University Press.

Hirsch, M. (1999), 'Projected memory: Holocaust photographs in personal and public fantasy', in M. Bal, J. Crewe and L. Spitzer (eds), *Acts of Memory: Cultural Recall in the Present*, Hanover: University Press of New England, pp. 3–23.

Hirsch, M. (2002), 'Marked by Memory: Feminist reflections on trauma and transmission', in N. K. Miller and J. Tougaw (eds), *Extremities: Trauma, Testimony and Community*, Urbana and Chicago: University of Illinois Press, pp. 71–91.

Hirsch, M. (2008), *The Generation of Postmemory: Writing and Visual Culture after the Holocaust*, New York: Columbia University Press.

Hjarvard, S. (2008), 'The mediatization of society: A theory of the media as agents of social and cultural change', *Nordicom Review*, 29(2): 105–34.

Höijer, B. (2004), 'The discourse of global compassion: The audience and media reporting of human suffering', *Media Culture Society*, 26: 513–31.

Hoskins, A. (2007), 'Ghost in the machine: Television and war memory', in S. Maltby and R. Keeble (eds), *Communicating War: Memory, Media and Military*, Suffolk: Arima Publishing, pp. 18–28.

Hoskins, A. (2009), 'Digital network memory', in A. Erll and A. Nünning (eds), *Mediation, Remediation, and the Dynamics of Cultural Memory*, Berlin and New York: Walter de Gruyter, pp. 91–106.

Hoskins, A. (2015), 'The mediatization of memory', in K. Lundby (ed) *Mediatization of Communication*, Series: Handbooks of communication science (21), Berlin, Boston: De Gruyter Mouton, pp. 661–80.

Hughey, M. W. and J. Daniels (2013), 'Racist comments at online news sites: A methodological dilemma for discourse analysis', *Media, Culture & Society*, 35(3): 332–47.

Hutchinson, J. (2006), 'Hot and banal nationalism: The nationalization of the masses', in G. Delanty and K. Kumar (eds), *The Sage Handbook of Nations and Nationalism*, London: SAGE, pp. 295–306.

Huyssen, A. (2003), 'Trauma and memory: A new imaginary of temporality', in J. Bennett and R. Kennedy (eds), *World Memory: Personal Trajectories in Global Time*, Basingstoke: Palgrave Macmillan, pp. 16–29.

Ivkovic, D. and H. Lotherington (2009), 'Multilingualism in cyberspace: Conceptualising the virtual linguistic landscape', *International Journal of Multilingualism*, 6(1): 17–36.

Janíčko, M. (2015), 'Misunderstanding the other and shy signs of openness: Discourse on the 1992–1995 war in the current Bosniak and Bosnian Serb media', *Central European Political Studies Review*, XVII(1): 28–56.

Jaworski, A. (1993), *The Power of Silence: Social and Pragmatic Perspectives*, Newbury Park, CA: Sage Publication.

Jaworski, A. and C. Thurlow (eds) (2010), *Semiotic Landscapes: Language, Image, Space*, London: Continuum.

Jaworski, A. (2014), 'Welcome: Synthetic personalization and commodification of sociability in the linguistic landscape of global tourism', in B. Spolsky, O. Inbar-Lourie and M. Tannenbaum (eds), *Challenges for Language Education and Policy: Making Space for People*, New York: Routledge, pp. 214–32.

Jones, G. M., B. B. Schieffelin and R. E. Smith (2011), 'When friends who talk together stalk together: Online gossip as metacommunication', in C. Thurlow and K. Mroczek (eds), *Digital Disocurse: Language in the New Media*, Oxford, New York: Oxford University Press, pp. 26–47.

Jones, R. H. (2005), 'Sites of engagement as sites of attention: Time, space and culture in electronic discourse', in S. Norris and R. Jones (eds), *Discourse in Action: Introducing Mediated Discourse Analysis*, London: Routledge, pp. 141–54.

Jones, R. H. (2010), 'Cyberspace and physical space: Attention structures in computer-mediated communication', in A. Jaworski and C. Thurlow (eds), *Semiotic Landscapes: Language, Image, Space*, London: Continuum, pp. 151–67.

Jones, R. H., A. Chik and C. A. Hafner (2015), *Discourse and Digital Practices: Doing Discourse Analysis in the Digital Age*, London and New York: Routledge.

Jones, R. and P. Merriman (2009), 'Hot, banal and everyday nationalism: Bilingual road signs in Wales', *Political Geography*, 28: 164–73.

Jugo, A. and S. Wastell (2015), 'Disassembling the pieces, reassembling the social: The forensic and political lives of secondary mass graves in Bosnia and Herzegovina', in E. Anstett and J. M. Dreyfus (eds), *Human Remains and Identification: Mass Violence, Genocide and the 'Forensic Turn'*, Manchester: Manchester University Press, pp. 142–74.

Juslin, N. and J. A. Sloboda (eds) (2011), *Music and Emotion: Theory and Research*, Oxford: Oxford University Press.

Kansteiner, W. (2002), 'Finding meaning in memory: A methodological critique of collective', *History and Theory*, 41(2): 179–97.

Karabegović, Dž. (2014), 'Što Te Nema? Transnational cultural production in the diaspora in response to the Srebrenica genocide', *Nationalism & Ethnic Politics*, 20: 455–75.

Karlander, D. (2016), 'Backjumps: Writing, watching, erasing train graffiti', *Social Semiotics*, 1–19.

Kellermann, N. P. F. (2001), 'Transmission of Holocaust trauma: An integrative view', *Psychiatry*, 64(3): 256–67.

Keinpointner, M. (1996), *Vernünftig argumentieren: Regeln und Techniken der Diskussion*, Hamburg: Rowohlt.

King, B. W. (2011), 'Language, sexuality and place: The view from cyberspace', *Gender and Language*, 5(1): 1–30.

King, B. W. (2012), 'Location, lore and language', *Journal of Language and Sexuality*, 1(1): 106–25.
King, B. W. (2017), 'Traversing the erotic oasis: Online chatting and the space/time continuum', *ACME: An International Journal for Critical Geographies*, 16(3): 475–99.
Kirmayer, M., J. P. Gone and J. Moses (2014), 'Rethinking historical trauma', *Transcultural Psychiatry*, 51(3): 299–319.
Kitis, D. E. and T. Milani (2015), 'The performativity of the body turbulent spaces in Greece', *Linguistic Landscape*, 1(3): 268–90.
Knudsen, B. T. and C. Stage (2016), *Global Media, Biopolitics, and Affect: Politicizing Bodily Vulnerability*, New York and London: Routledge.
Kollontai, P. (2010), 'Healing the heart in Bosnia-Herzegovina: Art, children and peacemaking', *International Journal of Children's Spirituality*, 15(3): 261–271.
Kordić, S. (2010), *Jezik i nacionalizam*, Zagreb: Durieux.
Kosatica, M. (2019), 'Sarajevo's War Childhood Museum: A social semiotic analysis of "combi-memorials" as spatial texts', in R. Blackwood and J. Macalister (eds), *Multilingual Memories: Monuments, Museums and the Linguistic Landscape*, London: Bloomsbury, pp. 161–84.
Kosatica, M. (forthcoming), 'Destroying monuments, unleashing wrath: The material disruption of contested memoryscapes', *Memory Studies*.
Kress, G. R. and R. Hodge (1979), *Language as Ideology*, London: Routledge & Kegan Paul.
Kress, G. R. and T. van Leeuwen (2001), *Multimodal Discourse: The Modes and Media of Contemporary Communication*, London: Arnold.
Kress, G. R. and T. van Leeuwen (2002), 'Colour as a semiotic mode: Notes for a grammar of colour', *Visual Communications*, 1(3): 343–68.
Kress, G. R. (2010), *Multimodality: A Social Semiotic Approach to Contemporary Communication*, London: Routledge.
Krzyżanowska, N. (2016), 'The discourse of counter-monuments: Semiotics of material commemoration in contemporary urban spaces', *Social Semiotics*, 26(5): 465–85.
Kupiszewski, M. (2009), 'Labor migration in southeast Europe: A review of the literature and a look at transversal issues', *Südosteuropa*, 57(4): 425–51.
Kwon, W., I. Clarke and R. Wodak (2014), 'Micro-level discursive strategies for constructing shared views around strategic issues in tea meetings', *Journal of Management Studies*, 51(2): 265–90.
Labov, W. and J. Waletzky (1967), 'Narrative analysis: Oral versions of personal experience', in J. Helm (ed), *Essays on the Verbal and Visual Arts*, Seattle: University of Washington Press, pp. 3–38.
Labov, W. (1972), *Language in the Inner City: Studies in the Black English Vernacular*, Philadelphia: The University of Pennsylvania Press.
Labov, W. (2006), 'Narrative pre-construction', *Narrative Inquiry*, 16(1): 37–45.
LaCapra, D. (1998), *History and Memory after Auschwitz*, Ithaca, NY: Cornell University Press.

LaCapra, D. (2001), *Writing History, Writing Trauma*, Baltimore: Johns Hopkins University Press.
LaCapra, D. (2016), 'Trauma, history, memory, identity: What remains?', *History & Theory*, 55: 375–400.
Lampe, E. (1988), 'Rachel Rosenthal creating her selves', *TDR*, 32(1): 170–90.
Landry, R. and R. Bourhis (1997), 'Linguistic landscape and ethnolinguistic vitality', *Journal of Language and Social Psychology*, 16(1): 23–49.
Langer, L. (1991), *Holocaust Testimonies*, New Haven: Yale University Press.
Lasswell, H. D. (1995), 'Propaganda', in R. Jackall (ed), *Propaganda*, New York: New York University Press, pp. 13–25.
Law, A. (2001), 'Near and far: Banal national identity and the press in Scotland', *Media, Culture & Society*, 23: 299–322.
Leclerc, J. (1989), *La Guerre des Langues dans l'Affichage*, Montréal: VLB éditeur.
Lefebvre, H. (1991), *The Production of Space*, Oxford: Blackwell Publishing.
Lennon, J. J. and M. Foley (1996), *Dark Tourism*, London: Continuum.
Levent, N. and A. Pascual-Leone (eds) (2014), *The Multisensory Museum: Cross-Disciplinary Perspectives on Touch, Sound, Smell, Memory, and Space*, Lanham, MD: Rowman & Littlefield.
Levin, M. G. (2006), *The Belated Witness: Literature, Testimony, and the Question of Holocaust Survival*, Stanford: Stanford University Press.
Levinson, S. (2003). 'Space in language and cognition: Explorations in cognitive diversity', *Space in Language and Cognition: Explorations in Cognitive Diversity*, Vol. 5.
Ley, D. and R. Cybriwsky (1974), 'Urban graffiti as territorial markers', *Annals of the Association of American Geographers*, 64(4): 491–505.
Leydesdorff, S., G. Dawson, N. Burchardt and T. G. Ashplant (2002), 'Introduction: Trauma and life stories in trauma stories book', in K. L. Rogers, G. Dawson and S. Leydesdorff (eds), *Trauma and Life Stories: International Perspectives*, London: Routledge, pp. 1–26.
Li, J. (2009), 'Intertextuality and national identity: Discourse of national conflicts in daily newspapers in the United States and China', *Discourse & Society*, 20(1): 85–121.
Lieblich, A. (1994), *Seasons of Captivity*, New York: New York University Press.
Linenthal, E. T. (2003), *The Unfinished Bombing: Oklahoma City in American Memory*, Oxford, New York: Oxford University Press.
Loke, J. (2012), 'Public expressions of private sentiments: Unveiling the pulse of racial tolerance through online news readers' comments', *The Howard Journal of Communication*, 23(3): 235–52.
Lomski-Feder, E. (1995), 'The meaning of war through veterans' eyes: A phenomenological analysis of life stories', *International Sociology*, 10(4): 463–82.
Lynn, N. and S. J. Lea (2005), 'Racist graffiti: Text, context and social comment', *Visual Communication*, 4(1): 39–63.
Machin, D. and G. Abousnnouga (2011), 'The changing spaces of war commemoration: A multimodal analysis of the discourses of British monuments'. *Social Semiotics*, 21(2): 175–96.

Machin, D. and A. Mayr (2012), *How to Do Critical Analysis: A Multimodal Introduction*, London: SAGE.

Machin, D. and J. E. Richardson (2012), 'Discourses of unity and purpose in the sounds of fascist music: A multimodal approach', *Critical Discourse Studies*, 9(4): 329–45.

Machin, D. (2013), 'What is multimodal critical discourse studies', *Critical Discourse Studies*, 10(4): 347–55.

Mannergren Selimovic, J. (2013), 'Making peace, making memory: Peacebuilding and politics of remembrance at memorials of mass atrocities', *Peacebuilding*, 1(3): 334–48.

Martín Rojo, L. (2014), 'Taking over the square: The role of linguistic practices in contesting urban spaces', *Journal of Language and Politics*, 13(4): 623–52.

Massumi, B. (2002), *Parables for the virtual: Movement, affect, sensation*, Durham and London: Duke University Press.

Mazzucchelli, F., R. van der Laarse and C. Reijnen (2014), 'Introduction: Traces of terror, signs of trauma', in R. van der Laarse, F. Mazzucchelli and C. Reijnen (eds), *Traces of Terror, Signs of Trauma: Practices of (re)presentation of Collective Memories in Space in Contemporary Europe*, Milano: Bompiani, pp. 3–19.

McCormick, R. (2014), *Croatia under Ante Pavelic: America, the Ustase and Croatian Genocide*, London: I.B. Tauris.

McDowell, S. and M. Braniff (2014), *Commemoration as Conflict: Space, Memory and Identity in Peace Processes*, New York: Palgrave Macmillan.

McIlvenny, P. and C. Noy (2011), 'Multimodal discourse in mediated spaces', *Social Semiotics*, 21(2): 147–54.

McMurtrie, R. J. and A. Murphy (2016), 'Penetrating spaces: A social semiotic, multimodal analysis of performance as rape prevention', *Social Semiotics*, 26(4): 445–63.

Media Plan Institute Available (2010), 'Internet–Sloboda bez granica?', Available online: https://mediaplaninstitut.files.wordpress.com/2017/05/internet-sloboda-bez-granica.pdf (Accessed 30 July 2018).

Metz, J. B. (1999), 'In the pluralism of religious and cultural worlds: Notes toward a theological and political program', *Cross Currents*, 49: 227–36.

Milani, T. (2015), 'Sexual citizenship: Discourses, spaces and bodies at Joburg Pride 2012', *Journal of Language and Politics*, 14(3): 431–54.

Milani, T., E. Levon, R. Gafter and I. Or (2018), 'Tel aviv as a space of affirmation versus transformation: Language, citizenship, and the politics of sexuality in Israel', *Linguistic Landscape*, 4(3): 278–97.

Milani, T., E. Levon and R. Glocer (2019), 'Crossing boundaries: Visceral landscapes of Israeli nationalism', *Sociolinguistic Studies*, 13: 37–56.

Milani, T. M. and J. E. Richardson (2021), 'Discourse and affect', *Social Semiotics*, 31(5): 671–6.

Ministry of Security Bosnia-Herzegovina (2019), 'Bosnia-Herzegovina migration profile for the year 2019'. Available online: file:///C:/Users/MAIDAK~1/AppData/Local/Temp/220720202.pdf (Accessed 30 August 2021)

Mohatt, N. V., A. B. Thompson, N. D. Thai and J. K. Tebes (2014), 'Historical trauma as public narrative: A conceptual review of how history impacts present-day health', *Journal of Social Science and Medicine*, 106: 128–36.

Moll, N. (2013), 'Fragmented memories in a fragmented country: Memory competition and political identity-building in today's Bosnia and Herzegovina', *Nationalities Papers: The Journal of Nationalism and Ethnicity*, 1–26.

Moreau, T. and D. K. Alderman (2011), 'Graffiti hurts and the eradication off alternative landscape expression', *The Geographical Review*, 101(1): 106–24.

Musil, R. (1987), 'Denkmale', in Gesammelte Werke, Hamburg, 1957. Quoted in H. E. Mittig (eds), *Dan Denkmal. Eine Geschichte der Kunst im Wandel ihrer Funktionen*, Munich: Funkkolleg Kunst series, pp. 480–83.

Navaro-Yashin, Y. (2009), 'Affective spaces, melancholic objects: Ruination and the production of anthropological knowledge', *Journal of the Royal Anthropological Institute*, 15: 1–18.

Neal, A. G. (1998), *National Trauma and Collective Memory: Major Events in the American Century*, New York: M. E. Sharpe.

Neiger, M. and K. Rimmer-Tsory (2012), 'The war that wasn't on the news: "In-group nationalism" and "out-group nationalism" in newspaper supplements', *Journalism*, 14(6): 721–36.

Nielsen, C. (2012), 'Newspaper journalists support online comments', *Newspaper Research Journal*, 33(1): 86–100.

Nietzche, F. (1899), *A Genealogy of Morals*, London: Fisher Unwin.

Nora, P. (1984), *Les lieux de mémoire*, Paris: Gallimard, I, La République.

Nora, P. (1989), 'Between memory and history', *Representations*, 26(1): 7–12.

Noy, C. (2015), *Thank You for Dying for Our Country: Commemorative Texts and Performances in Jerusalem*, Oxford, New York: Oxford University Press.

O'Brien, C. C. (1948), 'The paenellism of Sean O'Faolain', *Irish Writing*, July: 59.

Ochs, E. and L. Capps (2001), *Living Narrative*, Cambridge: Harvard University Press.

O'Connor, P. E. (1995), 'Introduction: Discourse of violence', *Discourse & Society*, 6(3): 309–18.

Open Society Foundations, (2012), 'Mapping digital media: Bosnia and Herzegovina'. Available online: https://www.opensocietyfoundations.org/sites/default/files/mapping-digital-media-bosnia-20120706.pdf (Accessed 30 July 2018).

Oppenheimer, L. (2005), 'The development of enemy images in Dutch children: Measurement and initial findings', *British Journal of Developmental Psychology*, 23: 645–66.

OSCE (2012), 'Tackling hate crimes: An analysis of bias-motivated incidents in Bosnia and Herzegovina with recommendations'. Available online: file:///C:/Users/MAIDAK~1/AppData/Local/Temp/107255-1.pdf (Accessed 30 July 2018).

Palmberger, M. (2006), 'Making and breaking boundaries: Memory discourses and memory politics in Bosnia and Herzegovina', in M. Bufon, A. Gosar, S. Nurković and A. L. Sanguin (eds), *The Western Balkans – A European Challenge. On the Decennial of the Dayton Peace Agreement*, Koper: Založba Annales, pp. 525–36.

Pauwels, L. (2012), 'A multimodal framework for analyzing websites as cultural expressions', *Journal of Computer-Mediated Communication*, 17: 247–65.

Peck, A. and C. Stroud (2015), 'Skinscapes', *Linguistic Landscape*, 1(1/2): 133–51.

Pennanen, R. P. (2010), 'Melancholic airs of the orient – Bosnian Sevdalinka music as an orientalist and national symbol', in RP Pennanen (ed), *Music and Emotions*, 9, Collegium: Studies across disciplines in the humanities and social sciences, Helsinki: Helsinki Collegium for Advanced Studies, pp. 76–90.

Pennycook, A. (2010), 'Spatial narrations: Graffscapes and city souls', in A. Jaworski and C. Thurlow, (eds), *Semiotic Landscapes: Language, Image, Space*, London: Continuum, pp. 75–88.

Pennycook, A. and E. Otsuji (2014), 'Making scents of the landscape', *Linguistic Landscape*, 1(3): 191–212.

Perlovsky, L. (2009), 'Language and cognition', *Neural Networks*, 22: 247–57.

Phillips, K. and M. Reyes (2011), *Global Memoryscapes: Contesting Remembrance in a Transnational Age*, Tuscaloosa: University of Alabama Press.

Pickering, M. and E. Keightley (2009), 'Trauma, discourse and communicative limits', *Critical Discourse Studies*, 6(4): 237–49.

Pietikäinen, S., P. Lane, H. Salo and S. Laihiala-Kankainen (2011), 'Frozen actions in the Arctic linguistic landscape: A nexus analysis of language processes in visual space', *International Journal of Multilingualism*, 8(4): 277–98.

Pink, S. (2007), 'Walking with video', *Visual Studies*, 22: 240–52.

Plate, L. and A. Smelik (2013), 'Performing memory in art and popular culture: An introduction', in L. Plate and A. Smelik (eds), *Performing Memory in Art and Popular Culture*, New York and London: Routledge, pp. 1–22.

Potter, J. and M. Wetherell (1987), *Discourse and Social Psychology: Beyond Attitudes and Behaviour*, London: SAGE.

Potter, J. (1996), *Representing Reality: Discourse, Rhetoric, and Social Construction*, London: SAGE.

Potter, J. and S. Wiggins (2007), 'Discursive psychology', in C. Willig and M. Stainton-Rogers (eds), *The Sage Handbook of Qualitative Research in Psychology*, London: SAGE, pp. 73–90.

Povrzanovic, M. (1997), 'Children, war and nation: Croatia 1991–4', *Childhood: A Global Journal of Child Research*, 4: 81–102.

Pratto, F., J. Sidanius, L. M. Stallworth and B. M. Malle (1994), 'Social dominance orientation: A personality variable predicting social and political attitudes', *Journal of Personality and Social Psychology*, 67(4): 741–63.

Reddy, W. (2001), *The Navigation of Feeling: A Framework for the History of Emotions*, Cambridge: Cambridge University Press.

Reich, Z. (2011), 'User Comments: The transformation of participatory space', in J. B. Singer, A. Hermida, D. Domingo, A. Heinonen, S. Paulussen, T. Quandt, Z. Reich and M. Vujnovic (eds), *Participatory Journalism: Guarding Open Gates at Online Newspapers*, New York: Blackwell Publishing, pp. 96–117. https://cris.bgu.ac.il/en/publications/user-comments-the-transformation-of-participatory-space (31 December 2021).

Reisigl, M. and R. Wodak (2001), *Discourse and Discrimination: Rhetorics of Racism and Antisemitism*, London and New York: Routledge.

Reisigl, M. (2017), 'The semiotics of political commemoration', in R. Wodak and B. Forchtner (eds), *The Routledge Handbook of Language and Politics*, New York: Routledge, pp. 368–82.

Renan, E. (1882), 'What is a nation?', in E. Geoff and S. R. Grigor (eds), *Becoming National: A Reader*, New York and Oxford: Oxford University Press, pp. 41–55.

Richards, J. (2016), 'Lived narratives, everyday trauma, and the aftermath of the Bosnian war: Human rights as living practice', PhD Thesis, The University of Utah.

Richardson, J. E. (2021), 'Holocaust commemoration and affective practice: A rhetorical ethnography of audience applause', *Social Semiotics*, 31(5): 757–72.

Ricoeur, P. (2004), *Memory, History, Forgetting*, Chicago: University of Chicago Press.

Ristić, M. (2013), 'Silent vs. rhetorical memorials: Sarajevo roses and commemorative plaques', in A. Brown and A. Leach (eds), *Proceedings of the Society of Architectural Historians: 30, Open*, pp. 111–122. SAHANZ.

Robinson, M. G., S. Engelstoft and A. Pobrić (2001), 'Remaking Sarajevo: Bosnian nationalism after the Dayton Accord', *Political Geography*, 20: 957–80.

Rubdy, R. (2015), 'A multimodal analysis of the graffiti commemorating the 26/11 Mumbai terror attacks: Constructing self-understandings of a senseless violence', in R. Rubdy and S. Ben Said (eds), *Conflict, Exclusion and Dissent in the Linguistic Landscape*, London: Palgrave Macmillan, pp. 280–303.

Santana, A. D. (2011), 'Online readers' comments represent new opinion pipeline', *Newspaper Research Journal*, 32(3): 66–81.

Sapolsky, R. (2004), 'Stressed-out memories', *Scientific American Mind*, 14(5): 28–33.

Savage, R. (2007), 'Disease incarnate: Biopolitical discourse and genocidal dehumanisation in the age of modernity', *Journal of Historical Sociology*, 20(3): 404–40.

Schiff, B., C. Noy and B. J. Cohler (2001), 'Collected stories in the life narratives of Holocaust survivors', *Narrative Inquiry*, 11(1): 159–94.

Schiffrin, D. (1996), 'Narrative as self-portrait: Sociolinguist constructions of identity', *Language and Society*, 25: 167–203.

Schiffrin, D. (2002), 'Mother and friends in a Holocaust life story', *Language in Society*, 31: 309–53.

Schiffrin, D. (2003), 'We knew that's it: Retelling the turning point of a narrative', *Discourse Studies*, 5(4): 535–61.

Schlesinger, P. (2000), 'Nation and communicative space', in T. Howard (ed), *Media Power, Professionals and Policy*, London and New York: Routledge, pp. 99–115.

Schmidt, B. E. and I. W. Schroder (eds) (2001), *Anthropology of Violence and Conflict*, London: Routledge.

Schramm, K. (2011), 'Landscapes of violence: Memory and sacred space', *History and Memory*, 23(1): 5–22.

Schwab, G. (2010), *Haunting Legacies: Violent Histories and Transgenerational Trauma*, New York: Columbia University Press.

Scollon, R. and S. W. Scollon (2003), *Discourses in Place: Language in the Material World*, London: Routledge.
Scrimin, S., U. Moscardino, F. Capello, G. Altoè, A. M. Steinberg and R. S. Pynoos (2011), 'Trauma reminders and PTSD symptoms in children three years after a terrorist attack in Beslan', *Social Science & Medicine*, 72(5): 694–700.
Shandler, J. (1999), *While America Watches*, New York: Oxford University Press.
Shaw, S. J. (1976), *History of the Ottoman Empire and Modern Turkey. Volume I: Empire of the Gazis: The Rise and Decline of the Ottoman Empire, 1280–1808*, New York and London: Cambridge University Press.
Sheller, M. and J. Urry (2006), 'The new mobilities paradigm', *Environment and Planning A*, 38(2): 207–26.
Shohamy, E. and D. Gorter (eds) (2009), *Linguistic Landscape: Expanding the Scenery*, London: Routledge.
Shohamy, E. and S. Waksman (2010), 'Building the nation, writing the past: History and textuality at the Ha'apala memorial in Tel Aviv-Jaffa', in A. Jaworski and C. Thurlow (eds), *Semiotic Landscapes: Language, Image, Space*, London: Continuum, pp. 241–55.
Shohamy, E. and S. Waksman (2013), 'Talking back to the Tel Aviv centennial: LL responses to top-down agendas', in C. Hélot, M. Barni, R. Janssens and C. Bagna (eds), *Linguistic Landscapes, Multilingualism and Social Change*, Frankfurt: Peter Lang, pp. 267–85.
Shohamy, E. (2015), 'LL research as expanding language and language policy', *Linguistic Landscape*, 1(1/2): 152–71.
Simic, O. (2017), 'Drinking coffee in Bosnia: Listening to stories of wartime violence and rape', *Journal of International Women's Studies*, 18(4): 321–8.
Skey, M. (2009), 'The national in everyday life: A critical engagement with Michael Billig's thesis of Banal Nationalism', *The Sociological Review*, 57(2): 331–46.
Smith, A. (2014), 'Drawing the line in Bosnia and Herzegovina: The advocacy of hatred constituting incitement to hostility, discrimination and violence', *Analitika*, Sarajevo: Center for Social Research. http://analitika.ba/sites/default/files/publikacije/drawing_the_line_-_discussion_paper_06_-_17martfinal.pdf (31 December 2021).
Softić, B. (2011), 'The music of Srebrenica after the war. Attitudes and practice among surviving Bosniacs, music therapy, and music works in the name of Srebrenica', *Narodna Umjetnost*, 48(1): 161–81.
Sokol, A. (2014), 'War monuments: Instruments of Nation-building in Bosnia and Herzegovina', *Politička Misao*, 5: 105–26.
Sontag, S. (1990), *Illness as Metaphor and AIDS and Its Metaphors*, New York: Doubleday.
Sontag, S. (2003), *Regarding the Pain of Others*, New York: Farrar, Straus and Giroux.
Spangler, M. (2009), 'Performing "the troubles": Murals and the spectacle of 100 commemorations of violence at free derry corner', in S. Brady, F. Walsh (eds), *Crossroads: Performance Studies and Irish Culture*, New York: Palgrave Macmillan, pp. 100–13.

Spillman, K. R. and K. Spillmann (1997), 'Some sociobiological and psychological aspects of images of the enemy', in R. Fiebig-von Has and U. Lehmkuhl (eds), *Enemy Images in American History*, Providence: Berghahn, pp. 43–64.

Staub, E. (1992), *The Roots of Evil: The Origins of Genocide and Other Group Violence*, Cambridge: Cambridge University Press.

Steinweis, A. E. (2005), 'The Auschwitz analogy: Holocaust memory and American debates over intervention in Bosnia and Kosovo in the 1990s', *Holocaust and Genocide Studies*, 19(2): 276–89.

Stroud, C. and M. Prinsloo (2015), *Language, Literacy and Diversity: Moving Words*, New York: Routledge.

Stroud, C. (2016), 'Turbulent linguistic landscapes and the semiotics of citizenship', in R. Blackwood, E. Lanza and H. Woldemariam (eds), *Negotiating and Contesting Identities in Linguistic Landscapes*, London, New York: Bloomsburry, pp. 3–18.

Stubbs, M. (2001), *Words and Phrases: Corpus Studies of Lexical Semantics*, Oxford: Blackwell.

Subašić, H. and N. Ćurak (2014), 'History, the ICTY's record and the Bosnian Serb culture of denial', in J. Gow, R. Kerr and Z. Pjanic (eds), *Prosecuting War Crimes: Lessons and Legacies of the International Criminal Tribunal for the Former Yugoslavia*, Abingdon: Routledge, pp. 88–103.

Tabeau, E. and J. Bijak (2005), 'War-related deaths in the 1992–1995 armed conflicts in Bosnia and Herzegovina: A critique of previous estimates and recent results', *European Journal of Population*, 21: 187–215.

Tannen, D. (2007), *Talking Voices: Repetition, Dialogue, and Imagery in Conversational Discourse*, Cambridge and New York: Cambridge University Press.

Taylor, M. and M. L. Kent (2000), 'Media transitions in Bosnia: From propagandistic past to uncertain future', *Gazette*, 62(5): 355–78.

Ten Bensel, T. and L. Sample (2014), 'Stories of wartime rape victims: The deconstruction of lived experiences in the balkan conflict', *Violence & Gender*, 1: 77–89.

Thompson, R. (2004), 'Trauma and the rhetoric of recovery: A discourse analysis of the virtual healing journal of child sexual abuse survivors', *Trauma and Rhetoric*, 24(3): 653–77.

Thurlow, C. (2001), 'Naming the "outside within": Homophobic pejorative and the verbal abuse of LGB high-school pupils', *Journal of Adolescence*, 24(1): 25–38.

Thurlow, C. and A. Jaworski (2011), 'Banal globalization? Embodied actions and mediated practices in tourists' online photo sharing', in C. Thurlow and K. Mroczek (eds), *Digital Discourse: Language in the New Media*, Oxford, New York: Oxford University Press, pp. 220–50.

Thurlow, C. and A. Jaworski (2014), '"Two hundred ninety-four": Remediation and multimodal performance in tourist placemaking' *Journal of Sociolinguistics*, 18(4): 459–94.

Tileaga, C. (2006), 'Representing the "Other": A discursive analysis of prejudice and moral exclusion in talk about romanies', *Journal of Community & Applied Social Psychology*, 16: 19–41.

Tileaga, C. (2007), 'Ideologies of moral exclusion: A critical discursive reframing of depersonalization, delegitimization and dehumanization', *British Journal of Social Psychology*, 46: 717–37.

Tirrell, L. (2012), 'Genocidal language game', in I. Maitra and M. K. McGowan (eds), *Speech and Harm: Controversies over Free Speech*, Oxford: Oxford University Press, pp. 174–221.

Torsti, P. (2004), 'History culture and banal nationalism in post-war Bosnia', *Southeast European Politics*, 2-3: 142–57.

Triandafyllidou, A. and R. Wodak (2003), 'Conceptual and methodological questions in the study of collective identity: An introduction', *Journal of Language and Politics*, 2: 205–25.

Truc, G. and C. Sánchez-Carretero (2019), 'Polarised topography of rival memories: The commemorations of the 11th March 2004 train bombings in Madrid', in M. L. Stig Sørensen, D. Viejo-Rose and P. Filippucci (eds), *Memorials in the Aftermath of Armed Conflict: From History to Heritage*, New York and Basingstoke: Palgrave Macmillan, pp. 33–60.

Tumarkin, M. (2001), 'Wishing you weren't here...: Thinking about trauma, place and the port Arthur massacre', *Journal of Australian Studies*, 25: 67.

Tumarkin, M. (2005), *The Power and Fate of Places Transformed by Tragedy*, Carlton, Vic.: Melbourne University Publishing.

Tumarkin, M. (2019), 'Twenty years of thinking about traumascapes', *Fabrications*, 29(1): 4–20.

Udovičić, Z., T. Jusić, M. Halilović, R. Udovičić and Media Plan Institute Research Team (2001), *The Media at a Turning Point: A Media Landscape of Bosnia-Herzegovina*, Media Online, https://www.researchgate.net/publication/320107509_The_Media_at_a_Turning_Point_A_Media_Landscape_of_Bosnia-Herzegovina (31 December 2021).

Unsworth, L. (2008), *Multimodal Semiotics Functional Analysis in Contexts of Education*, New York: Continuum.

Valenta, M. and S. Ramet (2011), *The Bosnian Diaspora: Integration in Transnational Communities*, Farnham, Burlington: Ashgate.

van der Laarse, R. (2013), 'Beyond Auschwitz. Europe's terrorscapes in the age of postmemory', in M. Silberman and F. Vatan (eds), *Memory and Postwar Memorials. Confronting the Violence of the Past*, New York: Pagrave Macmillan, pp. 71–92.

van Dijk, T. A. (1993), 'Principles of critical discourse analysis', *Discourse & Society*, 4(2): 249–83.

van Dijk, T. A. (2009), *Society and Discourse. How Social Contexts Influence Text and Talk*, Cambridge: Cambridge University Press.

van Leeuwen, T. (1999), *Speech, Music, Sound*, London: Macmillan Press.

van Leeuwen, T. and R. Wodak (1999), 'Legitimizing immigration – a discourse-historical analysis', *Discourse Studies*, 1(1): 83–119.

van Leeuwen, T. (2018), 'Moral evaluation in critical discourse analysis', *Critical Discourse Studies* 15:2, 140–153.

Vanderford, M. (1989), 'Vilification and social movements: A case study of pro-life and pro-choice movements', *Quarterly Journal of Speech*, 75: 166–82.
Violi, P. (2008), 'Beyond the body: Towards a full embodied semiosis', *Body, Language & Mind*, 2: 241–64.
Violi, P. (2012), 'Trauma site museums and politics of memory', *Theory, Culture & Society*, 29(1): 36–75.
Violi, P. (2017), 'Spaces of memory and trauma: A cultural semiotrumic perspective', in K. Bankov and P. Cobley (eds), *Semiotics and Its Masters*, Boston and Berlin: Walter de Gruyter, pp. 185–204.
Vulliamy, E. (1992), 'Shame of camp Omarska', *The Guardian*, August 7.
Waksman, S. and E. Shohamy (2016), 'Linguistic landscape of social protests: Moving from "open" to "institutional" spaces', in R. Blackwood, E. Lanza and H. Woldemariam (eds), *Negotiating and Contesting Identities in Linguistic Landscapes*, London and New York: Bloomsbury, pp. 85–98.
Wallis, M. and P. Duggan (2011), 'Editorial: On trauma', *Performance Research*, 16(1): 1–3.
Walter, T. (2001), 'From cathedral to supermarket: Mourning, silence and solidarity', *The Sociological Review*, 49(4): 494–511.
Walton, K. L. (1978), 'Fearing fictions', *Journal of Philosophy*, 75: 5–27.
Weber, C. (2015), *Social Memory and War Narratives: Transmitted Trauma among Children of Vietnam War Veterans*, New York: Palgrave Macmillan.
Wee, L. (2016), 'Situating affect in linguistic landscapes', *Linguistic Landscape*, 2(2): 105–26.
Weedon, C. and G. Jordan (2012), 'Collective memory: Theory and politics', *Social Semiotics*, 22(2): 143–53.
West, R. (1993), 'Tito and the rise and fall of Yugoslavia', *Journal of Croatian Studies*, 35: 235–51.
Wetherell, M. (2012), *Affect and Emotion: A New Social Science Understanding*, London: SAGE.
Whigham, K. (2014), 'Filling the absence: The re-embodiment of sites of mass atrocity and the practices they generate', *Museum & Society*, 12(2): 88–103.
White, C. J. (2015), 'Banal nationalism and belonging within the echoed imagined community: The case of New Zealand anthems on YouTube', *Journal of Language and Politics*, 14(5): 627–44.
Whitehead, N. L. (2004), 'Cultures, conflicts and the poetics of violent practice', in N. L. Whitehead (ed), *Violence*, Santa Fe: School of American Research Press, pp. 3–24.
Wieviorka, A. (1994), 'On testimony', in G. Hartman (ed), *Holocaust Remembrance: The Shapes of Memory*, Oxford: Basil Blackwell, pp. 23–32.
Williams, R. (1977), *Marxism and Literature*, Oxford: Oxford University Press.
Wilson, J. Z. (2014), 'Ambient hate: Racist graffiti and social apathy in a rural community', *The Howard Journal of Crime and Justice*, 53(4): 377–94.

Wodak, E. and J. E. Richardson (2009), 'On the politics of remembering (or not)', *Critical Discourse Studies*, 6(4): 231–5.

Wodak, R. (2006), 'Discourse-analytic and socio-linguistic approaches to the study of nation(alism)', in G. Delanty and K. Kumar (eds), *The SAGE Handbook of Nations and Nationalism*, London, New Delhi: SAGE, pp. 104–17.

Wodak, R. and G. Auer-Borea (eds) (2009), *Justice and Memory. Confronting Traumatic Pasts. An International Comparison*, Vienna: Passagen Verlag.

Wodak, R. and R. de Cillia (2007), 'Commemorating the past: The discursive construction of official narratives about the "rebirth of the second Austrian Republic"', *Discourse & Communication*, 1(3): 337–63.

Wodak, R. (2008), '"Us" and "Them": Inclusion and exclusion – Discrimination via discourse', in G. Delanty, R. Wodak and P. Jones (eds), *Identity, Belonging and Migration*, Liverpool: Liverpool University Press, pp. 54–78.

Wodak, R., R. de Cillia, M. Reisigl and K. Liebhart (2009), *The Discursive Construction of National Identity*, Edinburgh: Edinburgh University Press.

Wodak, R. (2011), *The Discourse of Politics in Action: Politics as Usual*, Basingstoke: Palgrave.

Wodak, R. and S. Boukala (2015), 'European identities and the revival of nationalism in the European union: A discourse historical approach', *Journal of Language and Politics*, 14(1): 87–109.

Wodak, R. (2018), 'Discourses about nationalism', in J. Flowerdew and J. E. Richardson (eds), *The Routledge Handbook of Critical Discourse Studies*, Abingdon: Routledge, pp. 403–20.

Young, A. (2005), *Judging the Image: Art, Value, Law*, London: Routledge.

Zaimakis, Y. (2015), 'Welcome to the civilization of fear: On political graffiti heterotopias in Greece in times of crisis', *Visual Communication*, 14(4): 373–96.

Zbikowski, L. (2013), 'Listening to music', in K. Chapin and A. H. Clark (eds), *Speaking of Music: Addressing the Sonorous*, New York: Fordham University Press, pp. 101–19.

Žižek, S. (2006), *The Parallax View*, Massachusetts: MIT Press Cambridge.

Index

affect 5, 6, 19, 32, 42, 44, 57, 68, 103, 114, 124, 149, 154
affective regimes 30, 32, 41, 43, 47, 154
atrocities 7, 9, 11, 36, 39, 51, 90, 98, 114, 155

banal nationalism 3, 80, 81, 155

commemoration 1, 17, 20, 21, 34, 50, 54, 55, 56, 57, 58, 59, 61, 62, 63, 64, 65, 66, 67, 70, 71, 73, 74, 75, 76, 90, 97, 103, 150, 151, 152, 154, 155
concentration camp 7, 10, 25, 49, 50, 57, 89, 90, 91, 101, 113, 122, 125, 127, 146

dehumanization 59, 60, 95, 96, 106, 107
denial 5, 51, 52, 62, 66, 67, 70, 73, 74, 75, 82, 101, 151, 152, 155
diaspora 70, 71, 84, 112, 113, 118, 119, 122, 125, 131, 133, 136, 139, 140, 145, 146, 148, 156
discourse of violence 30, 136

embodiment 47, 57, 63, 140, 147
empathy 62, 63, 91, 139, 151
emplacement 20, 33, 34, 35, 36, 37, 41, 42, 44, 45, 47, 62, 67, 71
ethnic cleansing 9, 36, 37, 42, 52, 57, 101

genocide 1, 2, 3, 5, 9, 21, 22, 25, 34, 42, 43, 45, 57, 61, 65, 66, 70, 76, 79, 88, 90, 94, 98, 101, 123, 127, 143, 149, 151, 152, 157
graffscape 27, 30, 31, 32, 36, 42, 45, 46, 47, 48, 118, 154

hate 7, 27, 30, 31, 32, 33, 34, 35, 42, 44, 47, 78, 83, 106, 125, 134, 152
healing 16, 21, 23, 118
historical trauma 45, 114, 115, 116, 117, 119, 146, 147, 156

linguistic landscape 18, 19, 29, 30, 32, 36, 47, 48, 57, 84

linguistic violence 30, 34, 35, 36, 44, 45, 47, 48
living memorial 54, 55, 63, 64, 65, 66, 75, 150, 154, 155
loss 5, 10, 17, 25, 28, 47, 64, 68, 72, 76, 78, 85, 117, 123, 133, 136, 146, 147, 156, 157

mediation 14, 18, 21, 69, 76, 103, 146, 156
memoryscape 13, 26, 57, 75
monument 5, 16, 18, 19, 26, 27, 45, 50, 51, 52, 53, 54, 62, 63, 64, 66, 69, 70, 75, 76, 80, 81, 94, 104, 106, 124, 128, 147, 150, 153, 156, 157, 158

Omarska 49, 50, 51, 54, 59, 61, 64, 101
oral narrative 119, 120, 146, 147, 156

performance 54, 56, 57, 58, 59, 60, 62, 65, 66, 67, 68, 71, 73, 74, 75, 76, 144, 154, 155
postmemory 72, 116

remembrance 13, 17, 19, 54, 104, 151, 155
revenge 7, 44, 45, 92

semiotic landscape 16, 18, 19, 27, 55, 57, 74, 80, 103, 147, 155, 156
semiotic resources 18, 20, 54, 58, 106
siege 36, 67, 69
silence 54, 58, 62, 63, 71, 114, 122, 127, 138
social semiotics 20, 21, 54, 56, 58
spatial melancholia 124, 147, 156
Srebrenica 1, 2, 3, 4, 7, 9, 11, 25, 34, 43, 44, 45, 46, 57, 65, 66, 70, 72, 73, 79, 98, 101, 112, 123, 127, 143, 144, 149, 151, 152
storytelling 23, 24, 114, 115, 116
suffering 4, 5, 17, 19, 22, 28, 54, 73, 92, 113, 114, 117, 120, 147, 152, 154, 157

transmission 18, 74, 117, 120, 146, 156
The White Armbands Day 59, 61, 62, 63, 64, 66, 67, 88, 90

www.ingramcontent.com/pod-product-compliance
Lightning Source LLC
Chambersburg PA
CBHW061832300426
44115CB00013B/2348